READING RESISTANCE

Disability
Studies in
Education

Susan L. Gabel and Scot Danforth
General Editors

Vol. 1

PETER LANG
New York • Washington, D.C./Baltimore • Bern
Frankfurt am Main • Berlin • Brussels • Vienna • Oxford

Beth A. Ferri & David J. Connor

READING RESISTANCE

Discourses of Exclusion in Desegregation & Inclusion Debates

PETER LANG
New York • Washington, D.C./Baltimore • Bern
Frankfurt am Main • Berlin • Brussels • Vienna • Oxford

Library of Congress Cataloging-in-Publication Data

Ferri, Beth A.
Reading resistance: discourses of exclusion in desegregation
and inclusion debates / Beth A. Ferri, David J. Connor.
p. cm. — (Disability studies in education; vol. 1)
Includes bibliographical references and index.
1. Segregation in education—United States. 2. Inclusive education—United
States. 3. Students with disabilities—Education—United States.
I. Connor, David J., 1961- II. Title. III. Series.
LC212.52.F47 2005   371.9'046—dc22   2005006782
ISBN 978-0-8204-7428-1
ISSN 1548-7210

Bibliographic information published by **Die Deutsche Nationalbibliothek**.
Die Deutsche Nationalbibliothek lists this publication in the "Deutsche
Nationalbibliografie"; detailed bibliographic data are available
on the Internet at http://dnb.d-nb.de/.

Permission to reproduce Jacob Lawrence's *Untitled,* 1947 (© Gwendolyn Knight
Lawrence/Artists Rights Society [ARS]) is by courtesy of Gwendolyn Knight
Lawrence. The four eugenics images appearing in chapter 2 are by permission
of the American Philosophical Society. Editorial cartoons appearing in chapter 4
are by courtesy of *Atlanta Journal-Constitution, Greensboro Daily News,
Clarion-Ledger/Jackson Daily News, Chicago Sun Times, Afro American
Newspaper Archives and Research Center, Nashville Banner, Memphis
Commercial Appeal, Star Tribune (Minneapolis-St. Paul), Richmond (Virginia)
Times-Dispatch, New York Times* and Mrs. Edith Knox. Every attempt was made
to secure permissions from remaining newspapers that are no longer in print or
from individual artists who could not be located through the newspaper or
through the *Society of Illustrators.*

Cover design by Sophie Boorsch Appel
Cover art by David J. Connor

To Vivian and John

CONTENTS

ACKNOWLEDGMENTS

We both have so many wonderful people to thank for their contributions to this book. Early on in the process we had two of the best research assistants anyone could hope for. Marisa Nealon, who spent hours pouring through newspapers and microfiche, and later Ji-Ryun Kim, who secured permissions and did countless other tasks, were invaluable to the project. We also had wonderful support from reference librarians, interlibrary loan staff, and research assistants at the Schomburg Center for Research on Black Culture, the New York Public Libraries, Millbank Library at Teachers College, Butler and Lehman Libraries at Columbia University, and Bird Library at Syracuse University. We also wish to thank Yin Wah B. Kreher and support staff at Faculty Computing at Syracuse University, who worked magic with scanning and cleaning up all of our visual images in preparation for publication. Each of these people has left an indelible mark on the book and we are so thankful for their professionalism and enthusiasm.

From 2003 to 2005 we presented various parts of the book at academic conferences, including the *Second City Conference in Disability Studies in Education, American Educational Research Association, Journal of Gender, Race and Justice Symposium* at University of Iowa Law School, *The Impact of the Brown Decision on American Education and Society* at Teachers College, Columbia University, and the *Brown Plus 50* conference at New York University. At each of these venues, colleagues shared their insights and offered invaluable feedback that helped strengthen this project. We would like to particularly thank James Rolling Jr., V. P. Franklin, and Ellen Brantlinger for reviewing portions of the manuscript and offering their sage advice, as well as Nancy Lesko for guidance with our initial book proposal. In addition, we thank Welton L. "Tony" Sawyer, Superintendent of Schools, Topeka, Kansas, for writing the foreword of this book. We are also grateful for our many supportive colleagues at Syracuse University and Teachers College. We want to particularly thank D. Kim Reid, Steve Taylor, Doug Biklen, Arlene Kanter, Bob Bogdan, Corinne Smith, Joe Shedd, and Louise Wilkinson for their support and mentoring. We also wish to acknowledge the much-needed financial support we received from Dean Wilkinson and Ben Ware at Syracuse University and Dean Darlyne Bailey at Teachers College.

We are also completely indebted to Scot Danforth and Susan Gabel for their careful reading and thoughtful editorial suggestions. Their visionary leadership was instrumental in getting this book series off the ground and we could not have hoped for a better editorial team. We would also like to thank our publishing team at Peter Lang for all of their support and patience.

Finally, we want to thank our family and friends, particularly our partners, Vivian and John, who understood the time, effort, and level of commitment involved in undertaking this project. We are so grateful for their support and encouragement.

W. L. Sawyer
Superintendent of Schools, Topeka, Kansas

FOREWORD

In the aftermath of the 50th anniversary of the *Brown v. Board of Education* decision in 2004 and the 30th anniversary of the *Individuals with Disabilities Education
Act* in 2005, the publication of *Reading Resistance: Discourses of Exclusion in Desegregation and Inclusion Debates* could not be more timely. Ferri and Connor ask that
the reader question: Are these celebrated legal policies actualized in practice, or
have other structural systemic methods that qualify as segregation behind the veil
of mental disability been retained in spite of our legislative efforts? In this context,
these authors have demonstrated the salience of labels such as ADHD,[1] LD,[2]
"challenging child," and multiple congruent terms employed to perpetuate historical patterns of exclusion within the American educational system.

The anthology of this text moves from a questioning of the previously stated
paradox to an exploration of the institutional application of such policies and their
impact on marginalizing the quality of education for African American children.
The book's historical context provides a multidisciplined critical approach to conceptualizing the long-term ramifications of substandard education. As James Bald-
win wrote, "The paradox of education is precisely this: that as one begins to become conscious, one begins to examine the society in which he is being educated."
Hence, Ferri and Connor's research provides the cultured foundation for exploring

1. (ADHD) Attention Deficit Hyperactivity Disorder
2. (LD) Learning Disabled

how American educational policies and ethnocentric social values and norms have contributed to resegregation coupled with continued unequal education.

Unlike other scholarly writings within the field of education, this work by Ferri and Connor has incorporated a theoretical framework that is often ignored: Black Feminist Thought. This particular theoretical framework not only provides an historical context for exclusionary policies and cultural systemic behaviors, but also investigates the role of race, class, and gender on the structural ritualization of resegregating children of color by standards that are culturally biased.

As the superintendent of a diverse school community which shall forever be regarded as the springboard for the judicial apocalypse that would transmogrify political and social thought in America, I appreciate the urgent need for literature like *Reading Resistance: Discourses of Exclusion in Desegregation and Inclusion Debates* for educators, scholars, and researchers. I commend Ferri and Connor for their innovative approach to the study of race, class, and gender within the academy. It is my sincere hope that this book will ignite our educational commitment to address the intended spirit of a half century of legislative effort.

1

INTRODUCTION

1

INTRODUCTION

Commemorating Anniversaries

This first decade of the 21st century marks two important milestones in educational history: the 50th anniversary of the *Brown v. Board of Education* decision in 2004 and the 30th anniversary of the *Individuals with Disabilities Education Act* (*IDEA*) in 2005. It is hard to overstate the significance of either of these milestones in terms of educational policy and practice. Both *Brown* and *IDEA* assert the need for increased educational opportunities for previously excluded groups of students. Moreover, each shares a more sweeping legacy of expanding notions of access beyond educational settings. *Brown,* for instance, paved the way for the passage of the landmark *Civil Rights Act* in 1964. Similarly, *IDEA,* following on the heels of the *Rehabilitation Act* of 1973, helped fuel the momentum for sweeping disability rights legislation, the *Americans with Disabilities Act* (*ADA*) in 1990. Despite these important legacies, however, the outcomes of both *Brown* and *IDEA* suggest that their promises have yet to be fully realized.

Anniversaries are often a time for reflection and taking stock. Throughout 2004, for example, conferences, lecture series, publications, and events commemorated the 50th anniversary of the *Brown* decision. The 2004 annual meeting of the American Educational Research Association (AERA) included the strand *Brown v. Board of Education—50 Years Later*. In one of the sessions, distinguished historian Lamar Miller described how he had been involved in commemorating the *Brown* decision with a conference every ten years on its anniversary.[1] He remarked that at this 50-year milestone he did not feel much like celebrating. In fact, Miller said he felt more pessimistic than ever before. On the following day, noted scholar Gloria Ladson-Billings, in weighing the progress of the *Brown* decision, echoed Miller's disappointment at the current state of "hypersegregation" between racial groups in schools. As these scholars note, although *Brown* is widely considered one of the legal milestones of the 20th century, racial integration in America's schools has not come very far, and by some accounts has actually regressed in terms of students having the opportunity to learn with peers of different races (Orfield, 2004).

Twenty-one years after *Brown,* with the passage of P.L. 94–142, students with disabilities were finally guaranteed access to a free and appropriate public education in the "least restrictive environment." This law, *IDEA*, built on the legacy and legal strategies of *Brown,* was seen by many to be an obvious extension of the idea that separate classes and schools were inherently unequal. In the years following *IDEA*, scholars have debated what should be considered "least" restrictive—and many now define the general education classroom as the only setting that should be considered the least restrictive. As we commemorate the 30th anniversary of *IDEA*, it is critically important to take stock of the progress made toward integrating students with disabilities into inclusive classrooms. Considering its 30-year history, we cannot help but acknowledge that students with disabilities continue to be taught in separate and highly restrictive classrooms, isolated from their nondisabled peers. The predominant model for service delivery in special education continues to be either pull-out services or self-contained classes (A. Smith, 2001). Moreover, by labeling disproportionate numbers of students of color and placing them in restrictive placements, special education undercuts desegregation efforts and legitimizes the ongoing segregation of students from nondominant backgrounds (A. Smith). In other words, one of the ways schools maintained segregated classrooms after *Brown* is by placing large numbers of students of color in special education classrooms and in nonacademic tracks. Thus, rather than simply thinking about *IDEA* as a proud legacy of *Brown,* we must also consider the role special education has played in the failure of *Brown.*

Special Education and Overrepresentation

One long-standing critique of special education practice centers on the disproportionate placement of students of color in special education programs, referred to in education literature as overrepresentation. The data on overrepresentation of students of color are consistent and robust (Hosp & Reschly, 2004). The United States Office of Civil Rights (OCR) has reported a persistent problem of overrepresentation of minority children in certain disability categories since it began collecting relevant data in the 1970s. It is not that the problem of overrepresentation has gone unnoticed. For example, early on, Dunn (1968) critiqued the overrepresentation of ethnic/racial minorities in special education, particularly in the category of mental retardation. His critique should have signaled the need for public outcry and educational reform. Yet, more than 35 years later, the problem of over-representation has not diminished.

In the most recent report from OCR, Black students remain the most over-represented of all groups in the majority of disability categories in nearly every state. However, Southern states continue to have the most disproportionate numbers of students of color identified for special education (Parrish, 2002). Although figures between states vary, in some states the risk of a student of color being overrepresented in special education is extreme. For example, a Black student in Montana is 5.44 times more likely to be labeled learning disabled (LD) than a White student; in Connecticut, a Black student is 4.76 times more likely to be labeled emotionally disturbed (ED); and in Nebraska, a Black student is 6.06 times more likely to be labeled mentally retarded (MR) than his or her peers (Losen & Orfield, 2002). Averaging data from all 50 states, Black students remain 3 times as likely to be labeled MR as White students, almost 2 times as likely to be labeled ED, and almost 1.5 times more likely to be labeled LD (Losen & Orfield). Among all disability categories, MR remains the most likely to be assigned to Black students, particularly Black males (Parrish, 2002). In addition, Black students who attend school in wealthier communities are actually *more* likely to be labeled MR than those attending predominantly Black, low-income schools (Oswald et al., 2002). This finding contradicts the commonly held assumption that the achievement differences of students of color can be explained by poverty (Salend et al., 2002).

The problem of overrepresentation is complicated and not confined to Black students. Latino and Native American students are more likely to be overrepresented in special education in states with high proportions of these ethnic/racial groups. Once labeled, students from racial, ethnic, and linguistic minority groups are all more likely to be placed in more restrictive/segregated classrooms in comparison to their White peers (Fierros & Conroy, 2002). Moreover, students from these groups who attend school in large urban districts are placed in the most segregated and restrictive of placements (Fierros & Conroy). Because these figures include education systems from across the country and illustrate a wide-ranging problem of overrepresentation, these statistics are cause for immense concern.

The Purpose of This Study

Our thinking about this book began with the nexus of two questions: Given the data on overrepresentation, how has special education ignored the intersection of racism and ableism and in so doing contributed to the failure of *Brown*? And, how did *Brown* fail to consider disability as a mechanism for resegregating students of color within otherwise desegregated schools? Because of the shared history of segregation and the continued overrepresentation of students of color in special education, we feel a pressing need to connect debates about inclusion, or the practice of educating students with disabilities in general education classrooms, to the larger sociohistorical contexts of desegregation (Oliver, 1996). As scholars have yet to fully engage with the ways that exclusion is framed between and among these various histories, we wanted to explore what could be learned by critically attending to the various types of resistance to integration in each of these discourses.

Although there are very few in-depth analyses connecting school desegregation and special education, it is not uncommon to find at least a passing reference to the *Brown* decision by scholars writing about the history of disability rights legislation or current debates about inclusion. The *Brown* decision is even included in lists of important disability-related laws in introductory special education textbooks. We assert that it is not enough, however, to draw analogies between race and disability or between desegregation and inclusion. An inherent problem with analogy is that it requires conceptual separation: when we compare A (desegregation) to B (inclusion), each is presumed to be distinct or separate. Differences *between* A and B either collapse and become indistinguishable or are thought of in additive or compounding terms. This is not to say that one cannot learn from analogy, but that its paradoxes must always be recognized and respected. As Elizabeth Spelman (1997) writes, "a danger in assuming [or appropriating] the experiences of others is that they as subjects of such experiences will be erased, a danger in *refusing* to do so is that one may thereby deny the possibility of a shared humanity" (p. 131). Our intent, therefore, is to create a dialogic space where "contradictions and ambiguities [between desegregation and inclusion] do not merge but stand alongside each other" (Tanaka, 1997, p. 261). In other words, our goal is to explore connections without erasing differences between the ways that power recirculates across and through particular categories of difference and histories of exclusion.

In this book, we explore how special education, designed to provide support for previously excluded students, has, paradoxically, participated in maintaining rather than minimizing racial inequities. As stated, the complicated relationship between resegregation and special education reflected in the problem of overrepresentation highlights a glaring problem with making a simple analogy between *Brown* and *IDEA*. Moreover, because we are studying *exclusion* rather than inclusion, our work runs counter to traditional progress stories of the field. Instead, our approach focuses on what was left unsaid, masked, obscured, and silenced in the stories of inclusion and desegregation. Critiquing long-standing exclusionary practices in public schooling, we hope to challenge conventional and overly simplistic approaches to these complex issues. In tracing the discourse of segregation, for example, we seek to uncover how certain rationales exerted enormous power in shaping schools and schooling practices, but, at the same time, to uncover important seeds of resistance. Most importantly, we aim to think beyond current practice and challenges to consider how, as professionals in the field, we might "be in ways we have not [yet] been" (Kendall & Wickham, 1999, p. 30).

A central concern of this book is to explore how the rhetorics of ability and race have been used to maintain and justify segregated education. Although these histories are often seen as one civil rights struggle building upon another, by attending to their overlapping histories we reveal the interconnected workings of power operating in both. By examining discursive productions of race and disability in the public imagination as they have emerged over time, we seek to understand how they have been mobilized *against* individuals—used as tools to separate and disempower. By reconceptualizing race and disability within a sociocultural-historical framework, we aim to uncover insights that will help us challenge exclusionary educational practices.

Situating Ourselves

Each of us comes to this project from a particular vantage point—influenced by our own experiences in school—as both teachers and students. I (Beth) recall how in my very first teaching position I was hired fresh out of my undergraduate studies to start a program for students with moderate cognitive disabilities in West Virginia. It was to be the first program of its kind in the district, since before that point all students with significant disabilities were bussed to an adjoining county. Because the county had nearly a dozen students who shared the label of TMI[2] and because students were spending an inordinate amount of their school day on a bus, the state required the district to begin to offer students a program.

When I arrived early in August to begin preparations, I was given a "tour" of the school and my new classroom. The principal was obviously proud of all of the arrangements that had been made in preparation for admitting the new students to the elementary school. I was shown how my classroom, which was the old art room,[3] had its own door to the outside. This meant, I was told, that "my" students could come straight into the "self-contained" classroom from their own "special" bus. They would also be able to exit to the playground at their own "special" time. Then I was escorted to the lunchroom, where a "special" table had been set up in its own "special" room adjoining the cafeteria so "my" students would have their own place to eat lunch. At this point in my "tour," I remember feeling a bit defensive for the students I had yet to meet! I told the principal that I didn't think all this "special" treatment was necessary or even desirable. He was firm that these arrangements were what K. M. Collins (2003) would call a "benign form of exclusion," and were in the best interest of the students. I looked around at the "special" table in the "special" lunchroom and quipped, "Well, since these students eat with 'normal' people at home, I am sure they'll be able to handle it here at school." He noted my impertinence, but did not budge from his position.

All of this "specialness" ensured that although the students were technically being "included" in the school, they were barely going to be breathing the same air as the other students. In reflecting back on this day, I know that it was a key point in politicizing my views about disability. I now understood that "special" and "separate" were designed for the comfort of general education students and teachers, and not for the benefit of students with disabilities. This was an example of inclusion that was designed to ensure that nothing would have to change—the students would come and go and most of the school would not even have to know. It, like tracking, allowed devalued groups of students to be quarantined—protecting general education students (and the curriculum) from their contaminating presence.

I was also significantly influenced by the experience of being bussed in the 1970s, which ensured that I received my middle and high school education with a diverse range of students. I know that I learned as much from the diversity of the student body[4] as from any of the textbooks I read or classes I attended. My worldview, growing up as a second generation Italian American, was made richer and more complex from these school experiences. I concluded from this experience that the real purpose of education was not to reinforce what a child brings from home, but rather to provide for each child what they could not or would not receive in their family context. The repeal of bussing nationwide, however, has meant that my own nieces and nephews, living only miles from where I grew up, are missing out on this vital lesson in living in a diverse world. Most likely they will have to wait until they get to college or into the workforce to find out that they missed out on an education. Of course, their story is not unusual and no one in my family seems particularly concerned. White, suburban students are now the most racially isolated group of students in America (Orfield, 2001). These students, because they grow up in racially isolated neighborhoods, are in the most need of diverse schools and they are the least likely to attend them. Moreover, students today continue to be isolated from their disabled peers, who are still not included in general education in any widespread fashion.

Most recently, as a teacher educator, I also witness firsthand the failures of schools of education to attract a diverse teaching corps, both in terms of race and disability. Nationwide, although our student population is becoming increasingly diverse, our teaching force is becoming even more disproportionately White[5] (National Education Association, 2003). Moreover, schools of education that *do* attract a racially diverse student body face the damaging effects of racial bias in high-stakes teacher examinations. During my first years in a university position in Texas, for example, all of the historically Black colleges as well as the few universities with large numbers of Latino and Black students were faced with losing accreditation because minority students were not testing well on the state teacher exam. When we as a faculty met with our students to go over test practice questions, one student remarked, "Maybe we should just answer these questions like we're White!" This student, astute to the politics of knowledge, understood that the answers were not necessarily right—they were simply White.

As a former high school teacher who is currently a teacher educator in the New York City public school system, I (David) likewise see the legacy of racial divisions in my everyday work. Black and Latino students, along with recent immigrants, many from Asia, with a trickle from Europe, predominate most inner city schools. Whites, by and large, are concentrated in a few of the "best" schools, confined to a handful of geographic areas, or educated in private institutions. For the students of color in public schools, the enormous discrepancies in facilities, teaching staff, availability of supplies and materials, and parental involvement, have been widely chronicled over the years (Kohl, 1967; Kozol, 1991, 1995). People within the system—teachers, administrators, teacher aids, and service providers—rarely acknowledge that they are working within an educational apartheid. However, the situation does not *always* go unnoticed. At a recent workshop I gave, one Black teacher spoke, unsolicited, about how the only White people most of "her" children knew were their schoolteachers. She concluded, "The education system is still Jim Crow." Not one person in a room of 40 people followed up on her comment. A familiar complacency seemed to make everyone glaze over, politely waiting for the uncomfortable moment to pass. I still do not know whether to attribute failure to acknowledge her statement as a tacit acceptance of the situation or as reflecting feelings of powerlessness in the face of a long history of resistance to integrated education.

In a similar vein, there is a tacit acceptance, particularly in large urban centers, of public school classes for the disabled being filled predominantly with students of color. Before I became a high school teacher of students labeled LD or ED, I lived in vibrant, multicultural, racially mixed New York City for two years. Yet, upon entering the schools, I immediately noticed that all of the special education classes were filled with Black and Latino students, an inaccurate reflection of society, the city, and the school. When I became the point person for admission of students with disabilities, I noticed how even admissions to special education classes within the school were filtered. On two separate occasions, general education administrators commented to me, "Don't take him"—indicating the darkest skinned student in the room—and "Make a note of the girls' earrings. The bigger they are, the bigger the troublemakers they'll be." I share these private remarks to illustrate subtle and not-so-subtle ways students of color labeled disabled were viewed before being engaged in a conversation or taking an entrance examination. Seemingly innocuous to the speaker, the reference to jewelry indicated large imitation gold earrings that were in vogue particularly among the Black and Latina girls. In terms of the dark-skinned youth, the administrator had never seen him before and knew nothing of his academic record, and yet felt justified in such an assessment of him.

As I grew to know many of the students, they shared their feelings about being ashamed and embarrassed to be in special education. I was also quick to learn that not only were the students stigmatized, but special education teachers were too. Many general education teachers viewed "special" and "general" education as two different (hierarchical) worlds, which carried over into professional expectations and social groupings. As my sense of understanding disability as a political category was coalescing through these experiences, it was further crystallized by the inclusion movement.

Following a mandate from the local education authority, schools were expected to begin to transition students with "mild" disabilities into general education classrooms. As part of the nationwide Regular Education Initiative (REI), I was one of the first staff members assigned to be a team teacher. In retrospect, we were all chosen judiciously, not to rock the boat. However, the majority of staff, both special and general, did not like this idea. The students involved, by and large, liked being in a mainstream class for part of the day. As semesters passed, the REI never gathered momentum. It was a highly circumscribed approach, giving only a few students access to general education. Departmental administrators admitted they did not believe in it, but "it had to be done." Never a priority, the REI was generally seen as an inconvenience contingent upon changeable funding formulas that would likely be withdrawn. But the thrust to include students with disabilities did not disappear, and, despite resistance, eventually snowballed into the inclusion movement.

After accepting a position as a staff developer, I worked in a regional office that oversaw 40 high schools, and I developed a specialty in inclusive education. I experienced resistance to inclusion from all sides—principals, assistant principals, general and special educators. However, parents or students were generally supportive of the idea. As years went by, I noticed some important changes, especially in newer schools. On the other hand, while giving many presentations and workshops, I habitually experienced various degrees of anger, hostility, and derision from the participants. Oftentimes, I would be met with palpable apathy. In some cases, there was genuine interest and an eagerness to engage in the issues, celebrate successes, and further explore ways in which to support students with disabilities in mainstream classes. However, I found most teachers feared inclusion and simply did not want change. For example, before students were designated to be included, teachers would demand that the "right" students be selected—ones who were "ready," or "as close to functioning on grade level as possible." Their selections reveal a preference for leaving the status quo undisturbed. Ironically, according to many administrators, the litmus test of a successful inclusion class was that you wouldn't be able to tell any difference between students. Once again, teaching all students in identical ways with the same methods prevailed.

In addition to this work, I have taught as a part-time college professor, specializing in inclusive education. Although I find that students in teacher education programs almost unanimously agree with inclusion in theory, conditions in most schools steadily challenge their beliefs when it comes to practice. What this indicates, sadly, is that much of my experience has exposed me to the pervasive resistance to the integration of people with disabilities and students of color in our society.

As disability studies scholars, we both come to the issue of racial segregation with disability as an important and interconnecting lens. Our shared disciplinary background in special education, however, is historically rooted in assumptions about the value of educational stratification and a dual system of education based on "ability" and "disability." Like many critical special educators, however, we do not share these foundational assumptions within the field. Furthermore, because disability classification intersects with race, special education has inadvertently exacerbated the exclusion of students of color. Despite these overlapping exclusions, disability segregation is often thought of as a separate issue from racial segregation. Even within civil rights–conscious circles, disability always seems to be at the end of "the social contract" (Russell, 1998). In other words, whereas racial segregation is considered discriminatory to most people, segregated placements for students with disabilities are still perceived as necessary and benevolent. We were not surprised, therefore, when we noticed that AERA did not dedicate a strand to *IDEA* this year to commemorate its 30th anniversary. Similarly, we do not expect many college campuses to organize conferences and lecture series to explore the progress of *IDEA*. Although as a society we are still hypersegregated according to disability, this division does not seem to be a priority (or even, at times, a concern) to the majority of nondisabled people.

When we began this project we suspected that segregation according to race and exclusion according to disability were branches of the same poisonous plant, and, as such, they would share the same discursive roots of power, fear, misunderstanding, and intolerance. By not recognizing the connection between different forms of exclusion, neither *Brown* nor *IDEA* has been able to curb the problem of overrepresentation of students of color in special education. Their shared failures have resulted in an urban special education system filled almost exclusively with Black and Latino students. In this current system, few students graduate and the majority of those who do receive an IEP (Individualized Education Program) diploma, a qualification insufficient for entry into state and city colleges and universities.

Attending to issues of race and disability simultaneously, we can clearly see how schools play a major role in social reproduction. In our society, Black students are valued less than White students; disabled students are valued less than able-bodied students; working class students are valued less than middle class students.[6] American schooling patterns clearly reflect these values. Thus, the fewest students *removed* from regular classes are White, middle class, and nondisabled students (unless, of course, removal means being placed in classes for the gifted and talented) (Losen & Orfield, 2002). Resistance to heterogeneous classrooms by White, middle class parents has been well documented by Brantlinger (2003). She explains that the familiar lamentation of White parents that their children are not being challenged or that they are bored or not being stimulated are simply *"euphemism[s]* for their not being separated into advanced or accelerated tracks" (p. 49). It is clear that dominant-group parents expect schools to mirror, rather than disrupt, the social stratification in the larger community.

The problem of social stratification in schools is compounded by the current national push for standardized testing, in which those students who "count" the most are those who score the highest. Students who have been segregated into low-tracked classes (mainly Blacks and Latinos) and children in segregated special education classes (again, mainly Blacks and Latinos) typically do not "perform" at the same academic levels as their White and nondisabled counterparts (Heubert, 2002). Because principals are assessed based on their pass rate statistics, in the interest of self-preservation, they prefer to admit and cultivate students without significant academic problems. Students considered to be at risk of failure in effect are positioned as less worthy and even as a threat. As schools are increasingly rewarded and punished based on student scores on standardized assessments, dropout rates have risen among low-income and minority students (Orfield, 2000). Is it any wonder that in the majority of the 30 or so high schools I (David) have visited in my career, the 12th grade exiting class is only *half* the size of the 9th grade entering class?

Likewise, the practice of referring and placing large numbers of Latino and Black students in special education prior to statewide testing in order to bump up pass rates was commonly known among Texas educators that I (Beth) knew. Data now confirm that coinciding with instituting statewide assessments in Texas, for example, the "percentage of students enrolled in special education grew tremendously" (Losen & Welner, 2002, p. 184). Once the courts started to demand higher participation rates among special education students in statewide assessments, dropout rates for Black and Latino students soared to disturbingly high levels (Losen & Welner). Nationally, graduation rates of Black and Latino and Native American students in comparison to White and Asian students is strikingly poor, as are the graduation rates of disabled students compared to their nondisabled peers. Because in the daily operation of schools, race, disability, and class overlap, we must ask: Are these students dropping out, or are they being pushed out?

A fact that is difficult to ignore is that schools find multiple ways to segregate students along existing lines of inequality. Even when integration was court ordered after *Brown,* segregation simply took on different forms, such as stratified academic tracking and segregated special education placements that mirrored previous racial hierarchies. As a result, our school system continues to mirror the racial hierarchies constructed by 19th-century scientists (Gould, 1996; Lesko, 2001) and early 20th-century eugenicists (Ferri & Connor, 2004), with working class and poor Black and Latino students firmly entrenched at the bottom of the pyramid. Ayres (2004) facetiously claims that because we live in a society that is apathetic about moving toward racial equality, our country should be called "The United States of Amnesia." He questions whether we as a society are self-deceiving, telling ourselves that change has already occurred, or whether we are self-satisfied, believing that change is simply not worth pursuing? In either case, the ideals of social justice and truly democratic education continue to appear as a mirage, glistening on the horizon, but always out of reach. Although we may embrace equality and justice as a basic value, we do not expect to see it in practice.

What is clear is that the most powerless students in the current system fall between the cracks of *IDEA* and *Brown.* They are the large percentage of minority children confined to self-contained special education classes. To borrow a phrase from Bell (1992), these are the students who are "at the bottom of the well" (p. ix). And although *Brown* dismantled *legal* educational apartheid in this country, it was beyond the scope and power of *Brown* to compel one group to accept another as social or academic equals. Nor did *Brown* counteract the ability of schools to find new ways or new justifications to segregate students through tracking and special education. Like *Brown, IDEA* opened the doors to disabled children, but unlike *Brown,* it has only encouraged, not *required,* schools to educate disabled children with their nondisabled peers and only to the extent the school deems possible or appropriate. Moreover, neither *Brown* nor *IDEA* adequately predicted the multiple forms of resistance and reassertions of power that would emerge to keep general education an exclusive privilege for some, but not for all.

We believe that real change can only come about if we begin to think critically about all kinds of exclusions and how they work in tandem. When the teacher commented about the educational system being "Jim Crow," *we all knew* that she was right. Yet we also knew the situation was not usually talked about in those terms. Even in the discourse of inclusion, issues of race have been largely absent (A. Smith, 2001). Moreover, although we know that overrepresentation of students of color reflects bias, the problem remains. The question we must ask to push us from complacency is: What are we prepared to do about it? We must begin by challenging the beliefs, expectations, and habits of mind about what has come to pass as "normal" or "business as usual" in the field of education.

As critical special educators we do not feel at ease in either special or general education as they are currently configured. Although we believe the creation of special education was well meaning, by sustaining a *separate* system for students labeled disabled, the system runs counter to our beliefs about democracy. We likewise cannot reconcile the supposed beneficent view of special education with its deep implication in matters of both racism and ableism. We find that disability studies is a useful tool to bring out different perspectives, alternative histories, and marginalized voices, especially of those labeled disabled. Rather than embracing one particular perspective, disability studies encourages multiple standpoints from which to analyze and critique cultural practices and beliefs about schools and the world that creates them.

It is our hope that this book will have the power to influence people's thinking about human difference and encourage dialogue about the connections between race and disability. We believe that ideas can transform societal practices. However, if the educational system barely changes decade after decade, then it is not by accident but intention (or at least inattention). Uncovering the interconnections between race and disability requires us to go beyond the usual parameters of thought. We must look behind current practices and peel away the thick, protective skin of the status quo. We must do more than document glaring inequities. We must continue to ask hard questions: How did we get to this place? Who benefits from these arrangements? In what ways do various forms of privilege interconnect? What forces have shaped our education system to be this way? Where do forces of resistance originate? How do they operate? And, most importantly, what can be done? In untangling the various forms of resistance to integrated schooling, we strive to encounter new truths, new ways of thinking that offer the potential to shape and guide our words and actions in ways that shift practice to match our democratic ideals.

Theoretical Grounding

Our project is grounded in interdisciplinary and critical approaches to disability studies in education, which makes possible alternative models for understanding disability (Gabel & Danforth, 2002). Thus, we analyze disability as a social, political, cultural, and discursive phenomenon rather than an individual or medical one (Linton, 1998). A key idea within disability studies is that disability is constructed within social, cultural, historical, legal, and medical discourses, and is further complicated by race, ethnicity, gender, age, sexual orientation, and class. Because disability is always entangled with other social markers, a disability studies orientation requires that we attend to the ways that racism and ableism interdepend.

Our work is further influenced by feminist disability studies scholars such as Price and Shildrick (1998), who argue that to consider "every form of embodiment not as a fixed category, but as a fluid, shifting set of conditions" thwarts attempts to think in terms of pregiven, stable identity categories and binaries (p. 246). Thus, we consider all categories as porous and unstable, requiring constant reiteration by disciplinary regimes set in place in order to patrol their borders. Simply put, categories always function as artificially constructed dividers between self and other. These borders, however, are false, reducing complexity and ignoring differences among individuals in any one category. After borders are constructed, they must be maintained—individuals must be made to fit available categories of difference. Segregation, we argue, is one such form of containing diversity, fulfilling its purpose of reproducing and managing difference.

We draw particular insight from Black feminists, who have argued that because race and gender intertwine, an intersectional analysis is essential to understand the unique social location of Black women who experience simultaneous race and gender oppression (P. H. Collins, 1991). Building on these theoretical insights, we assert that only an intersectional analysis of ableism and racism captures the interactive social processes faced by students of color who are labeled disabled. Because racism and ableism are not single, isolated systems of oppression, but are interconnected and interdependent social forces, we focus on how racist notions of ability reinforce the classroom as a normative and exclusionary space.

Methods

Range of Data

To explore how the interconnected discourses of race and ability have been used to maintain and justify a segregated educational system, we collected editorials, opinion editorials (op-eds), political cartoons, and letters to the editor from a range of publications, in the years during and after the *Brown* decision, 1953–1956. Data included editorial pages from the *New York Times*,[7] *Atlanta Journal and Constitution*,[8] and the *Washington Post*,[9] as well as several important Black independent newspapers, including *Atlanta Daily World*,[10] *Richmond Afro-American*,[11] *Philadelphia Tribune*,[12] and *Chicago Defender*.[13] This range of papers represents northern and southern presses as well as "mainstream" and "independent" publications (not coincidentally divided along lines of race). Another key data source was the "What They Say" column in *Southern School News*. Financed by the Ford Foundation, this monthly publication synthesized coverage of desegregation in newspapers from around the country, providing access to a broad array of opinions across many states. In publication from 1954 to 1965 and boasting a circulation of 30,000 at its peak, *Southern School News* was considered the "bible" on school desegregation (Cumming, 2003).

In total, our data on desegregation collected from these papers included more than 800 photocopied pages of text. Approximately 389 of those pages were from the Black press, 315 pages from the three White presses and *Southern School News*, and the remaining pages comprise more than 100 editorial cartoons.

In an effort to explore the parallels and differences between debates about the implementation of inclusion and those about desegregation, we then collected editorials, op-eds, and letters to the editor from the same publications (except *Southern School News*) from 1987 to 2002 covering the inclusion of students with disabilities in general education classrooms. We chose this 15-year span because discussions about inclusion were arguably the most intense during this time period, particularly after the reauthorization of *IDEA* in 1997. In addition, because desegregation and inclusion were not comparable in terms of editorial coverage, we then cast a wider net and included other newspapers in the U.S., as well as some international publications, mainly from the U.K., which has a parallel history of inclusion. It is interesting to note that although there was a plethora of political cartoons relating to *Brown*, there were none that we found depicting inclusion. In our total data set for inclusion, we collected approximately 200 photocopied pages from the mainstream press and 45 from the Black press.

By focusing on editorial pages, we explored neither specific court actions nor professional debates in academic journals or other publications. We also did not focus our analysis on news stories, although occasionally we did take note of feature stories that included interviews or those that provided important context to various letters or editorials. Instead, we focused on how ideas about race and ability were manifest in the everyday discursive context of the editorial page at two important and somewhat parallel times in the history of American education. We describe editorial pages as everyday discourse for several reasons. First, the presumed readership of the newspaper as a whole is much broader than the anticipated audience of research reports, professional papers, or court briefs. Second, newspapers, particularly editorial pages, because they invite readers to respond in the form of letters to the editor, facilitate dialogue among various constituents. Finally, in everyday places from living rooms to front porches, bars to barbershops, beauty parlors to bodegas, newspapers are an important part of private and public conversations. By collecting editorials from both "White" and "Black" presses,[14] we aimed to gather a diverse range of opinions. We do not suggest that newspapers include every voice or perspective, but that within the editorial page there is typically a range of perspectives from a range of people—some journalists and professional writers and some everyday people who feel compelled to comment on the issue of the day. In our analysis, each voice is given equal weight—although we could not help but notice when we encountered letters and columns from such notable people as Mary McLeod Bethune, Langston Hughes, and Lillian Smith.

In summary, we focus on the editorial page as our unit of analysis: a unique social space where divergent opinions and voices are represented for (and sometimes by) a popular audience. By analyzing editorials, political cartoons, letters to the editors, and op-ed pieces usually written by columnists or contributing writers who are often considered experts, across a range of newspapers with different audiences, we create a space where no single point of view dominates or claims absolute authority (see Tanaka, 1997). In other words, we were less interested in attempting to document the "official" opinion of any particular newspaper or editor, and more interested in documenting a full range of complex and even contradictory public opinions on the issues of school desegregation and inclusion.

Analysis and Representation of Data

In mapping out ways to present the data for the book, we engaged in several methodological experiments with interruption, deliberately working to keep the lines between these two histories fluid and in play. Rather than collapsing one history into another, we wanted to explore how juxtaposition could offer a more nuanced understanding of segregation and inclusion. We found ourselves wanting to "move beyond the impulse to represent 'the real story'" and struggling with the impossibility of telling the whole story of desegregation and inclusion (Britzman, 2000, p. 31). We therefore sought a method that would highlight concurrence, complexity, multiplicity, and nonlinearity. We wanted our work to trouble official histories and origin stories, to acknowledge the dynamic interplays of power/ knowledge between racism and ableism, and to uncover how special education became one of "the conditions of possibility" (Kendall & Wickham, 1999, p. 37) for resegregating education. We considered a variety of metaphors for "staging" our work such as textual counterpoint, mosaic, and montage (Richardson, 2000, p. 157). Ultimately we settled on a nonparallel format that would enact Bakhtin's notion of a "word with a sideways glance" (P. Morris, 1994, p. 20) and which would also have the montage effect of an editorial page. Our goal was *not* to create a parallel structure to present our data, but to create a space where each discourse would interact with the other in a conversational or call-and-response manner.

Guided by Foucault's genealogical method, we attended carefully to discourse (Rabinow, 1984) to illustrate how the general public participated in exclusion through everyday language practices (P. H. Collins, 1998). We viewed discourse as "a way of representing knowledge about a particular topic at a particular historical moment" (Hall, 1997a, p. 44). We concur with disability studies scholar Susan Gabel (2001), who suggests that a discursive approach "holds great hope for . . . educational research because it has the potential to account for political, cultural, social, and economic contexts" (p. 2). In our analysis we note the various strategies of verbal and visual rhetoric that worked to shape and produce widespread understandings of race and ability. By analyzing how various people justified their beliefs and actions, our work builds on P. H. Collins (1991), who demonstrates the importance of everyday epistemologies and meanings as forms of social theorizing. Her work also helps us to see the importance of analyzing the matrices of domination across social categories and attending to everyday and institutional resistance to integrated education at the same time it points toward strategies for initiating change.

We also examine the rules that constitute the way things are, how they influence what can (and cannot) be said, and ascertain what forces influence new strategies that resist or maintain the status quo. We found it useful to think about Foucault's concepts of archeology and genealogy as complementary tools for working with discourse. Archeology is useful in excavating a "historical slice" and opening it up for further inquiry. Genealogy helps to *explain* a problematic aspect of present-day history—in this case, overrepresentation and segregated schooling—by examining the origins and functions of such practices. In other words, genealogy is concerned with how things have come to be the way they are, rather than unquestioningly accepting official stories (Rose, in Kendall & Wickham, 1999). Most importantly, genealogy emphasizes the inextricable link between power and knowledge in tracing how discourses change and shift over time.

To summarize our theoretical positioning, we consider racism and ableism not as discrete forms of oppression, but rather as interconnected and interdependent social forces. As stated earlier, however, our intention is not to draw a simple analogy between racist and ableist discourses, but rather to show how, for example, overlapping rhetorics of race and disability have been used to justify exclusion. Thus, we have focused on the ways exclusion and segregation were taken up in both contexts, recycling modes of power while redefining types of student-subjects and modes of educational practice. In addition, rather than try to tell a linear history, we focus on particular historical moments when, as old forms of segregation and pathologizing of race were being dismantled, new forms of exclusion were springing up to replace them.

Format of the Book

In the remaining chapters, we focus on specific themes that either emerged from our data analysis or extend our understanding of these findings. Although the chapters are interrelated to some degree, they can also stand alone. We conclude each chapter with a discussion of the implications of our findings in a section titled "Lessons Learned." In chapter 8, we summarize these lessons from each section and speculate on the importance of working across categories of difference. In the remaining section we briefly outline each chapter.

In chapter 2, *Strange Bedfellows: Race and Disability in U.S. History,* we place the problem of overrepresentation in a wider historical context. We focus on moments when the conflation of race and ability figured into the American psyche. Drawing a connection between disability and race in the scientific imagination and in educational practice, we review some of the long-standing perceptions that *Brown* attempted to disrupt. We contemplate how public perception about race and dis/ability was shaped by the eugenics movement. In keeping with our focus on everyday discourse, we examine eugenics posters and educational materials displayed at state fairs around the country, particularly during the 1920s and 1930s, to show how racialized notions of ability taught to the general public helped to further marginalize people of color.

We argue that unacknowledged vestiges of eugenics-based thinking provided the necessary justification for the overrepresentation of students of color in special education. These ideas became further rationalized by the widespread use of intelligence tests, which provided an authorized discourse for labeling students of color with the "official" categories of mental retardation and emotional disturbance. These labels relied on assumptions that associated people of color with feeblemindedness and criminality. We also illustrate how the testing movement authorized already-established public attitudes and stereotypes about racial hierarchies of ability.

In chapter 3, *Race, Ability, and (Re)segregated Education,* we begin to explore the interconnections between special education and school resegregation after *Brown.* Although previous scholars have implicated the use of ability tracking as a strategy to resegregate schools along racial lines after *Brown* (Mickelson, 2001; Oakes, 1985), we break new ground and extend this discussion by asserting that special education served a similar purpose.

In this chapter we focus primarily on ideas about change that were reflected in the public debates about desegregation and inclusion. A central lesson we take from this chapter is the futility of incremental or gradual change, which allowed those who were interested in maintaining the status quo to institute new strategies to circumvent or subvert change, rather than time to adjust or prepare for it.

We also note the danger and ineffectiveness of single-issue or categorical approaches to educational reform. Specifically, we highlight how *Brown* did not predict that schools would develop new forms of segregation based on biased notions of ability. Similarly, because *IDEA* did not address issues of racial inequity and bias, we interrogate how it too failed to consider how dominant ideas about ability would be used to maintain White, middle class privilege through the disproportionate placement of students of color in special education categories. In both cases, failing to consider the intersections of race and dis/ability allowed schools to maintain the status quo of segregated schooling.

In chapter 4, *Power, Race, and Re/presentation: Political Cartoons of the* Brown *Era,* we analyze 28 political cartoons published in the years around the *Brown* decision in both mainstream and Black-owned presses. We explore how these cultural images re/presented race. Using the work of Hall (1997a) to guide us in deconstructing political cartoons and Barthes's (1977) notions of denaturalizing mythical images, we explore racial representation within a social and political context. As cultural texts, political cartoons are artifacts in which meaning is constructed and/or contested. By using a discursive approach to race, we trouble the "natural order" of race not as a "real" distinction, but as a signifier of difference created by colonizing ideologies of Western culture. Hence, our concern is with "the *effects and consequences* of representation—its 'politics'" (Hall, 1997a, p. 6).

Using a three-pronged approach to analyze the signifier (material images, objects, sounds), signified (mental representation), and sign (associative total of image and concept), we first explore the relationships between knowledge and power in terms of "racial" identity. In the second phase we cross-analyze each set of images (White and Black presses) to examine how the visible/sayable and the invisible/unsayable in each of these contexts reified race in particular ways. This cross-analysis of cartoons from both mainstream and Black presses illustrates startling differences in terms of racial representation. We conclude by noting the significant impact cultural texts have in enforcing or challenging perceptions of people differentiated by social and political power.

In chapter 5, *Challenging Normalcy: Dis/ability, Race, and the Normalized Classroom,* we analyze both the hopes and fears of desegregation and inclusion by focusing on the predictions that were made in response to each of these watershed educational reforms. By carefully listening to some of the more resistant and hopeful of voices in the editorial pages, we explore what was perceived to be at stake in mandates of integration. In other words, we attend to both the threat and promise that race and disability posed to the normative space of the classroom.

Examining the emergence of the concept of "normalcy" in 19th-century European thought, we trace the relationship between schools and governmental desire to standardize students in preparation for a socially stratified workforce. The creation of average/normal citizens as a state imperative provided the impetus for developing mechanisms to sift out "problem" students from mainstream classrooms. By removing students who were seen as deviating from established norms, educators reinforced the classroom as a normative space. The response to desegregation and inclusion teach us important lessons about what happens when the "sacred space" of the classroom is challenged by those who have been positioned as outsiders. By juxtaposing these various predictions, we illustrate how the mainstream classroom, constructed through its exclusions, will always be a contested space.

In chapter 6, *The Power of Persuasion: Making (Non)Sense of Exclusion,* we focus on the specific rhetorical strategies and language games that proponents used to advance their arguments for or against integrated education. We point out specific strategies, including appeals to patriotism, morality, and intelligence, as well as the use of metaphors and imagery. Through a careful and critical reading of these letters, editorials, and cartoons and their presumed audience, we unearth the embedded assumptions about power, normalcy, and citizenship operating within these discourses.

In addition to the strategies used by the dominant group to maintain the status quo of segregated schooling, the specific strategies of resistance within outsider discourses illustrate how marginalized groups use particular language practices as powerful tools to enact social change. We draw on the work of Bakhtin to demonstrate how language, particularly within the dialogic space of the editorial page, is a site of ideological struggle infused with webs of power and resistance.

In chapter 7, *Shared Legacies:* Brown *and the Counterpull of Inclusion,* we focus more narrowly on the history and growth of special education. We describe how technologies associated with special education, such as constant redefinition of standards and norms, testing, labeling, and tracking *produce* new student types and new ways to justify exclusion. Redefining students of color within the discourse of disability thereby validates their removal from "general" education and their containment in special classes. The expansion of disability categories, particularly the "soft" labels of mental retardation, emotional disturbance, and learning disability, further facilitates the removal of students of color based on more subjective criteria.

In the second part of this chapter, we explore how the least restrictive environment clause of *IDEA* has been used not to facilitate inclusion but to justify the widespread exclusion of students with disabilities. We link the inclusion of students with disabilities as both an important legacy of *Brown* and an integral step in achieving the promise of *Brown*. Finally, by outlining a brief history of inclusion, we chart the movement's counterpull against the continued containment of students of color and students with disabilities.

In chapter 8, *Learning from* Brown: *The Future of Democratic Schooling,* we contemplate the potential contributions of disability studies and multiculturalism to debates about integrated education. We argue that in order to counteract persistent attempts to segregate and exclude marginalized students, a broader, all-encompassing, and intersectional vision of inclusion needs to be cultivated. The normative classroom, standardized curriculum, and traditional approaches to teaching and learning must all be reevaluated and made accountable in terms of inclusion and access. We argue the need for teacher education programs to place issues of difference, otherness, and social responsibility at the center of curricula and teaching. We must also recognize that despite our disappointments, the push for social justice is also evident in racially integrated schools and inclusive classrooms around the country. These spaces of possibility represent the promise of both *Brown* and *IDEA* and lay the groundwork for us to cultivate the discourses of inclusion.

2

STRANGE BEDFELLOWS: RACE AND DISABILITY IN U.S. HISTORY

2

STRANGE BEDFELLOWS: RACE AND DISABILITY IN U.S. HISTORY

Introduction

Brown v. Board of Education maintains a ubiquitous presence in our ideas about educational access and inclusion, and there remains much to learn from its 50 years of struggle. To tell the origin story for this project, we must begin with a "big glossy"[1] special education textbook. This particular textbook was not distinct in form or content from the barrage of similar course books that arrive in departmental offices from major publishers each year. Leafing through it, however, a particular chart came to the fore, a reprint from a U.S. Department of Education publication titled, "Selected legal cases related to special education" ("National agenda," 1993, pp. 6–8). Like the textbook, the chart was not unusual; similar graphic representations show up in many introductory texts. What was interesting about this chart (and others like it) is that it included *Brown v. Board of Education* as the first legal case related to special education. The remaining list included cases that, unlike *Brown,* were all decisions that specifically related to students with disabilities. The precedent that *Brown* offers special education is the idea that segregating any "class" or group of children, even if done in equal facilities, is inherently unequal under the 14th Amendment of the U.S. Constitution because of the unavoidable stigma associated with separating students from the mainstream. Of course, *Brown* was *not* a special education decision, per se. Nonetheless, our thinking was piqued: What *is* the relationship between *Brown* and special education? Is it as easy as one civil rights movement building upon another—or is the history far more complicated than this tidy chart implies?

Early in our research into newspaper coverage of the *Brown* decision, we came across a letter to the *New York Times* editor written by noted author and activist, Lillian Smith. In her letter Smith (1954) celebrates *Brown* as "every child's Magna Charta" (p. 10E). We were particularly interested in her correspondence, because it was the first explicit link we were able to find between *Brown* and students with disabilities. In her letter Smith writes:

> There are perhaps five million children in the United States who are colored. There are close to five million other children who will be directly affected by this decision. I am not speaking of the majority of White children, many whom have undoubtedly been injured spiritually by the philosophy and practice of segregation. I am speaking of disabled children, who . . . we have also segregated. (p. 10E)

In the letter she also criticizes the 40 states that then had laws enforcing the exclusion of students who were blind, deaf, "crippled," or who had epilepsy, cerebral palsy, speech defects, and "those that we call 'retarded'" (p. 10E) from attending public schools. Smith writes that many disabled children are kept out of school not because they are "unable to attend, but because there are teachers who do not want to teach them" (p. 10E). Here Smith communicates an emerging social view of disability, that students are excluded not because of their impairments, but because teachers are unwilling to teach them. She also understands that the term "retarded" is a label, not an inherent quality or attribute. Her letter might be understood as prophetic about the impact of *Brown* on students with disabilities, although 20 years would elapse before disability-focused legislation would be passed.

Once enacted, however, disability legislation *did* draw heavily on the logic set forth in *Brown*. The major disability law in education, P.L. 94–142 (now referred to as *IDEA*), used *Brown* as its legal precedent. In making the case, lawyers employed a similar strategy of arguing for the rights of students with disabilities to a free and appropriate public education as an issue of equal protection under the 14th Amendment. Yet, because special education largely developed as a parallel system of education, with separate funding streams, teaching certifications, methodologies, and classrooms—reinforced by specialized academic departments, professional organizations, and publications—it could also be seen as a throwback to *Plessy v. Ferguson* (1896) or as a Jim Crow endeavor. In other words, although the law ensured access to education, it simultaneously created the possibility for two entirely separate school systems—as separate as Jim Crow water fountains and White and Black schools. Thus, while legislation, like *Brown* and *IDEA,* demanded access to public schooling, the access for students with disabilities often stopped short of the general education classroom door. Later special education reforms, like inclusion, drew quite self-consciously not simply on the logic, but also on the spirit of *Brown* to argue that *all* forms of segregated schooling, including segregated special education classes, were inherently discriminatory. From this vantage point the inclusion movement is certainly a testament to *Brown*'s wide-reaching and continued influence on matters of educational access and equity. Unfortunately, because inclusion *is* in many ways a legacy of *Brown,* it is also subject to the same risks of subversion and failure that have undermined school desegregation. On both accounts, however, *IDEA* and inclusion have much to learn from their older legal sibling.

And yet, it is not so easy to draw straight lines when it comes to history. To do so requires erasing or ignoring moments of backlash and negative momentum, as well as times when histories get crossed or entangled. For example, to talk only about special education as a legacy of *Brown* ignores ways that special education, like academic tracking and ability grouping, was used to resegregate *within* schools after court-ordered desegregation. Also erased is the *continued* problem of over-representation of students of color in special education (Losen & Orfield, 2002) and the increased restrictiveness of placements that students of color experience in schools (Fierros & Conroy, 2002). Thus, we argue that the past and present experiences of students of color in special education illustrate how special education has actually hindered the progress of racial desegregation set in motion by the historic *Brown* decision.

Moreover, when we collapse these two histories we also ignore ways that even critical educators, who find the continued racial segregation in schools a failure of *Brown* and overrepresentation of students of color a failure of special education, maintain that segregating students with "real" disabilities is justified. From their perspective, disability (unless it is a function of racial or ethnic bias) is a "real" reason for segregating students, whereas race or ethnicity is not. Although recognizing the social construction of race, these scholars continue to regard disability as an ahistorical, apolitical, and asocial marker of difference (Mitchell & Snyder, 2003). This explains why race is often understood as a group identity, whereas disability is perceived to be an individual one (Mitchell & Snyder). In other words, the "tendency has been to view people with disabilities as a) victimized by a disabling condition, and b) in need of treatment—not of rights" (Biklen, 1988, p. 128).

Similarly, we have yet to see sufficient scholarly attention paid to the intersection of race, class, and dis/ability beyond simply documenting the continued problem of overrepresentation of students of color in special education. Although documentation is an important precursor to increased understanding of the problem, this increased understanding must lead to the implementation of large-scale solutions to overrepresentation. There also remains a lack of recognition and an undertheorizing of how various forms of exclusion interconnect. As a result, we have little insight into how to enact real change across categories of difference and oppression. One of the lessons we take from *Brown* is that individuals and institutions must address complicities and inconsistencies between our stated ideologies and our actual practices. We must adopt more synergistic models for school reform to fully address multiple and intersecting inequalities and exclusions (A. Smith, 2001).

In this chapter we take a more detailed look at what we consider an important and usually overlooked (or for obvious reasons, downplayed) aspect of U.S. history, namely, the eugenics movement. We focus on eugenics because of its influence in "shaping educational thought and practice" and justifying school segregation (Valencia, 1997, p. 9). Because it exerted so much influence in the first decades of the 20th century, and because of its "disastrous legacies" (Mitchell & Snyder, 2003, p. 845), eugenics deserves a more critical analysis in terms of both race and disability. Scholars in many fields of study, including disability studies, have argued that "scientific" thinking has long been privileged over all other forms of knowledge. Conceptualizations of race and disability, which dovetailed during this era, illuminate how misinformed and dangerous so-called "objective" knowledge claims can be.

Eugenic thinking was a mindset that fused ideology and science (Valencia, 1997) in ways that fortified existing modes of racism and ableism. It permeated the curriculum, influenced social policy, and swayed public opinion. Eugenic circles in the U.S. included a tight-knit and powerful group of scientists (Valencia, 1997)—all White and upper class—who were intent on promulgating notions of racial purity, ability, and superiority. Tragically, support for eugenics culminated in Nazi Germany, where a self-proclaimed master race sanctioned the imprisonment and genocide of Jews, homosexuals, Gypsies, and disabled people. Although these extreme actions did not take place in the U.S., they were born nonetheless of American and British scientific thought and illustrate what can happen when the humanness of a particular group is called into question.

Race and Disability in the Scientific Imagination

Steven Selden (1999) traces the history of the eugenics movement in the United States during the early decades of the 20th century. The term *eugenics* is derived from the Greek term meaning "well born" (Dwyer, 2003, p. 107). As a social and scientific movement, first developed by Sir Francis Galton (cousin of Charles Darwin), eugenics blended ideas from Darwin's theory of natural selection with turn-of-the-century ideas about genetics and heredity (Selden, 1999). Historically, the movement had two major aims: first, to restrict the breeding of individuals considered to be "unfit"; and, second, to encourage selective breeding of society's most "fit." The social engineering of "careful" breeding was postulated as necessary for the "betterment of society" (Pfeiffer, 1994, p. 493). To accomplish their goals, eugenicists "lobbied to keep racial and ethnic groups separate, to restrict immigration from southern and eastern Europe, and to sterilize people considered 'genetically unfit'" (Dolan DNA learning center, last visited August 2004).

Leaders of the eugenics movement, influenced by Social Darwinism, located all manner of social ills, including degeneracy, poverty, criminality, and immorality in heredity (Selden, 2000; Valencia, 1997). At its most fundamental level eugenics was steeped in deficit thinking, which traced all perceived inferiority to genetic pathology (Valencia, 1997). The category of "feeblemindedness," in particular, was used to denote any number of real and supposed mental disabilities. It was a catch-all term, commonly attributed to members of ethnic and racial minority groups, as well as poor and working class Whites (Valencia, 1997). The category of "unfit" was elastic and slippery. It relied on grouping a whole cast of social others, including racial and ethnic minorities, as well as other "classes" of people—epileptics, alcoholics, disabled people, poor people, prostitutes and others—into one "distinct class" of defectives (Snyder & Mitchell, 2002). Blamed for their own inequality, those labeled unfit were seen as a "'disease' plaguing society," eliciting a sense of both fear and urgency in dominant classes about the "spread" of feeblemindedness (Carey, 2003, p. 412). People were divided into either healthy or diseased classes, and the unfit were characterized as a "cancer" or a "parasite" on society (Proctor, 1995, p. 173). Eugenics, of course, became the cure of choice—a vaccine aimed to prevent the spread of dis/ease and to disinfect the nation's gene pool. Because the unfit were perceived as a menace or threat to the health and wealth of the nation, they were subject to various forms of state-sanctioned control.

Eugenics was first imported to the U.S. from Britain and later exported to Germany to become the basis of Nazi ideology and genocide (A. Shapiro, 2000). It could be said that eugenics was one of the first examples of a global discourse (Baker, 2002) or a "multi-national conversation" (Mitchell & Snyder, 2003, p. 845). In a "mutual project of human exclusion," eugenicists in the U.S., Europe, and Canada aimed to banish deviance from the trans-Atlantic gene pool (Mitchell & Snyder, p. 844). Their strategy included various interconnected phases, including sterilization, incarceration, euthanasia, and taken to the extreme, even genocide (Proctor, 1995).

In Germany, the Nazis began their so-called euthanasia program (called T4) by first killing disabled children and institutionalized adults, who were considered "unworthy of life" (A. Shapiro, 2000, p. 222). In 1939, Hitler declared the beginning of what would become the Final Solution as the year of the "duty to be healthy" and all those who were institutionalized were first targeted to either be "cured or killed" (Proctor, 1995, pp. 170–171). Defined as a financial drain on society, disabled people were referred to by the Nazis as "useless eaters" (Proctor, p. 171). In the Nazi worldview, "mental infirmity, moral depravity, criminality, and racial impurity" were all interconnected in one lethal and expansive discourse (Proctor, p. 181). Tragically, between 1939 and the end of the war, 240,000 people with disabilities were systematically murdered by the Nazis (Mitchell & Snyder, 2003). The progression from eugenics to euthanasia to full-scale genocide of the Holocaust is an important chapter in the history of race and disability that warrants further study.[2] In keeping with our interest in everyday discourse, however, our focus will be on the public information campaigns of the eugenic era in the U.S., which were popularized in the decades leading up to the *Brown* decision.

The center of American eugenics research from the 1920s to the 1940s was the Eugenics Record Office at Cold Spring Harbor on Long Island, New York.[3] Selden (1999, 2000) illustrates how leaders of the eugenics movement sought out public venues during the so-called Progressive Era to influence public opinion about the dangers posed by certain classes of people. In a "carefully orchestrated public relations campaign" (Mitchell & Snyder, 2003, p. 856), eugenicists enlisted the "pedagogical power of visual displays" (Wilson, 2002, p. 52) and developed a wide range of materials for educational conferences (including the

National Education Association conference). In addition, they sought to sway the public by influencing curriculum in high school and college textbooks, promoting quasi-educational films[4] and religious sermon contests, and by printing pamphlets, which were widely disseminated. They also created traveling exhibits that were displayed at state fairs around the country.[5] Designed with rural farmers in mind, eugenic "lessons" purposely drew "parallels between human reproduction and livestock breeding or crop production" to emphasize how a litany of negative traits such as feeblemindedness or mental deficiency, shiftlessness, criminality, insanity, alcoholism, pauperism, epilepsy, and even prostitution were the result of bad heredity (Wilson, 2002, p. 61).

Analogously, meritorious traits such as intelligence, morality, leadership, and physical strength were thought to result from the selective breeding of "good" genes (Selden, 1999). It should be no surprise that White individuals from upper and middle classes were deemed "fit," whereas those of other races and social classes were seen as potentially "unfit." Thus, exhibits and educational materials upheld eugenic ideas about biological determinism and constructed "merit, race, and disability" in ways that "further empower[ed] the already powerful" (Selden, 2000, p. 236). Certainly, the seduction of "eugenics was embodied in the simplicity of [its] empirical schema"—one was either normal or defective (Snyder & Mitchell, 2002, p. 84). Furthermore, the binary schema of fit and unfit, normal and defective, matched existing social hierarchies and established ideas about race and ability operating in society. In gaining such widespread currency, eugenics solidified heredity as the dominant explanation of human difference during this time (Valencia, 1997). Fueled by social anxieties about an increasingly diverse population resulting from urbanization, industrialization, immigration, and migration of African Americans (Valencia, 1997), eugenics was not simply an academic endeavor. Merging science and politics, eugenics legitimized existing power relations between dominant and nondominant groups. Proponents also used eugenic thinking to exert direct political, material and social consequences on those deemed unfit (Selden, 1999; Valencia, 1997).

Eugenics infused scientific legitimacy to racism by affiliating with and influencing the developing field of mental measurement. To do this they drew on a concept borrowed from early mathematics, the error or bell curve, which was used to predict errors in astrological sightings and for explaining games of chance. An important link in the chain between Galton's use of the bell curve and the early mathematicians' concept of the error curve, was Quetlet, a quantitative social scientist, who first applied the error curve to social phenomena to come up with the concept of the "average man" (Goertzel, n.d.). In coming up with this idea, however, Quetlet ignored that the social world rarely fits simple mathematical formulas and many human attributes are not normally distributed. Moreover, he failed to account for an inherent flaw in the error curve, which states that the greater the amount of error, the greater likelihood you will end up with a normal distribution (Goertzel, n.d.). Nonetheless, in Quetlet's formulation, the mean distribution for any physical human attribute was taken as the ideal. Galton continued to ignore these methodological flaws and applied the error curve to a host of human traits including intelligence, and then converted his data into standard scores, which could then be averaged together even though the variables would be unrelated and unduly influenced by social forces. Galton and others would continue to use the bell curve to bolster eugenic ideologies, ignoring methodological flaws and inappropriately applying it to social and clinical contexts (Goertzel, n.d.).

Newly designed tests[6] helped to validate the idea that mental ability was innate and "normally" distributed, an idea that remains "one of the most entrenched assumptions in psychology" (Valencia, 1997, p. 60). After Binet's intelligence test was translated, it quickly became the "cornerstone of Goddard's research" (Pfeiffer, 1994, p. 492). It also helped to launch a host of school reforms, such as academic tracking and differentiated curriculum based on a student's predicted "educability" (Valencia, 1997). Of course, the fact that these tests yielded intellectual hierarchies between ethnic and racial groups was not thought to reflect cultural bias in the tests, but rather to "prove" the superiority of the dominant White and upper classes (Oakes et al., 1997; Valencia, 1997).

In what Snyder and Mitchell (2002) call a "frenzy of assessment," a whole host of new professional disciplines "flocked to participate in the identification, 'care,' and training of those labeled 'feebleminded'" (p. 82). Interestingly, many of the most prominent eugenicists of the time "were employed by or worked in association with state institutions for individuals with disabilities" (Kliewer & Drake, 1998, p. 99). The emergence of the "helping" professions greatly expanded the ability of professionals to control the lives of people with disabilities. Many of these same therapeutic professions, such as medicine, psychology, social work, and special education, as well as various humanitarian agencies and charities, continue to dominate the management of disability today (Mitchell & Snyder, 2003).

Professionals entrusted with the tasks of care and treatment of disability, however, took on the new role of social engineer (Carey, 2003). They participated in various ways in a significant shift in psychology from studying commonalities to a sustained hyperfocus on difference (Valencia, 1997). Schools, in particular, played an important sorting function through their "systematized watching" and sorting of students (Baker, 2002). In a merging of medicine and education, schools became critical sites for this surveillance and school officials were increasingly entrusted with controlling, diagnosing, and policing difference (Baker, 2002; Carey, 2003; Snyder & Mitchell, 2002; Valencia, 1997). Once identified with one of an ever-expanding list of disability labels, "defective" students were segregated in ungraded classes—a precursor to modern-day special education (Snyder & Mitchell, 2002). These lower tracked classes were designed to prepare students for manual and low wage labor (Danforth & Smith, 2005).

More than simply a descriptive or even an explanative model of difference, eugenics was also seen as having predictive and even prescriptive value (Valencia, 1997). Thus, Terman advocated the use of formalized assessments to determine which type of curriculum (i.e., vocational or academic) students would have access to depending on their level of educability (Baker, 2002; Valencia, 1997). Of course, any differences in performance on these assessments were attributed to heredity and innate inferiority. Language or cultural differences, for example, were dismissed as irrelevant variables for "Latin" students, a group that included Mexicans, Portuguese, and Italians (Valencia, 1997). Even today, in its categorical approach to disability, special education pays scant attention to contextual or sociocultural factors (K. M. Collins, 2003; A. Smith, 2001). As data on tracking and overrepresentation of students of color in special education suggest, schools perform an important gatekeeping function, sorting children in ways that mirror the social stratification of the larger society. K. M. Collins refers to the ranking and sorting function of schools as a form of "ability profiling" that marks students of color as particularly suspect. Thus, rather than equalizing opportunities between marginalized and privileged groups, education serves instead to legitimate the status quo (Valencia, 1997). Despite the long-standing knowledge of the problem, the fact that schools continue to segregate students along lines of race, class, and gender is perhaps the most submerged aspect of public schooling (Baker, 2002).

Eugenicists in the U.S. were also the first to push for the legalization of forced sterilization of those deemed unfit. Well into the 20th century, sterilization continued to be considered a "common remedy for 'feeblemindedness'" (Pfeiffer, 1994, p. 482). In an important early test case for legalizing involuntary sterilization, *Buck v. Bell* (1927), a 17-year-old woman named Carrie Buck, who became pregnant after being raped by a member of her foster family, was admitted to the Virginia Colony for Epileptics and Feeble Minded (Selden, 1999). This was the same institution where her mother had been placed for prostitution. When Carrie's child, Vivian, was mistakenly deemed mentally deficient based solely on her physical appearance, the state sought to sterilize Carrie. Delivering the Supreme Court decision in 1927, which upheld the state of Virginia's right to sterilize Carrie Buck, Oliver Wendell Holmes, Jr. proclaimed, "Three generations of imbeciles are enough" (Selden, 1999, p. 130). Similar legislation was enacted in 33 states and an estimated 63,000 Americans were sterilized without their own or their family's consent (Pfeiffer, 1994). Neither Carrie Buck, who was released from the institution after she was sterilized and later got married and worked as a care worker, nor her daughter, who turned out to be an honor student, was ever found to be mentally retarded (D. J. Smith, 1999). Although Carrie Buck was White, many of those sterilized were African American women. In fact, in 1973, "*Essence* magazine published an exposé of forced sterilization practices in the rural South, where racist physicians felt they were performing a service by sterilizing Black women without telling them" (Malveaux, 2001, p. 10).

Goddard lectured widely about the threat of feeblemindedness, advocating that all "weak-minded" children be segregated by statute and not released until they were "voluntarily" sterilized. He once claimed, "every feebleminded child is a potential criminal" (in Carey, 2003, p. 417). Goddard was particularly worried about women like Carrie Buck, labeled "high-grade Moron, who appeared normal and were therefore, capable of attracting a man and bearing children" (Selden, 1999, p. 97). Mirroring this view, Terman once wrote, "every feebleminded woman is a potential prostitute" (in Oakes et al., 1997, p. 487) and Fernald claimed that "feeblemindedness" was the "mother of crime, pauperism, and degeneracy" (in Pfeiffer, 1994, p. 493). Eugenicists also attempted to capitalize on the fear that "imbeciles, weaklings, paupers and hoboes" were breeding at a faster rate than those destined for leadership and genius (Selden, 1999, p. 86). Their ultimate goal was to increase the birthrates of the upper classes, whose privileged position was seen as proof of their meritocracy, and diminish (even by force) the birthrates of those deemed unfit by virtue of their ethnic/racial group membership, presumed disability status, or social class (Shakespeare, 1998).

Eugenicists argued that because of social progress, humans were no longer subject to the laws of natural selection. In other words, they argued that advances in civilization were creating an artificial buffer to the starker realities of the survival of the fittest. Social and educational programs, in particular, were seen as interrupting this "natural" selection process. Thus, eugenicists saw a whole host of social programs, including compulsory education, as "at best a waste of time and at worst a threat to society" (Selden, 1999, p. 90). Leta Hollingworth, a leading gifted educator and eugenicist, criticized schools for being "preoccupied with the incompetent" and too supportive of society's least able students (Selden, p. 101). Likewise, Margaret Sanger, an early feminist who was instrumental in founding Planned Parenthood and was an early advocate of birth control, argued against "spending more in maintaining morons than in developing the inherent talents of gifted children" (Wilson, 2002, p. 62). In her 1922 book, Sanger wrote:

> Every single case of inherited defect, every malformed child, every congenitally tainted human being brought into this world is of infinite importance to that poor individual; but it is of scarcely less importance to the rest of us and to all of our children who must pay in one way or another for these biological and racial mistakes.

Because for the eugenicist every social problem was located in heredity, the only intervention that made sense was to carefully select who should and should not reproduce and strictly enforce these policies. In addition to working to lower "the threshold for exclusion" in U.S. immigration law (Baynton, 2001, p. 45), and advocating involuntary sterilization requirements, as well as marriage and voting restrictions (Carey, 2003), eugenicists saw public education as a key to furthering their cause. Although public education of eugenics took place in multiple venues, we focus specifically on campaigns aimed at the general public. The next section provides detailed descriptions from a selection of some traveling exhibits that the American Eugenics Society displayed at state fairs around the U.S.

Informing the Public: Taking Eugenics on the Road

One of the goals of the American Eugenics Society was public education, and state fairs and expositions were the venue of choice for these campaigns. For instance, an

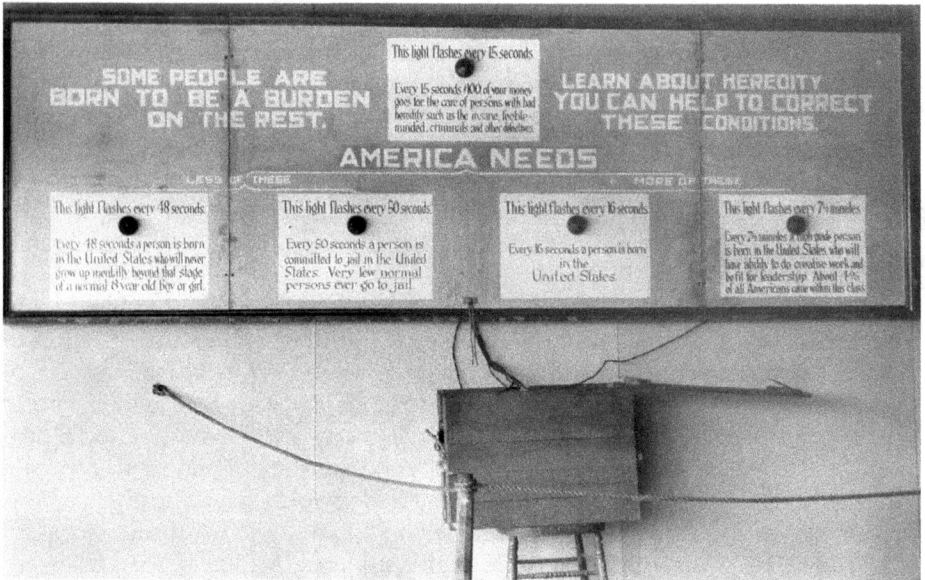

FIGURE 1.

exhibit of the American Eugenics Society displayed at the Sesqui-Centennial Exposition in Philadelphia in 1926 (Selden, 2000, p. 239) provided fairgoers with specific suggestions for improving the nation on its 150th birthday. The display warned that the "rising tide of bad heredity is endangering the nation's well being" (Selden, 1999, p. 24). The display used flashing lights to teach the audience to connect poor heredity and feeblemindedness with crime and a concurrent financial drain on society (see figure 1). This particular exhibit featured a light that flashed every 48 seconds to mark the rate at which a person who will "never grow up beyond the stage of an 8 year old boy or girl" was born in the U.S. (Selden, 2000, p. 239). Another light flashed every fifteen seconds to mark the rate at which crime cost the nation one hundred dollars. Finally, a light flashed every 50 seconds to designate the rate at which a person goes to jail. In parentheses the display explained that very few of these criminals are "normal." Thus, the message linked the nebulous category of feeblemindedness with criminality and societal burden.

In the same exhibit titled, "Some people are born to be a burden on the rest" (see also figure 1), again in flashing lights, the poster explained that America needed both positive and negative eugenics. In this section, a light flashed every 16 seconds to mark the nation's birthrate. At a slightly faster rate (15 seconds), the participants learned that the birthrate for those with bad heredity, including "the insane, feebleminded, criminals, and other defectives" was outpacing the national average (Selden, 1999, p. 25). Those viewing the poster would have to stay around awhile to see the light in the bottom right-hand corner, which flashed only once every seven and one-half minutes to mark the rate that a person of "high-grade inheritance" was born in the U.S. Clearly the exhibit was designed to elicit fear that "lower classes" of people were reproducing at a much faster rate than people who were considered to be the most "fit."

Another display from the 1929 Eugenic and Health Exhibit Building at the Kansas Free Fair in Topeka repeated this message about the dangers posed by differential birthrates (see figure 2). The posters to the left and right of the building framed the problem of American illiteracy in terms of differential birthrates. If read left to right the audience learned again that the nation's "upper 50 percent" had a lower birthrate (represented by a light that flashed every 40 seconds) than the lower 50 percent (represented by a light that flashed every 17 seconds). The poster prominently displayed to the right of the stage instructed the audience that the ratio of literate to illiterate between native-born citizens and immigrants was 49:1, yet the nation's literacy rate was only 17:1. This disparity was explained by immigrant literacy rates, which were listed as 8:1, and Black literacy rates, which were listed as only 4:1. Thus, the poster warned that the increase in immigrants and African Americans was the cause of the nation's falling literacy rates. Of course, the eugenics "lesson" does not consider the influence of compulsory illiteracy instituted after the slave rebellions or public school closings in the wake of *Brown* in the South. Thus, by ignoring social context,

FIGURE 2.

illiteracy becomes the "proof" of genetic inferiority in the quasi-science of eugenics. A smaller poster in this same exhibit emphasized the inheritability of intelligence. It read, "Wooden heads are inherited, but wooden legs are not."

One exhibit titled, "Triangle of Life," displayed at the Kansas Free Fair in 1929, promised the audience that three generations would be all that it would take to rid the nation of criminality, insanity, alcoholism, pauperism, and feeblemindedness. The second part of the poster (see figure 3) posed the futility of educational social programs. It suggested that "[even if you] improve your education, and even [if you] change your environment . . . what you really ARE was all settled when your parents were born." Such conceptions of intelligence were quite influential and would remain so (Valencia, 1997). Thus, the idea that intelligence was innate, fixed, one-dimensional, and easily assessed would persist in the public imagination long after such ideas would come to be seen as teetering on "shaky empirical ground" (Gould, in Oakes et al., 1997).

Another exhibit of the American Eugenics Society displayed at the Kansas Free Fair provided, in simple Mendelian terms, the mathematical outcomes of fit and unfit parentage. The poster (see figure 4) evoked the specter of tainted and abnormal births if marriages were not carefully controlled. In this poster, the audience learned that marriages of "pure + pure" would produce normal children, but that

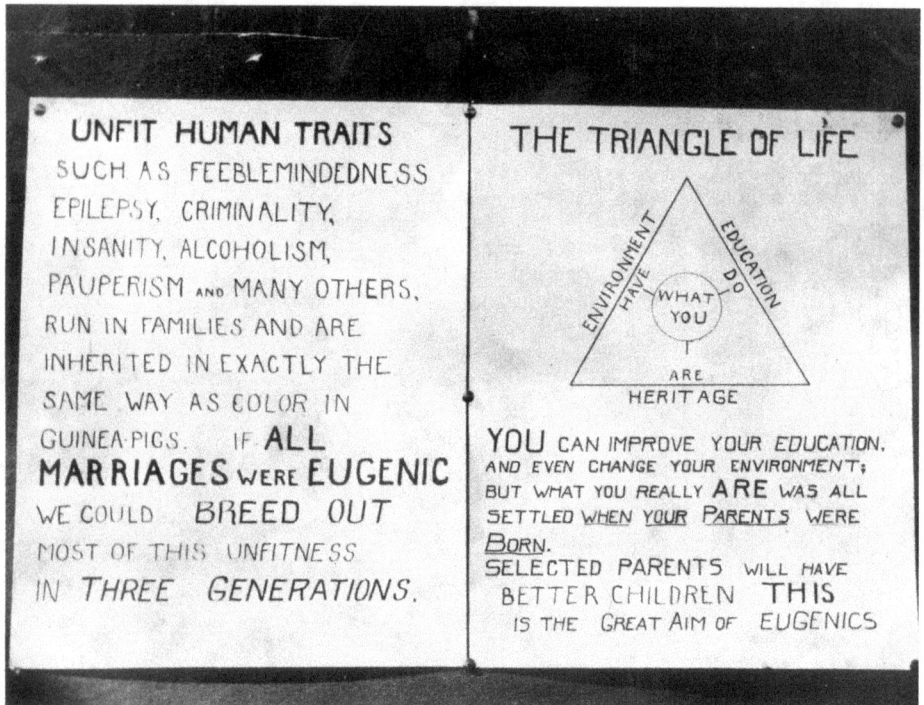

FIGURE 3.

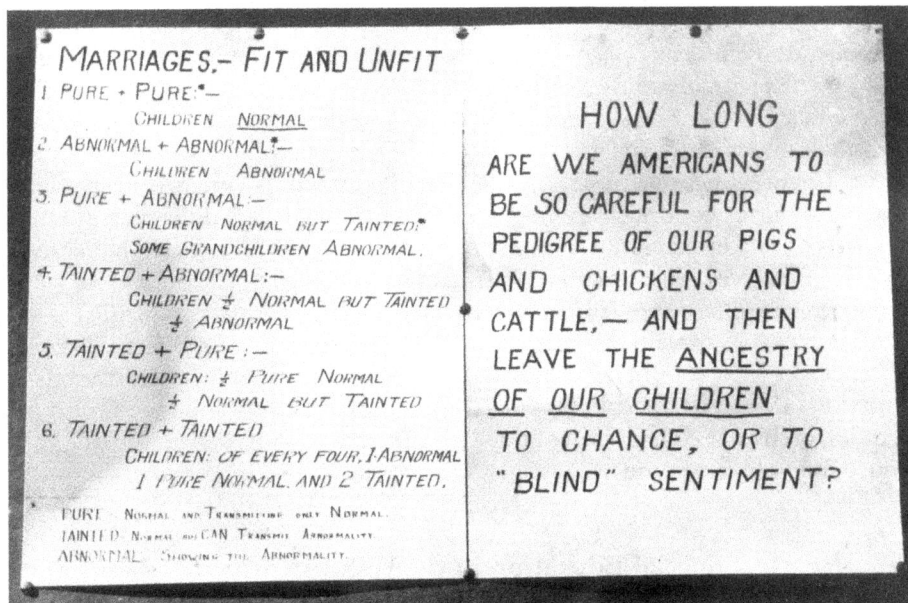

MARRIAGES.- FIT AND UNFIT

1. PURE + PURE:—
       CHILDREN   NORMAL
2. ABNORMAL + ABNORMAL?—
       CHILDREN   ABNORMAL
3. PURE + ABNORMAL.—
       CHILDREN   NORMAL   BUT TAINTED.*
       SOME GRANDCHILDREN ABNORMAL.
4. TAINTED + ABNORMAL:—
       CHILDREN ± NORMAL BUT TAINTED
               ± ABNORMAL
5. TAINTED + PURE :—
       CHILDREN: ± PURE NORMAL
               ± NORMAL BUT TAINTED
6. TAINTED + TAINTED
       CHILDREN: OF EVERY FOUR, 1-ABNORMAL
               1 PURE NORMAL, AND 2 TAINTED.

PURE   NORMAL AND TRANSMITTING ONLY NORMAL.
TAINTED NORMAL BUT CAN TRANSMIT ABNORMALITY
ABNORMAL SHOWING THE ABNORMALITY

HOW LONG
ARE WE AMERICANS TO
BE SO CAREFUL FOR THE
PEDIGREE OF OUR PIGS
AND CHICKENS AND
CATTLE,— AND THEN
LEAVE THE ANCESTRY
OF OUR CHILDREN
TO CHANCE, OR TO
"BLIND" SENTIMENT?

FIGURE 4.

a marriage of "pure + abnormal" would produce children that carry a "taint" of abnormality, which could then be passed on to children, some of whom would be abnormal. Eugenicists did not seem to care that Mendel's theories, upon which these notions about heredity were based, had been disproved by this time.

In 1928, at the Third Race Betterment Conference in Battle Creek, Michigan, individuals were actually encouraged to compete for Race Betterment and Fitter Families awards. Similar competitions took place in Oklahoma, New York, Kansas, Arkansas, Massachusetts, Michigan, Georgia, and Texas. Prominent "citizen-judges" rated contestants according to "social and educational attainments and mental and physical status" (Evans, in Selden, 1999, pp. 30, 34). Of course, these judgments were highly subjective and reflective of the ideologies and biases of the dominant group, who, no surprise, were deemed especially fit. The utopia envisioned by eugenicists was that winners would marry other winners and thereby fulfill their social responsibility of producing more and more fit babies. Losers would also do their part by refraining, either voluntarily or involuntarily, from reproducing.

The combined message of the traveling eugenics public education campaign was threefold: (1) race, ability, and social class were intimately interconnected; (2) cognitive ability and social achievement were heritable; and (3) segregation and selective breeding, as opposed to social or educational reforms, were the only way to achieve a better society. Once eugenic ideas took root in the public imagination, support for segregation based on blurred notions of race and ability followed. In other words, we argue that vestiges of eugenic ideas about race and ability contributed to the disproportionate placement of students of color in special education after the *Brown* decision, as well as to the supposed need to segregate students with disabilities.

As Baker (2002) argues, eugenics should not be thought of as a discrete movement, but rather as a series of "transmogrified" discourses (p. 664). Thus, as eugenics began to fall out of favor, other deficit discourses emerged in its place. These discourses continued to pathologize racial/ethnic/class differences, but on the basis of perceived cultural, environmental, or familial deficiencies, rather than genetic differences (Valencia, 1997). As Brantlinger (2003) notes, during the 1960s and 1970s genetic theories fell out of favor and cultural deprivation emerged as the dominant way to explain the achievement differences in students. The shift from old eugenics to new forms of deficit thinking helps to explain why the overrepresentation of students of color in special education went largely unquestioned for decades, even after eugenics fell out of favor. In other words, deficit thinking continued, but scholars found a new explanation for it.

Special Education in the Wake of *Brown*

In the early years after *Brown,* teachers who were interviewed after their schools began to integrate Black students were quick to label them as slow learners (see chapter 3). Given the popularity of eugenics in the decades preceding *Brown,* it is not altogether surprising that White teachers would make this quick association between race and dis/ability. As schools became more diverse, the process of labeling students steadily increased during the late 1950s and throughout the 1960s, during which time the term learning disability (LD) was coined and the category of emotional disturbance (ED) gained increased usage in the field (Lipsky & Gartner, 1997). As the category of mental retardation became overpopulated with Black students, the new label of learning disabilities gave families of White, middle class children a different and less stigmatizing way to explain their children's difficulties and to gain access to special services. In other words, according to Sleeter (1987), the label allowed a new group of mostly White, middle class children to receive educational supports without being mixed into the existing pool of special education students. Moreover, the label of LD helped to solve the perplexing problem of White underachievement in ways that did not threaten assumptions about White supremacy. If White middle class children were not achieving, it was not because they were slow learners or because they were culturally deprived—both explanations that were reserved for Black and poor children. Thus, Sleeter (1987) contends that the LD label served a particular political purpose: "to differentiate and protect White middle class children who were failing in school from lower class and minority children, during a time when schools were being called upon to raise standards" (p. 212). Because students within special education were placed in classrooms according to their labels, special education classes became as racially segregated as general education ones.

Fortunately, schooling practices that mislabeled and segregated students in overly restrictive placements with fewer opportunities did not go unnoticed in the courts. *Diana v. California State Board of Education* (1970) and *Larry P. v. Riles* (1979) became landmark legal cases when they successfully confronted racial and cultural bias inherent in standardized tests and special education procedures. The first case, *Diana,* was a class action suit filed on behalf of nine Latino children who had been forced to take an individually administered intelligence (IQ) test in English, and were thus misclassified as educable mentally retarded. Once these same students were retested, this time by a Latino examiner and in Spanish, scores of eight of the nine children showed that they had been inappropriately labeled. In the second case, *Larry P.,* plaintiffs claimed that the overrepresentation of minority children in classes for children with mild mental retardation throughout San Francisco was due to unfair and biased educational practices. These two cases clearly revealed the critical role of school personnel, tests, and testing practices in deciding who received the label of "disability." They also attributed the disproportionate labeling of racial and linguistic minorities in segregated special education classes to school personnel and biased assessment procedures. They also publicly highlighted how special education, along with ability tracking, was unofficially serving as a tool to resegregate classrooms despite the *Brown* ruling that determined that racially segregated schools were unconstitutional.

Of equal importance, the cases drew attention to how special education labeling and placement decisions were based in large part on stereotypic beliefs about White intellectual superiority. *Diana* and *Larry P.* called into question the widespread use of purportedly "scientific" objective tests to gauge intellectual ability. The IQ score that had once been viewed as innate, fixed, one-dimensional, and naturally distributed along racial and class lines, would now be cast in a different light. It became increasingly clear that evaluation instruments and the manner of their implementation served to reinforce intellectual hierarchies among racial and ethnic groups. Although many continued to view these tests as relatively neutral and valid, others came to view them as mechanisms of institutionalized racism. Critics, for example, began to call attention to the ways that assessments contained cultural and linguistic biases and were based on norms that were predicated upon values and expectations of White, middle class culture (Selden, 1999). As Kwate (2001) argues, even when tests are normed "appropriately," an African American, Asian American, or Latino child is typically measured against norms based on a sample that is 70 percent White. Because of increased attention to this kind of bias, the conflation of race and dis/ability is increasingly seen as political rather than inherent or natural.

Conclusion

According to Garland (1995), history is always a conversation between the past and the present. Thinking about history as a conversation rather than a linear progression helps us to see moments when past and present collide or bleed into one another. Hence, thinking about history as a conversation enables us to place the present-day problem of overrepresentation of students of color in special education alongside long outmoded pseudoscientific notions of eugenics. Moreover, attending to scientific perceptions and popular portrayals of race and ability contextualizes the various responses to desegregation. We would argue that the current place in which we find ourselves in terms of the racial makeup in special education *must* be seen in a larger historical, cultural, and ideological context. To fully understand how easily Black students and other racial minorities were labeled as mentally deficient, we must consider the assumptions about race and ability underlying these actions. In these assumptions we find the traces of a troubling past.

Thinking about history as a conversation helps us to connect various strategies of political resistance that emerged as well. Greatly influenced by the civil rights movement forged by Blacks in the 1950s and 1960s, for example, people with disabilities galvanized into their own movement and made significant strides toward gaining access to schools, services, jobs, and housing, which were all viewed as essential to improving the quality of their lives (Fleischer & Zames, 2001; Russell, 1998). Like critical race activists and scholars, those in the disability rights movement fought for inclusion on many fronts. As Linton (1998) pointedly notes, "The enormous energy society expends in keeping people with disabilities sequestered in subordinate positions is matched by the academy's effort to justify that isolation and oppression" (p. 3). In response to both of these exclusions, the academic discipline of disability studies evolved to forge new and political understandings of disability. Within this model, disability is understood as interacting with social, cultural, historical, legal, and medical discourses, as well as race, ethnicity, gender, age, sexuality, and class. As a result, the term disability has come to represent "a lynchpin in a complex web of social ideals, institutional structures, and government policies" (Linton, p. 10). Many people with disabilities, therefore, have claimed the status of disability as a significant marker of their own individual identity, while adopting a "minority model" of their shared identity. The purpose of identifying with the minority model is to unite around a common identity and, along with allies, influence change leading to a more equitable society.

Advocating for a social model[7] of disability, scholars and activists have attempted to counter medical model and deficit approaches to disability and to focus instead on everyday societal practices that are disabling and prevent people with disabilities from fully accessing all aspects of life. One important aspect of life is schooling, and scholars in the field of disability studies in education, in particular, have questioned the damaging taken-for-granted practices within special education. For example, one of the usually unquestioned practices in special education is a seemingly perpetual expansion of disability categories. These categories, which become reified as "natural" are socially constructed designations, created in response to particular needs of the dominant group within society (Brantlinger, 1997; Danforth, 2002; Ferri, 2004; Gabel, 2001; Reid & Valle, 2004; Ware, 2001; Watts & Erevelles, 2004). Thus, as each new category emerges, we should be compelled to ask how the new label fills a particular social need at this time.

Despite the power of each of these civil rights and scholarly movements, like Watts and Erevelles (2004), we seek out possibilities for a coalitional politics between disability studies and critical race studies. Yet, we still see too little critical attention to disability in those advocating or writing about race and too little critical attention to race in those advocating or writing about disability. Perhaps because we are disability studies scholars studying *Brown* we cannot help but see the overlap of race and disability. But, if the history of desegregation and overrepresentation teaches us anything, it is that strategies of exclusion are elastic and flexible—when one falls away another can pick up its slack. It is this shared understanding of exclusion that could be the starting point for an intersectional approach to desegregation and inclusion.

Lessons Learned

In this chapter we contextualize the various forms of resistance to *Brown,* including the overrepresentation of students of color in special education, to ideas about race and disability within scientific thought. With a wide lens we take various snapshots of history and place them alongside one another. We place eugenic posters displayed at state fairs around the country, alongside the continued practice of disproportionately labeling Black students as mentally retarded. Of course, much is left out of our retelling, but what we gain is a better understanding of how supposedly scientific theories and practices can be both harmful and seductive, depending on their cultural context.

An important lesson in this chapter is that science is always *inside* culture. Thus, part of the popularity of eugenics can be explained by how well eugenic ideas dovetailed with commonly accepted notions about race and ability operating at the time. Unfortunately, these assumptions, once given scientific credibility, have been extremely difficult to overcome. Such is the circle of science and culture. Thus, because Blackness was associated with mental deficiency, tracking and segregated classes for slow learners must have seemed to many like a reasonable response to racially diverse schools. A related lesson is that despite its claim to neutrality, science can be harmful. Practices like assessment and labeling, like sterilization and segregation, regardless of their supposedly scientific justification or rationale, can have horrific consequences. Moreover, if we understand science as always inside culture we can no longer disclaim cultural bias in assessment, referral, or any other educational practice. To do so is to practice willful ignorance about how race, as well as disability and social class, permeates all aspects of education (A. Smith, 2001). Finally, a lesson of this chapter is to continue to ask what parts of our past continue to haunt our present? In the next chapter, we begin to examine the relationship between a nascent special education and school resegregation immediately after *Brown.*

3

RACE, ABILITY, AND (RE)SEGREGATED EDUCATION

3

RACE, ABILITY, AND (RE)SEGREGATED EDUCATION

Introduction

In this chapter we begin to explore the interconnected relationship between special education and school resegregation in the years following the 1954 landmark Supreme Court decision, *Brown v. Board of Education*. Although previous scholars have implicated the use of ability tracking as a strategy to resegregate schools along racial lines after *Brown* (Mickelson, 2001; Oakes, 1985), we break new ground and extend this discussion by highlighting how special education served a similar purpose. In the everyday discursive context of the newspaper, we examine how public response to court-ordered integration involved calls for delay and gradual compliance, as well as outright refusal. We argue that gradualism functioned to maintain rather than disrupt the status quo of segregated schooling. Moreover, we connect the current problem of overrepresentation of racial minorities in segregated special education classrooms to the ineffectiveness of incremental approaches to reform.

As discussed in the introduction to this book, we chose editorial pages as our unit of analysis for several reasons. First, we were interested in how ideas about segregation manifest in everyday discursive contexts. Although no discursive space is completely open, we view newspapers as everyday discourse because the presumed audience of a newspaper is much broader than the anticipated audience of research reports, professional publications, or court documents. Second, editorial pages invite dialogue. Space is given to both editors and guest editors, but also to the range of people who feel compelled on any given day to write letters to the editor. Because editorial pages elicit a range of opinions, we found them to be a fertile place from which to gather a range of perspectives from a particular time and place. Indeed, because of the range of authors and their opinions typically represented in the editorial page, no particular voice or perspective dominates.

In the following sections of this chapter we first explore the shared histories of desegregation and inclusion, noting both lines of connection and dissonance between these two watershed educational reforms. After providing this important historical context, we then present our findings, taken from hundreds of newspaper editorials, op-eds, and letters to the editor written in response to school desegregation and inclusion. In this chapter our findings are organized around several broad themes related to change or pace of change. We conclude with a discussion of the problems of gradualism as a strategy to implement reform.

History Lessons: Connecting Desegregation and Inclusion

In the landmark *Brown v. Board of Education* decision, Justice Earl Warren writes that the practice of segregating students by race creates in Black students "a feeling of inferiority as to their status in the community that may affect their hearts and minds in a way very unlikely ever to be undone" (in Williams, 1987, p. 34). Direct or indirect references to *Brown*'s contention that segregated schooling is inherently unequal are not uncommon in current debates about the inclusion of students with disabilities in general education classrooms. For example, Harlan Hahn (1997) echoes the *Brown* decision when he writes, "Since separation on the basis of disability is apt to leave an enduring imprint on the *hearts and minds* [italics added] of disabled young people, desegregation or inclusion is a fundamental component" of sociopolitical approaches to disability (p. 321). Likewise, Lipsky and Gartner (1996) argue, "The continuation of the current special education system—*separate and unequal* [italics added]—violates" standards of equal opportunity and integration (p. 146). The *Brown* decision is even listed as an important piece of special education legislation in many introductory disability texts. In some respects these parallels are justified, since, although *Brown* did not speak to segregation based on disability, special education legislation owes its legal precedence and thinking to *Brown*'s strategy of placing segregation as counter to the equal protection guaranteed by the 14th Amendment of the Constitution.

Other similarities can be drawn. For instance, both *Brown* and later disability legislation were criticized for vague terminology. From the beginning, *Brown* (or more accurately, *Brown II*) was critiqued for not setting deadlines for states to comply with desegregation orders.[1] Obtuse language in *Brown II*, requiring states to proceed with "all deliberate speed," opened the door for "obstructionism, foot-dragging, and outright refusal to begin the process of school desegregation" (Irons, 2002, p. 195). Likewise, various "escape routes" (Clotfelter, 2004, p. 8), such as freedom of choice statutes, pupil placement laws, vouchers, and "voluntary" desegregation plans were all strategically designed to "deliberately delay court orders" (Patterson, 2001, p. 96) and appease White parents. Similarly, P.L. 94–142 (now *Individuals with Disabilities Education Act* or *IDEA*) included highly contested terminology. For example, *IDEA* required that placement decisions for students with disabilities consider on a case-by-case basis the "least restrictive environment" (LRE). Although *IDEA* has been enormously successful in giving students with disabilities access to public education, the high percentage of students (particularly students of color) placed in more rather than less restrictive placements has led some to characterize LRE as a "loophole" that has contributed to two largely segregated and unequal education systems: general education and special education (Linton, 1998; Lipsky & Gartner, 1997; Taylor, 1988).

The historical connection between special education and resegregation is complex. As stated earlier, special education and tracking were used as tools to resegregate Black and White students within desegregated schools after the passage of *Brown* (Mickelson, 2001; Parrish, 2002). Acknowledging that schools were resegregating students of minority racial groups from White students, *IDEA* aimed to break race-based "patterns of segregation" (Fleischer & Zames, 2001, p. 185). Unfortunately, disproportionate numbers of students of color continue to be identified for special education services and given the most restrictive of placements[2] (Artiles et al., 2002; Fierros & Conroy, 2002; Lipsky & Gartner, 1997; Osher et al., 2002). Drawing on the logic set forth in *Brown*, and responding to the criticisms of overrepresentation of minority students and poor transition outcomes for students in special education, advocates in the late 1980s and early 1990s began to push harder for more inclusive placements for all students with disabilities.

To fully understand the connection between present-day inclusion and the ongoing history of racial desegregation in schools, it is useful to look back to the origins and growth of what has come to be known as special education. During the 1950s, as *Brown* was becoming a reality, a sharp rise in standardized testing helped to establish a set of rigid norms based on White, middle class American experiences, values, and expectations. As an institutionalized practice, the testing movement simultaneously identified and created groups of students who deviated from the "normal" or "average" student. The result was the seemingly beneficent provision of separate classes. One newspaper editor notes, "as school[s] became more diverse, teaching became more challenging. Separating children by ability was one way to make it easier" ("All of our children," 1995, p. 8A). However, as diversity and ability became conflated, "special" classes became increasingly populated by minority, immigrant, and other already marginalized students.

Earlier in the first half of the 20th century and coinciding with the U.S. eugenics movement, facilities and programs for children deemed slow or retarded flourished (Franklin, 1987). Later, the emergence of new categories, such as slow learner, mentally retarded, emotionally disturbed (ED), and culturally deprived, further rationalized the practice of removing certain students, especially those from non-White, immigrant and poor backgrounds, from general education (Sleeter, 1987). Labeling dramatically increased during the 1960s, when the term learning disability (LD) was coined and increasing numbers of students were labeled as ED (Gartner & Lipsky, 1987). During this time students who were labeled disabled were likely to receive most if not all of their education in separate classrooms (Wang et al., 1986). Moreover, it became increasingly obvious that disability labels were being disproportionately assigned to historically marginalized students of color, facilitating their removal from mainstream classrooms (Sleeter, 1987). Conversely, students belonging to racial minority groups were underrepresented in categories denoting exceptional ability or giftedness, whereas White students were overrepresented for these programs[3] (Ford, 1998; Salend et al., 2002). Both types of labels functioned to separate White students from students of color who were attending otherwise desegregated schools.

Like school desegregation, the inclusion movement elicited strong opposition in the press. Despite the simple premise that inclusion would ensure equal access to general education classrooms in which appropriate accommodations and supports would be provided for students with disabilities, descriptions of inclusion in the press are frequently cynical and even hostile (see chapter 6). Negative comments from a variety of stakeholders, including editors, parents, politicians, administrators, and teachers, frame inclusion either as unrealistic or unnecessary and unwanted. This pervasive ridicule and dismissal of inclusion exposes an unwarranted fear that an increase of students with disabilities in general education classrooms makes teaching and learning difficult, if not impossible.

Although Albert Shanker (former President of American Federation of Teachers) and others predicted that inclusion would bring catastrophe ("Special focus," 1996, p. 6B), the experiences of students with disabilities taught in segregated settings have already been described as such (Brantlinger, 1997; Karagiannis, 2000). While reviewing a documentary on inclusion, journalist Walter Goodman (1994) asks whether inclusion is a "real educational approach" (p. C18), but fails to ask the equally pertinent question: "Is exclusion a real educational approach?" The cheerful optimism implied by the name "special" education obfuscates the reality of segregation and stigma. Imparato (2001), for example, draws from Department of Education data to show that the "national graduation rates for students who receive special education have stagnated at 27 percent for the last three years, compared to 75 percent for students who do not rely on special education" (p. 14). He notes the hypocritical posturing of policies such as *No Child Left Behind* (federal policy enacted in 2002) for students in special education who have three times the chance of failing in their pursuit of a diploma compared with their nondisabled counterparts. Some of the most negative outcomes are associated with students identified with high incidence or "mild" disabilities (Arnold & Lassmann, 2003). These same categories are associated with the highest levels of disproportionate placement of students of color. As Orfield (2000) finds, in the current push for standards-based school reform, we have actually lost ground in many areas such as minority graduation rates, postsecondary attainment, and the achievement gap.

Resistance to desegregation and inclusions merit closer analysis, if only to begin to untangle the reasons why certain students are so unwanted in the "mainstream." How does resistance to integration manifest itself in both explicit and tacit ways in both debates? How do schools appear to accommodate legislation, while actively seeking to keep things the way they are? These are the questions that initially framed our analysis for this chapter.

Analytical Format

In the following sections, we present our findings in a call-and-response format that requires the reader to consider the connections between desegregation and inclusion, without resorting to easy parallels between the two. Enacting Bakhtin's notion of a "word with a sideways glance" (P. Morris, 1994, p. 20), we place each of these social discourses in dialogic contact with the other. We also placed the excerpts from newspaper editorials, op-eds, and letters in rapid succession with minimal discussion in order to simulate a montage of the opinions found in the editorial pages from the years we studied. As stated in the introduction, we collected editorial pages primarily from the following papers: *New York Times, Atlanta Journal and Constitution, Washington Post, Atlanta Daily World, Richmond Afro-American, Chicago Defender,* and the *Philadelphia Tribune.* We also gathered data from *Southern School News,* which was a monthly compilation of coverage on desegregation financed by the Ford Foundation. Coverage on desegregation focused on the years 1954 to 1956, whereas data on inclusion covered a 15-year period, 1987–2002. These newspapers represent both White and Black presses from a range of geographic locations. The data aligned to the left margin feature writings about desegregation; the data aligned to the right margin highlight responses about inclusion. In the commentary that follows each section, we draw connections—including parallels and dissonances—between the two discourses.

As discussed in chapter 1, we chose this format for several reasons. First, we sought to deliberately disrupt the way data are typically represented in qualitative research. Rather than a summary of findings where dissonant voices are relegated to the margins if they are recognized at all, we hoped to stimulate a back-and-forth dialogue between various points of view on both sides of each debate. Resisting the impulse to collapse our data, either from within each data set or from one data set to the other, we selected a format where connections could be established without erasing differences. In other words, we sought to create a structure where "contradictions and ambiguities do not merge but stand alongside each other" (Tanaka, 1997, p. 261). "Back-and-forthing" within a nonlinear text invites (and even requires) the reader to contemplate the intertwined discourses of race and dis/ability, made complex through a multiplicity of similarities and differences. Such a reading requires a willingness to enter a space of polyphonic openness, a space where each reader potentially can create new understandings and connections.

Variations of formats used by other researchers, most notably Tanaka (1997), Lather (1997), and Lather and Smithies (1997) were useful in helping us to think through ways to present our data.

Like the editorial pages we were studying, we sought to create a space where "no single point of view dominates" (Fanger, in Tanaka, 1997, p. 259), including our own. Presenting multiple perspectives privileges Bakhtin's (1936/1984) notion of unfinalizability over linear notions of closure. By simultaneously attending to the rhetorical justifications for segregation as well as for integration, we hoped to gain insight into the "networks of what is said and what can be said of [the] social arrangements" in and around schooling (Kendall & Wickham, 1999, p. 25). Although the data are *organized* around broad themes, each theme contains a degree of ambiguity and discord, which we have left intact. Embracing a lack of unity or one-to-one correspondence between desegregation and inclusion, this format purposely disrupts our desires to draw easy analogies or parallels or to spin linear progress narratives of schools becoming ever more democratic over time.

The data are organized broadly around three categories related to change, or more specifically, resistance to change: (1) *Evolution or Revolution* focuses on attitudes about the speed of change; (2) *Not Here, Not Now, Not Ever* documents vehement opposition toward change; and (3) *Progress Reports From the Field* charts the progress of change.

Findings

Evolution or Revolution: The Limits of Gradualism

The *New York Times* (*NYT*), widely considered "the acknowledged newspaper of record and thus the most powerful editorial voice in the nation," published a series of report cards at 10-year intervals following the *Brown* decision (Martin, 1998, p. 199). Although these four editorials (reprinted in Martin, 1998) were published beyond the years of our data collection, we include them because they illustrate in snapshot form the slow progress of desegregation.

Reflecting on the 10th anniversary, the *NYT* editor calls *Brown* a "great turning point in the battle for civil rights [although] the battle is far from won . . . the commitment to equal opportunity is irrevocable, the outcome certain" (*New York Times* editor, cited in Martin, 1998, p. 224).

Likewise, the Black press, "lauded the decision as heralding a new age in race relations" (Martin, 1998, p. 33).

At the 20th anniversary, the *NYT* editor writes that *Brown* "[set in motion an] irreversible social revolution . . . moving [the nation] irrevocably toward its integrated goal" and "dual school systems are no more" (cited in Martin, 1998, p. 226).

The editor of the *Washington Post* concurs: "Twenty-six years after the Supreme Court declared school segregation unconstitutional, separate education for Blacks and Whites still predominates outside the south" (in Morgan, 1980, p. A6).

At the 30th anniversary, the *NYT* editor acknowledged a "continued resistance" to desegregation, and as standing "rock solid as a matter of law" and a "cause for celebration" (cited in Martin, 1998, p. 228).

At the 40th anniversary, the *NYT* editor calls the decision "an occasion both for national pride and national shame . . . [faulting court decisions as well as] suburbanization, white flight, industrial decay, and political ennui [all contributing to] an unacceptable number of minority students still attending all-minority or nearly all-minority schools" (cited in Martin, 1998, p. 228).

"It took us most of the twentieth century to throw off the legal shackles that had bound Blacks as closely as possible to slavery. . . . *Brown* was the key event in that struggle. Facing up to the enduring racism at the center of our culture . . . is an even bigger challenge. . . . A strong hundred-year effort would be a modest estimate of the time required. After all it took us 375 years to get into the hole we now occupy. It's been only forty years since *Brown*" (Wilkins, 1995, p. 618).

Editorial coverage of inclusion also illustrates the slow progress being made in integrating students with disabilities. Even though children with disabilities were ensured a free and appropriate public education (FAPE) by law in 1975, they were not guaranteed a general education placement. Over the years, as parents and advocates of students with disabilities became more dissatisfied with segregated classes, they began to argue that the LRE clause in *IDEA* should be understood to mean that the general education classroom, with appropriate supports and services, is the least restrictive educational setting. As pressure from these groups increased, the inclusion debate garnered more attention in the press. Critics of inclusion were quick to cite a lack of research supporting inclusion; however, these same critics failed to account for the lack of efficacy studies supporting segregated placements. Detractors also cautioned against the unfettered growth of inclusion, ignoring the fact that a full 20 years would elapse between *IDEA* and any serious push for inclusion.

"More than 30 years ago, the civil rights movement ushered our nation into a more enlightened era. Thanks to those who struggled for justice then, few people question the moral imperative of integration—that is, except, when it comes to children with disabilities" (Head et al., 1996, p. C8).

"The lack of specific data [on inclusion] has fueled the controversy, allowing critics to charge that the nation is rushing headfirst into something it little understands" (Evans, 1996, p. 4H).

"Inclusion programs are being tried in all 50 states, but there's scant national research to show what really happens when disabled students are included in regular classrooms" (Evans, 1996, p. 4H).

"Chicago was woefully neglectful . . . in fulfilling its obligations to afford handicapped children their federally mandated 'meaningful' access to an education" (Bratcher, 1988, p. 6).

One judge ruled that a 16-year-old student, "would be isolated socially and academically . . . his [segregated school] constitutes the least restrictive environment" ("Transfer of disabled," 1988, p. B6).

Although not a unified group in terms of support for inclusion, many parents were critical of the progress being made in including their children with disabilities in the general education classroom. They contended that even when school systems were pressured by law to shift to more inclusive practices, the results were often cosmetic.

As parents Margo and Doug Ellis conclude, the state government of Massachusetts' "commitment to mainstreaming is shallow" (Nealon, 1991, p. 1).

Another parent writes of her son: "Even now, Patrick spends most of the school day in a corner of a classroom, working with a teacher instead of being integrated into the classroom with other students" (Evans, 1996, p. 4H).

"[A] group of parent advocates . . . have sued on behalf of the most severely handicapped, [along with] the principals and teachers who work with those children. Citing a federal law requiring schools to provide special services for disabled children, the group has argued that any changes would reduce services for children" (Belluck, 1996, p. A1).

Another parent asserted, "It's essential to keep a Centralized government for children who need it" ("Parents protest," 1991, p. A1).

Despite growing frustration over the slow pace of change, school officials continued to advocate for additional time and/or resources before instituting integration. Often the concern was not necessarily when to desegregate, but rather how to avoid or delay it. One of the more common themes in letters and editorials at the time of *Brown* was the appeal for more time as a key to the "problem" of desegregation. With time, many would suggest, southern Whites could adjust to the "social upheaval" involved. A similar strategy was emerging in the inclusion debate. Here the call was not for more time, but for additional resources and teacher training. Thus, both inclusion and desegregation were perceived to require a host of adjustments. Unfortunately, most schools, when given more time, failed to institute any serious plans or policies. Instead, in both debates we see a shift from "should we" to "if we have to do it, how or when should we," the message is clear: Proceed with caution.

"[F]ears of an extremely volatile Southern white response to an immediate implementation decree . . . [made] gradualism the only viable option" (cited in W. E. Martin, 1998, p. 31).

Justice Stanley Reed believed segregation should "be dismantled gradually rather than all at once" (Williams, 1987, p. 33).

Of course, others saw through these calls for more time. "When the National Association for the Advancement of Colored People says it opposes 'gradual' because there are communities where 'gradual means never' it is being wholly realistic" (Krock, 1956, p. 34).

"There must be a strong teacher training component to avoid both teachers and students being overwhelmed by frustration" ("Expand inclusion in proper way," 2002, p. 14).

"Mainstreaming might have a chance if we have small classes and prepared teachers" (Young-Hawthorne, 1990 p. B6).

Paul Alberto, a special education professor at Georgia State University, claims: "While social and communication skills improve for these students, more work is needed to determine if self-help and job skills can still be taught in an inclusive setting" (Jacobson, 1994, p. C1).

"The high court showed profound wisdom in not setting a definite time limit . . . [directing] integration as soon as practical. That won't be anytime soon in many counties in the South. The public in general simply isn't ready for that monumental change" ("Arkansas," 1955, p. 8).

Of course, even early on many saw these calls for delay as simply strategies for avoidance. "As a matter of fact, 'prompt' means now, immediate, during the present. Therefore it can be concluded that, while the court has not set a deadline for the conclusion, it has unequivocally set a deadline for the beginning . . . that deadline being now" ("What they say," 1955, July, p. 5).

"In a 1994 national survey by the American Federation of Teachers, only 11 percent of teachers said they were trained adequately [for inclusion]" (Evans, 1996, p. 4H).

"[M]any schools push the disabled into crowded classrooms where they compete with nondisabled peers under uncertified teachers who cannot meet their needs" ("Battle over special education," 2001, p. A30).

"Gradual compliance . . . [would give] the South the opportunity to adjust itself" ("South's editors," 1955, June 1, p. 4).

"[More time is needed] to prepare both the minds and the attitudes of both children and parents" ("More time," 1956, p. 9).

"Well, they [the White community] are not satisfied with desegregation and are not ready to enter into it right at the present time. . . . I believe if we were given sufficient time we could work the problem out but at the present time we have no plan" ("Interview," 1956, p. 14).

"Often, children are left behind and alone, getting little or no individualized attention" (Reback, 1994, p. A17).

A project director of an inclusion grant stated, "I think inclusion is going to grow. . . . But I'm afraid that there is going to be a rapid shift to do it wrong" (Jacobson, 1993, p. J1).

Some of the editorial coverage signaled that *Brown* and inclusion were not the end of segregated education, but rather the beginning of a long and protracted struggle. Often predictions were made about the amount of time that would be required to integrate the schools. Many in the inclusion debate predicted a loss of funding, diminished services, and an inevitable slide into chaos. Unfortunately, even those voicing the most pessimistic predictions underestimated the degree of resistance that integrationists and inclusionists would encounter.

As one person remarked, "We are simply passing through another phase of the fight" ("Greenville," 1955, p. 9).

Another letter warns, "those of us who look forward to the early end of segregation in all areas of our national life might do well to prepare for something less than what we seek" (Brown, 1955, p. 16).

"People who advocate [full inclusion] should listen to teachers in mainstream schools, where there is uncertainty, lack of confidence, concern, and, sometimes, I'm sad to say, indifference to the needs of our pupils. I don't disagree with mainstream provision, but it's a considerably long way off" (Revell, 2001, p. 6).

"Integration is still a long way off where we are" ("Focus on education," 1956, p. 8).

"[I]t is going to be many years before there is any end to segregation in Georgia schools. . . . [I]t will be many years before the schools in most communities of the South are desegregated" ("Georgia editors," 1955, p. 4).

"Dr. Lawrence Jones of the small Piney Woods school for Negroes in Mississippi, said desegregation will take at least 50 years" ("Raps Supreme Court," 1956, p. 7).

> "[T]he state would attempt to wring savings from the program by putting disabled students back into regular classroom settings without providing the services those students needed" (Hernandez, 1999, p. B1).
>
> "[There is] frustration and dissatisfaction with public education's failure to provide all students the kind of high quality education they need. . . . The backlash [against special education] is unlikely to diminish without a major shift in our thinking about school accountability and community" (O'Neil, 2002, p. 17).

> "I cannot see how integration can possibly be accomplished on any major scale in Alabama any time soon" ("Negro responsibility," 1957, p. 15).
>
> "It [desegregation] may be feasible in Florida in the next fifty to 100 years. No one could say it's feasible now" ("South reacts," 1955, p. 30).

Those who desired to maintain special education as an exclusive system stressed the vast differences between the needs of students with disabilities and their nondisabled peers.

> "Seventy-five percent of students at the New York Institute for Special Education were once in public school placements. . . . [They were not] having great success in passing statewide tests—because the specialization they needed could not be achieved in their public school setting" (McMahon, 2002, p. 24).
>
> "It is beyond dispute that disabled children require more time with the teacher than non-disabled children, often with a heavy emphasis on behavior modification" (Kastens, 1995, p. A15).

Several letters and editorials suggested that, given enough time, Black schools would be equalized, despite the fact that *Plessy v. Ferguson* (passed into law in 1892) had guaranteed equal facilities in the first place. The extremely costly last ditch efforts to equalize schools in the South were not based on good will or even fairness, but on the assumption or hope that if Black schools were finally equalized, Black parents would not fight for integrated schools. Blacks were told to be patient and to put their trust in the courts or in the states to do the right thing.

> Even some Black educational leaders acknowledged the "one good [albeit overdue] by-product of the controversy [had] been the building of some excellent schools for Negroes in the South" ("Raps Supreme Court," 1956, p. 7).
>
> "[A] new 12-room Negro school . . . will go far toward equalizing school facilities" ("Georgia is building," 1954, p. 4).

Opponents of inclusion argued that only segregated special education placements would meet the very specialized needs of students with disabilities. Some go as far as to imply that students would be disadvantaged in integrated settings. In either case, there is a fear about instituting change too quickly or before everyone involved is ready.

> "I have seen, time and again, that . . . [inclusive placements] turn out to be more restrictive, because almost nobody is capable of giving these kids attention, consideration, and respect that they need" (Kent, 1998, p. 6).
>
> "Special education children often have very different needs than the average child. . . . [T]he parents want their children in an environment in which that student's needs are being met" (Strausberg, 1992, p. 3).

> "In due time it will have worked out, as evidenced by the building of good schools for both races and staffing them with competent teachers within each of the races, which will work to the best interest of all" (Yates, 1956, p. 26).
>
> "Georgia's accelerated school building program . . . emphasizes equal facilities for Negroes. Throughout Georgia, one can see them going up—splendid new structures to replace ramshackle, frame firetraps. We have been slow in rising to the obligation of equal educational opportunities, but once having raised we are moving fast" ("Negro school dedication," 1954, p. 4).

> For example, the President of the Missouri Chapter of The Association for Persons with Severe Handicaps comments: "The discussion, rather, should focus on individuals and their choices" (Renner, 1994, p. 7B).

"Even children with the same disability often have very different needs. You can't say that all Autistic children should be educated in the general education classroom. . . . It depends on the severity of their disability and the parents' desires" (Moore & Hayasaki, 2002, p. 1).

"As for me, I say to h—l with patience. That's all we've had for 300 years and what did it get us?" (H. Morris, 1954, p. 4).

"Nobody needs to explain to a Negro the difference between the law in books and the law in action" (Williams, 1987, p. 35).

"[T]he doctrine of 'gradualism' . . . has it really been working as well for our Negro schools? Have we yet equalized opportunities . . .?" (Mitchell, 1955, p. 4).

"I think families should have a range of choices" (C. Johnson, 2001, p. 2).

"It is important to understand there are some types of disabilities . . . which require special services . . . and these special services are better provided to groups of children with these conditions" (Barker, 1991, p. A16).

"It's nerve-wracking, as a parent, to choose between inclusion and self-contained [or segregated placements]" (Brett, 2002a, p. 1JF).

Handed down by the Supreme Court a year after *Brown, Brown II* ordered schools to begin desegregation plans with *all deliberate speed*. Two decades after the *Brown* decision, P.L. 94–142 (*IDEA*), was passed by Congress. It guaranteed a public education for all students with disabilities in the LRE. Although the social revolution of both *Brown* and *IDEA* may have been seen as irreversible, they were both met with enormous resistance. Thus, at the 20-year anniversary of *Brown*, many schools across the nation remained firmly segregated (Irons, 2002; Orfield & Eaton, 1996; Patterson, 2001). Similarly, 20 years after the passage of *IDEA*, students with disabilities, particularly students of color, remained largely segregated in special "self-contained" classes (Fierros & Conroy, 2002; Lipsky & Gartner, 1997; A. Smith, 2001).

Advocates of *Brown* and *IDEA* stressed the grounding of integration in the democratic principles of a free society. As time passed, initial optimism was tempered by the slow progress that has, as yet, yielded only incremental change. As these excerpts illustrate, the pace of implementation was contested. The slow pace of change can be partly attributed to decisions made either on a district-by-district or grade-by-grade basis for school desegregation or on a case-by-case basis for placement decisions for students with disabilities. In each instance, gradualism was seen, even by many advocates, as the only way to bring about institutional change. However, others grew increasingly frustrated and cynical. Although civil rights had been encoded within the law, the same legal system allowed detractors to contest and delay integration. As Wilkins (1995) points out, centuries of oppression cannot be expected to dissipate within decades, so gradualism may have been accepted as inevitable. Yet, in retrospect we can see how gradualism, in both instances, allowed the educational system to counteract and subvert rather than institute the intended change. The acceptance of gradualism also enabled schools time to reconfigure testing, tracking, and other policies that resulted in resegregation. Practices such as ability tracking and special education allowed schools to maintain segregation within otherwise integrated schools.

The pertinence of Martin Luther King's (1963) phrase (originally adapted from William Gladstone) "justice too long delayed is justice denied" can be seen in both of these histories. In response to *Brown* and *IDEA,* institutions complied with laws without necessarily believing them right or just. Thus, integration and inclusion appear to begin on paper with minimal, if any, mixing of physical bodies. Parents and advocates were quick to note the hollow nature of the law if not supported by individuals who share a sincere desire for social change. More disturbingly, subsequent court rulings undermined the original intent of the law. For example, many courts ruled against inclusive placements despite parental preferences, thereby maintaining district policies based on rationales of exclusion. Failure to institute bussing across district lines and more recent legislation that has challenged affirmative action at the university level, have both undermined the progress of racial integration and access.

Sometimes resistance came from within each community. For example, some parents of students with disabilities invoked *IDEA* to uphold their legal right to chose to have their children in segregated settings, which they believed were preferable, even superior, to inclusive classes. Likewise, some of the resistance to *Brown* came from within the Black community; some parents and others rejected the idea that integrated schools were inherently better than Black-run and -taught schools. Instead they sought equal resources for all schools (Mondale & Patton, 2001) or a more expansive notion of equality (Prendergast, 2002). Still others saw the issue as more complex than a simple either/or debate would allow (Baker, 2002; Crenshaw, 1998; Gallagher, 2001).

Considering the pervasive and ongoing resistance to change, we must remember that advocates of *Brown* and inclusion positioned segregated schooling against the democratic principles of a free society. However, transforming public education by ensuring access and equal opportunities for previously segregated groups of students has proven more difficult than perhaps anyone predicted. In both debates, integration was viewed as an imposition of dramatic change forced upon groups who constitute the "majority" (Whites and nondisabled people, respectively). While recognizing most members of the dominant group did not ask for or desire change legislated by *Brown* and *IDEA,* the government failed to address the fears and apprehensions of those opposing integration or the underlying biases behind such resistance.

In both cases, detractors characterized integration as ill advised and even dangerous. In terms of desegregation, there were predictions of violence and, unfortunately, in some cases these predictions would come to pass. In terms of inclusion, opponents often predicted that students with disabilities would be neglected, taunted, or worse, and that they would lash out at nondisabled students as a result. In other words, either the general education classroom was characterized as hostile territory, potentially damaging to students with disabilities, or the students themselves were thought to pose a serious risk to others. Because of these perceived differences, integration was thought to require either inordinate time (in the case of desegregation) or training (in the case of inclusion). Clearly, in both instances, students who were previously segregated were thought to be so radically different and deficient that it was believed that incorporating them into the everyday workings of the classroom would cause unprecedented upheaval and potential chaos. The great number of calls for either more time or more training to adjust, underscores the perceived difficulty integration was thought to entail. Moreover, promoting integration without working to dispel the bias behind such attitudes has proven ineffective.

Despite calls for time and training, however, few districts instituted specific plans to prepare teachers, parents, or students for implementation of either *Brown* or inclusion. Instead, time was used to delay or strategize how to circumvent the law. From the beginning there was pessimistic speculation about the ability of *Brown* or *IDEA* to transform education. *Brown's* phrase "with all deliberate speed" led to predictions of a half or a full century for implementation. Many denied that changes would occur at all. Typically these denials were marked by a stubborn insistence that integration would *never* occur ("Georgia editors," 1955, p. 4). Some of the most resistant voices were politicians, such as a former governor of Georgia, who said flatly, "those who do not agree with the Court need not comply" ("Supreme Court decision, 1954, p. 4). Moreover, tactics such as last-ditch efforts to finally equalize existing Black schools were clearly a ploy to appease the Black community. In the case of inclusion, teachers claimed that they were not ready and did not have the necessary expertise needed to educate disabled students. Ironically, although many teachers continue to make this claim, very little has changed in terms of schools or universities requiring all teachers to be trained to meet the needs of a diverse range of students.

Those opposing integration often portrayed education as a competitive arena in which students of color or those with disabilities would be overlooked, fall through the cracks, or "drown." In addition, many parents and advocates worried that hard-won services for students with disabilities would be lost. Likewise, many in the Black community worried that White schools would fail to maintain high expectations of Black students or to instill in them a sense of cultural pride. Thus, exclusion was sometimes described as a preferable option for students' own best interests. However, benefits reaped by White and nondisabled students remain obscured by these arguments. Thus, the needs and desires of the general education system for homogeneity are left unstated and unacknowledged, because only certain students are seen as having "special needs."

In both debates the issue of choice was often invoked. Some warned that by choosing an integrated or inclusive setting, parents risked placing their children in a potentially hostile environment. And, it is true that historically general education has been unwelcoming to both groups. Thus, there remains a substantial imbalance of power in terms of whether individuals can choose to attend public institutions, or whether public institutions allow individuals to attend. Furthermore, neither *Brown* nor inclusion required substantive changes to the existing structures of the schools. In other words, students with disabilities and students of color were simply to be integrated into an already established system—a system that did not see itself as in need of change or in any way lacking. As many students have experienced, simply being included in a school or a classroom does not guarantee full participation or true integration. Moreover, we would argue that choice requires two (or more) equally viable options, which are not typically afforded to marginalized groups.

As the previous section illustrates, some of the resistance encountered by both reforms is framed in very indirect ways. Couched in language that suggests that schools will get around to integration in due time or once they get everyone ready, belies the fact that decades later, schools (and teachers) would continue to claim that they were not yet ready. In contrast, the examples in the next section speak in more direct tones. Here we analyze examples of outright refusal or overt defiance contained in the most outwardly resistant voices that we encountered. They were important for us to include because they illustrate the depth of resistance that both *Brown* and inclusion would have to overcome.

Not Here, Not Now, Not Ever

Perhaps the most shocking of all of the data that we collected, besides threats of violent retaliation, were the letters and editorials contending that the only reasonable response to desegregation orders was outright refusal. Some officials even went as far as to threaten to abolish public education altogether rather than desegregate the schools.

"The private school . . . deserves the award of 'Nonsense of the Year'" (C. J. Smith, 1954, p. 4).

Voucher plans would "divert public money into subsidies for specialized groups—namely, the proprietors of so-called private schools. Of course, these schools would not really be private. They would be free schools for White children to which

Negro children would not be admitted" ("Georgia v. U.S."
1954, p. 20).

"[D]esegregation would bring the 'reluctant' abandonment of
public schools in this state" ("South reacts," 1955, p. 30).

Those who defended segregated placements for students with disabilities also warned that inclusive practices would cause disastrous effects. Inclusion, like desegregation, was characterized by its opponents as impossible and even dangerous. Described as a catalyst for destruction, inclusion was perceived as annihilating support services and threatening academic standards and codes of behavior.

"Albert Shanker, president of the American Federation of Teachers, says a lot of dumping is going on. The AFT believes that many teachers are either afraid or skeptical of the inclusion policies. An AFT poll of West Virginia teachers shows that 78 percent of respondents think that disabled students won't benefit from the inclusion policy; 87 percent said other students wouldn't benefit either" (Leo, 1994, p. 22).

"[Inclusion] tosses the disabled child into an environment in which the child cannot possible develop, and in fact, may regress, while simultaneously depriving the remainder of the class of critical instructional time" (Kastens, 1995, p. A15).

One Southern governor proclaimed, "There will be no . . . mixing of the races in any of the state-operated educational institutions. . . . With all due respect to the mighty power of the United States government, it will never be able to force racial integration" ("Nothing to fear," 1956, p. 15).

"[T]here will be no integration South Carolina" ("What they say," 1956, January, p. 5).

"Tuscaloosa was a powder-puff compared with what could happen here. . . . Negroes are not going to school with Whites in Marshall" (Segregation groups," 1956, p. C6).

"Rep. Monique Davis (27) . . . agreed with members of the Ada S. McKinley Foundation who likened mainstreaming children with disabilities into the public school system to an

act of 'terrorism,' [referring to the dismantling of special education as] 'a terrorist attack against education'" (Strausberg,
1992, p. 3).

"The students and teachers might not know how to react if
the handicapped student had a nervous breakdown or became
deranged. Only with the help of uniquely-trained and caring
teachers, should mentally handicapped students be allowed
into the regular high school environment" (Grady, 1989, p.
M6).

"[T]he fact remains that Georgia will never permit integration
in its public schools. . . . [T]hey will never accept it" ("Georgia
editors," 1955, p. 4).

"[T]hey'll run out of grits in Georgia before the White politicians pay heed to the court's declaration that racial segregation
is . . . unconstitutional" (Lahey, 1954, p. 23).

One parent asserted, "Our children and special education
have been wed and there cannot be a divorce" (Strausberg,
1992, p. 3).

"Parents should seek assurances that their children will never
be forced to sit near, or be left alone with, another child
known to have been violent towards other children or adults,
or known to be a regular disrupter of classes" (Inson, 2000,
p. 33).

Making dire predictions of disaster and destruction, opponents of desegregation threaten to abolish public schools rather than institute court orders. In
stating their resistance, opponents do not articulate *why* they are so opposed to
integration, appearing to operate from an unquestioned standpoint of right-
eousness of their "way of life." Similarly, opponents of inclusion describe public education as being under siege from enemy forces seeking to destroy the existing social order. The interests of the normative student is placed in
opposition to a "threatening" other who challenges the status quo, which is assumed to be normal and natural.

Drawing on problematic stereotypes, opponents of integration and inclusion conjure images of invasion and disruption. Desegregation is commonly referred to as "mixing," a thinly veiled euphemism for miscegenation. Outraged

White fathers deplore the idea that their little (White) girls would be forced to sit next to a Black boy. Such unexamined fears evoke the myth of the Black rapist, ironically obfuscating the history of the physical and sexual exploitation of Black women by White male slave owners.

Children with disabilities are typically portrayed as behaviorally disordered to the point of derangement, harboring desires to injure "normal" children. Again, parents of nondisabled students suggest that their children should be protected from these dangerous and disabled menaces. Many expressed fear of disabled children being "dumped" (like trash) into the general classroom. Clearly some students are positioned as more valued than their excluded counterparts. The message behind this resistance is clear: the purity of the normative student body would not be contaminated by racial or disabled others.

In the final section we include several follow-up reports on the successes of integration. In these reports, advocates hoped to demonstrate that integration need not be feared. These were clearly designed to counter some of the negative predictions that were being made about integration. It is important to note that although *Brown* caused quite a stir in 1954, integration did not begin in earnest in many schools until the late 1960s (O. L. Davis, 2004; Wells et al., 2004).

Progress Reports From the Field

Southern School News and several high-profile papers, including the *New York Times,* published follow-up reports from schools, mostly in the border states, that had begun to implement desegregation. Many of these reports included interviews with teachers and principals. Editorial coverage and letters to the editor regarding the progress of inclusion often cite educational research, school success stories, and positive individual experiences from parents of disabled and nondisabled children. These reports provided a counternarrative to the multitude of letters and editorials claiming that desegregation was not feasible.

> "[Principals of several schools reported that] everything had gone along smoothly this past year and that teachers and pupils were working together without friction. . . . Desegregation in the Baltimore public schools had progressed in a most satisfactory manner. . . . All in all it has been an excellent example of American democracy at work" ("What they say," 1956, June, p. 9).
>
> Any "anticipated friction did not develop and . . . the opening was 'amazingly successful' because of cooperative efforts by parents, children, and teachers" (Huston, 1956, p. 2C).

"A 1993 study by the Department of Education found disabled students taught in inclusive classes were more likely to hold jobs and participate in their communities after high school" (DeFord, 1998, p. W8).

"Studies have shown that students without disabilities are still achieving at the same rate and, in fact, may be learning more than their peers who don't have this opportunity" (McMullen, 1994, p. 7B).

"Our experience has been that the integration of disabled and non-disabled students benefits everyone. The atmosphere of the school is tolerant and compassionate. The self-esteem and academic performance of physically disabled students in the general education setting rise dramatically. Their non-disabled peers develop a level of caring and understanding that is remarkable" (Gest, 2002, p. 23).

A representative of one Catholic school commented, "We haven't had any kind of problem. Everything has been most satisfactory. You would never know there was any difference in color on the playground or any place" ("Parochial school," 1955, p. 14).

One principal described two "threatening phone calls" after several White boys danced with Black girls at "an afternoon Soc Hop" ("Parochial school," 1955, p. 14).

"It [putting their child back in a segregated class] would be like putting him back to sleep" (Evans, 1996, p. H4).

In an article featuring the experiences of a mother and her son, one reporter noted: "Once she believed he would always be dependent; today she foresees 'a self-sufficient young man who is not going to need a group home or supported work environment.'" (DeFord, 1998, p. W8).

"St. Louis School board president Burton Sawyer . . . regards the first year's experience as a decided success, and proof that integration will gain acceptance despite a community's initial reluctance to approve it. . . . Taking the year as a whole, we feel integration has worked remarkably well. . . . [The principal] and teaching staff say the biggest problem has been the scholastic disparity between the Negros and Whites" ("First year a 'success,'" 1955, p. 19).

As one teacher states, "The Negroes in her room were slower in almost all subjects than the Whites. They seemed to have poor work habits and a tendency to inattention. The result, she felt, was to lower the academic achievement of the whole class" ("Study made," 1956, p. 12).

"Collin is now a student in a regular education class. He is starting to 'show what he knows,' as he calls it—not only the basic kindergarten fare of shapes and numbers but also how to spell and read. These skills are never demonstrated in a segregated classroom" (Jacobs, 1999, p. B8).

" 'I was one of the scared parents,' said Alicia Pizza, whose 10-year-old autistic son had been at the Ridge School for several years before moving to a special class at Kingsville Elementary in September. She says her son's progress is considerable. 'I used to walk him to the school bus, holding his hand. Now I open the door and he's gone. The children in our neighborhood look at him differently now. They don't say, 'Kevin, you can't play.'" (Maushard, 1994, p. 1B).

In published follow-up reports on school desegregation and inclusion teachers, parents and school officials share their experiences regarding integration. These reports from the field seemed to serve the purpose of calming the fears of those who continued to oppose integration. Often individuals spoke of their initial apprehension and subsequent relief that their predictions had not come to pass. On the whole, reports published after *Brown* are positive, with examples of smooth implementation and benefits to all involved. Follow-up reports on inclusion, however, tend to run the gamut. Many include statements from parents who relayed in emotional tones about how their child benefited from the experience—although the converse was also true.[4] Parents reporting negative experiences tend to focus on the loss of supports for their children, which were not adequately provided in the general education setting. Often teachers admitted feeling nervous initially, but find the experience positive both for them and their students. Teachers who report negative experiences tend to either focus on a lack of supports in the classroom or difficulties handling challenging behavior. Students with behavioral disabilities are overrepresented in these reports and are described as presenting extremely challenging and unpredictable behaviors. Students with less severe and nonbehavioral disabilities, who represent the vast majority of students with disabilities, are typically not the focus of these reports.

In the initial follow-up reports after *Brown,* there is a direct conflation of race and dis/ability. Just as students with behavioral problems are the focus of follow-up reports on inclusion, students of color who are underachieving are typically the sole focus of follow-up reports on desegregation. In these reports we took note of the hyperfocus on academic differences between White and Black students. In one report, a principal claims that although students are getting along "famously," very few of the Black students are "rated by standard tests in the above average group. . . . Most [are] low average or below average" ("Missouri," 1955, p. 19). Elementary teachers in this school are also interviewed. A sixth grade teacher describes most of the Black students in her class as "definitely slow to learn . . . [and] slower physically and mentally" (p. 19). Her colleague, a fourth grade teacher, agrees, calling the "scholastic differences . . . dreadful" (p. 19). She tells the reporter that the "individual needs of the very inferior Negro students just cannot be met in a class of this size." She stresses that White and Black students learn differently and Black students "have trouble following detailed instructions" (p. 19). Finally, a first grade teacher reports, "The five Negroes are all below average, and the lowest in the class" (p. 19).

The difficulties mentioned in these reports are attributed solely to the children being integrated or to their cultural and familial backgrounds, which are assumed to be lacking. Differences in achievement are *not* seen as a failure of the school or to bias in the measures of achievement, none of which are cited. Many of the follow-up reports after *Brown* include student comparisons on every dimension imaginable, and "ability" is increasingly enlisted to justify segregation and tracking within schools. A sharp rise in standardized testing at this time further codified these reported differences between groups of students within integrated schools and justified various ways to regroup students.

Schools in St. Louis were followed in the first and second years after integration in the *Southern School News.* The high school enrollment jumped from 900 to 1400 in the first year of integration with the addition of 500 Black students. As a result, after one year, a third of the high school students in the previously all-White school were Black ("First year of desegregation," 1956, p. 3). Although desegregation in St. Louis schools proceeded "without a single incident of identifiable racial friction," in the first year teachers report vast differences between their White and Black students. For example, teachers claim that Black students are "tardier to school, tardier to class, more prone to skip an afternoon's classes, more inclined to absenteeism" (p. 3).

Teachers and administrators in these reports seem to have come to a consensus that the "biggest problem [posed by integration] is the difference in academic aptitude and achievement" between White and Black students ("Missouri," 1955, p. 19). Charts are commonly featured to document comparisons in various subjects along racial lines, carefully listed in percentages. Reporters are careful to mention that teachers compared students, "without reference to racial prejudice, and attributing the facts solely to differences in cultural, social and economic background" ("First year of desegregation," 1956, p. 3). As this statement illustrates, there is some care taken with the ways student differences are explained. We find similar statements about differences in ability or achievement not being racial, per se, in this and other articles. Of course, although teachers are not willing to attribute differences to race, they have no problem pathologizing students' cultural or familial backgrounds. Thus, we see a shift from regarding achievement differences between different groups as genetic to seeing them as cultural.

The following year, in an article entitled, "The Second Year is Harder," St. Louis teachers state that, "now the novelty has worn off" ("Second year," 1956, p. 1). The teachers report that in the second year the "scholastic disparity remains just as great . . . [but that these differences are] now complicated by feelings of frustration and defensiveness on the part of the Negroes" (p. 3). The fact that Black students must deal with the indignity of being called "slow learners" and "below average" in their local paper is not seen as having anything to do with these "feelings of frustration and defensiveness" (p. 1). Again this year, the principal is careful to say,

> They are not racial differences. . . . They are differences of cultural background, family habits, educational level, interest in and capacity for learning, and parental concern and direction, and so on. It is not the color of the skin that makes these differences. . . . The fact is we now have in our school one group of youngsters so very different in all these ways that the teaching problem is complicated and the social results in the classroom difficult. ("Second year," 1956, p. 1)

Although she is careful not to attribute differences to race, her words are contradicted by an accompanying chart, which lists numbers of students who are White and Black and then divides those groups into average, below average, and above average ("Second year," 1956, p. 1). The chart does not explain, however, how the school came up with these numbers or what criteria they used to determine these categories. Moreover, on this list only one Black student is rated above average out of a total of 59 Black students (less than 2 percent), whereas 27 percent of White students in the school are deemed above average. In fact, more Black students are rated as below average (62 percent) than in the average or above average categories combined! Only 21 percent of the White students are rated in below average range. No text accompanied the chart—the figures are reported simply as fact.

In this second-year report, teachers are again interviewed. One teacher claims that the "majority of Negro pupils in her class are slow learners, need special attention, [and] may ultimately affect the quality of education available to others" ("Second year," 1956, p. 1). She also finds Black parents "uncooperative and unresponsive to suggestions." She concludes from her observations that, "Negroes have a poorly developed sense of responsibility, apparently due to neglect at home" (p. 1). Another teacher explains that Black students are experiencing a "conflict between *traditional* [italics added] standards for middle class White children and lower standards, which Negroes in a segregated school and at home had been accustomed to" (p. 1). Again, we find an almost unrelenting focus on differences between White and Black students and, similarly, differences are not attributed directly to race. Some of the interviewers go as far as to inquire about differences in "hygiene and cleanliness" ("First year of desegregation," 1956, p. 3) or "health and sanitation problems" ("Parochial school," 1955, p. 14) between White and Black students, even though teachers did not report any differences in these areas. The fact that hygiene and sanitation is even questioned reflects an assumption about the depth and scope of presumed racial differences. Concerns about sanitation and health also show up in arguments against including students with disabilities in the general education classroom, particularly students who are considered to have more severe disabilities or more significant physical needs.

Teachers in these follow-up reports are often asked to reflect on the impact that increased diversity among students is having on themselves and other teachers. In one article two teachers give very different responses to this question. One teacher reflects, "Negroes may benefit from integration, but at this stage the teacher is drained of vitality due to strain of managing differences in academic standards, cultural background, behavior patterns, personality" ("Second year," 1956, p. 1). The reporter contrasts this teacher's experience with another teacher who has a very different experience. The reporter describes:

> one new teacher who had just come out of university, where she studied alongside Negroes in a wholly integrated situation, did not report nearly so many problems and disappointments as some of those who had been teaching for many years in an all-white school. She accepted integration from the start and began her teaching career within that frame of reference. (p. 1)

At least in this example we can see some hint that the problem of diversity may lie in perceptions and attitudes of teachers and administrators, or even White students and families, as opposed to Black students.

Because in follow-up reports on desegregation and inclusion students are held responsible for their so-called shortcomings, there is no need to consider how classroom practices failed to change in order to accommodate diversity. We see, for example, no discussion of "changes in curriculum, teacher expectations, school buildings, social structures, and classroom organization" (Gabel, 2002, p. 188). Moreover, without significant reflection and changes in understanding the philosophical, moral, and ethical dimensions of integration or inclusion, educational institutions and the educators within them remain calcified in ideologies prioritizing sameness over difference. Such attitudes and unwavering commitment to the status quo create formidable barriers to integration.

In these follow-ups, teachers and school officials claim to support desegregation and inclusion in theory, but maintain the need of special provisions for *some* students. This argument echoes the familiar appeal for a gradual implementation of integration. It is grounded in the belief that there is a need for special classes, but only for *some* students. It should come as no surprise that students from nondominant racial, cultural, and disability groups are characterized as the ones who "cannot" be assimilated. This continues to play out in current practice where students of color with disabilities are overrepresented in special education and educated in the most restrictive of special education placements (Losen & Orfield, 2002).

Perhaps the most disturbing aspect of any of these reports is the second follow-up from St. Louis, in which a teacher states that "segregation within integration" is developing this year, not on racial lines but those of ability and cultural background ("Second year," 1956, p. 1). Apparently, the same students who, a year ago, were "getting along famously" are now resegregating themselves in accordance with school-based definitions of ability. The teacher describes the students as "voluntarily" segregating themselves. The teacher claims, "Neither group seeks out the other . . . [and] each seems to find it more comfortable to be with [his/her] own kind" (p. 5). After two years, [Mrs. Compton] agrees with these divisions and says that the most "retarded Negroes should be given special attention in classes for slow children, so that they would not burden the regular classes" (p. 1). This theme of diversity being a burden or drain on the system would surface again with the inclusion of students with disabilities. In both cases the normative space of the classroom is brought back to balance with the help of segregated classes for students with disabilities.

Discussion

In the final section, *Progress Reports,* we illustrate the various measures of success that are experienced as a result of desegregation and inclusion. Yet, these triumphs are juxtaposed with tensions among various stakeholders. While some schools seem ready to integrate, others are clearly not. For every parent who wants their child with a disability to be in an inclusive setting, there is another who demands segregated services. In the first section, *Evolution or Revolution,* we see how perceptions of the pace of change vary enormously. Many advocates call for significant change to begin immediately, but their calls are often met with delay or even refusal. The most vociferous opposition is charted in *Not Here, Not Now, Not Ever,* where the most resistant opponents urge group mobilization and noncompliance. Although these themes appear distinct, they coalesce around the broader theme of *when* and *how* to implement change. In the push-and-pull between opponents and proponents, the former managed to slow down the process of integration considerably. The "when" became synonymous with "soon," just as the "how" became viewed as euphemism for "slowly." Arguments favoring gradualism have prevailed in both discourses, leading us to reflect upon the merits and dangers of this approach.

Long-standing institutionalized racism and ableism is reflected in the pace with which actual change took place. After both *Brown* and *IDEA,* the shifting expectations of teachers toward their more culturally diverse classrooms and variously abled students caused considerable reactions that often negatively impacted students. Both groups are feared in terms of "tipping the scales" toward classes that would be considered too Black or too disabled. Teachers complain that they are not adequately prepared for impending changes, often becoming angry at their predicament. The fear of Black students or disabled students as unwanted elements, virtual borderline criminals, is openly expressed. While many Black teachers fear the loss of their jobs in the immediate post-*Brown* era, special educators likewise fear that their role will be diminished or eclipsed in inclusive classrooms.

The various responses to integration served to inhibit both the integration of African American students and the inclusion of children with disabilities. For example, immediately after the *Brown* decision, local education authorities offered more financial resources to existing Black schools; similarly, after *IDEA*, monies continued to be allocated to build separate schools for severely disabled children. Moreover, loopholes existed within the very legislation that was designed to forge change. *Brown II* contained the phrase "with all deliberate speed," subsequently interpreted by many states as "proceed gradually, if at all." Similarly, *IDEA* allowed for a continuum of services that were construed as synonymous with separate placements. Both laws created a wake of increased testing, tracking, and academic labeling predicated on notions of ability.

Lessons Learned

This tangled history of resegregation and special education illustrates the danger and ineffectiveness of single issue or categorical approaches to educational reform. Specifically, we highlight how, because *Brown* did not predict how schools might develop new forms of segregating students based on biased notions of ability, efforts toward school desegregation failed to foresee how special education would come to be used to circumvent the intent of the law. Similarly, because *IDEA* did not address issues of racial inequity and bias, it failed to consider how dominant ideas about ability would be used to maintain White, middle class privilege through the disproportionate placement of students of color in certain special education categories. In both cases, failing to consider the intersections of race and dis/ability allowed schools to maintain the status quo of segregated schooling.

A central lesson in this chapter is the futility of incremental or gradual change, which enables those who desire to maintain the status quo time to institute new strategies to circumvent or subvert change, rather than time to adjust or prepare for change. Gradualism, while ostensibly conciliatory, is vaguely located somewhere "in the middle," and thus appeases both sides to some degree, at least temporarily. However, as we have seen, such a compromise is usually a tactic for delay, allowing opponents time to think of ways to block progress. Thus, despite what is sometimes characterized as a sincere attempt at educational change, Hochschild

(1984) argues that incremental approaches to school desegregation have proven "little . . . help [to] either minorities or whites" (p. 91). By arguing that "Half a loaf, in this case, may be worse than none at all" (p. 91), Hochschild also suggests that incremental policies may be more damaging in the long run than no policy at all, because gradualism results in backlash and more subtle forms of resegregation. As DeCuir and Dixson (2004) argue, incremental change most "benefits those who are not adversely affected" (p. 29).

The alarmist, dire warnings that often contribute to the adoption of gradualist responses to change, are tantamount to scare tactics that usually predict worst-case scenarios. In the case of inclusion, the amount of coverage that is given to "violent" students far exceeds the proportion of students with emotional disturbance in the special education population. In addition, parents and schools who want children to receive certain services rely on legal remedies to achieve their goals. In schools, the subjective LRE clause is used to defend placements in restrictive settings. At the court level, judges have also interpreted the clause to favor special settings. Thus, on a case-by-case basis, and mobilizing the legal system to defend exclusion, widespread inclusion of students with disabilities has been significantly slowed.

Rather than claiming that working in inclusive classes is not feasible because of class size, materials, access to resources, and insufficient personnel, schools should work to change these variables. Instead, special educators and general educators alike stress the benefits of having a separate system. Yet this system seems to suit the purposes of teachers more than students. And although inclusion has been tremendously successful in many schools, it is likely to be viewed as a technical challenge that should aim to minimize any imposition on the existing system, rather than as a way of thinking and being that will require structural changes to the educational system.

Thus, a bifurcated system continues to exist, despite high-profile attempts to ameliorate inequities. For example, New York State Department of Education revised its initial statement that *all* students would have to take Regents exams in order to graduate high school. Students labeled disabled are now required to take either the general standardized tests or, if this was not appropriate, an alternative assessment. With the push for higher standards, only students with significant special education needs were eligible for such alternative assessments, and many students with high-incidence disabilities still do not qualify. Such accommodations, however, could be appropriate for a range of students for a variety of reasons (such as children of migrant workers or English language learners) and would provide a way for students who are at risk of failing traditional assessments to stay in school and graduate.

Unfortunately, the various reactions to *Brown* demonstrate how gradualism has been used to subvert the original intent of the law. It is important to remember that although *IDEA* mandates a free and appropriate public education for students with disabilities and stresses an environment as close to general education as possible, it does not mandate inclusion. This, in and of itself, allows a perpetual state of gradualism to exist—as *each* child's placement is debated separately. As a result, many of the same patterns of resistance, both subtle and blatant, emerged in response to inclusion. In the next chapter we shift our gaze to political cartoons from the *Brown* era, with the purpose of showing how human difference—in this case "race"—is discursively constructed, and used to further substantiate the rationale of separation within schools.

4

POWER, RACE, AND RE/PRESENTATION: POLITICAL CARTOONS OF THE *BROWN* ERA

4

**POWER, RACE, AND RE/PRESENTATION:
POLITICAL CARTOONS OF
THE *BROWN* ERA**

Preface

Race in the American Landscape

Atlanta Constitution (1954, May 22) p. 4.
The image is chilling (See Figure 1). A sturdy tree dominates the picture, replete
with human skulls. Inscribed on the trunk are the words "racial and religious prejudice" (p. 4). The limbs of the tree are laden with the fruit of suspicion, hate, bitter-
ness, bigotry, discord, and death. At the foot of the tree lies an axe that has been
used to cut a notch out of the trunk. The label attached to the axe reads, "Entertain
a brotherly affection and love for one another." It is signed, "Washington." Taken
together, the visual image and verbal text suggest that prevailing prejudicial racial
and religious beliefs are deeply rooted, beginning a growth cycle that ultimately
bears the fruit of death (a paradox, given that a tree usually symbolizes life). The axe
evokes the "true" intention and spirit of George Washington, regarded by many as
a founder of the nation and its greatest president. The axe also conjures the mytho-
logical tale of a young Washington chopping down a cherry tree. Because he "could
not tell a lie," Washington's words are invested with undisputed truth. The image of
the tree with "strange fruit hanging"[1] is associated with White terrorism in the
South that resulted in the lynching of Black men. Although the axe has been used
against the tree, it has not made sufficient progress to prevent the tree from yielding
a harvest of hatred. The caption signals the need to chop down the tree, thereby

An Unfinished Job

FIGURE 1. *Atlanta Constitution* (1954, May 22) p. 4.

stemming racial and religious prejudice. With its outstretched handle, the axe is a call to arms. Appealing to each reader, it urges us to pick up the axe to help complete the task and maintain the integrity of the founder of the country.

Political Cartoons of the *Brown* Era

Political cartoons are cultural artifacts that offer a glimpse into various points of view operating during particular times and places. Because of their primarily visual nature, cartoons can be "read" against, instead of, or in addition to the written text.

In a cartoon, even complex issues can be reduced to a single image with minimal writing. As such, cartoons have the ability to convey meaning in an extraordinarily concentrated manner. Although commonly cited as useful artifacts that capture the tenor of a particular time, cartoons are generally considered supplementary material to emphasize the news stories or editorials they usually accompany. Whether featured in a limited manner in history texts or sparingly in social science examinations, cartoons surface here and there, but rarely as a constellation of images and ideas that speak for a particular period in history.

To the best of our knowledge, no published research has been done using political cartoons as the primary corpus of data. In reviewing 92 political cartoons published between 1952 and 1957 in mainstream ("White") and independent ("Black") presses,[2] we analyzed how racial "differences" were discursively (re)constructed through such representations. In focusing on representation, we were particularly interested in interrogating the workings of power: Who is represented in the image? How are they represented? What are the implications for "others"? What knowledge is being generated/obscured in the representation?

Political cartoons are overtly *political* because they focus essentially on operations of power. As political images they have the potential to exert significant influence. In the political cartoons we analyzed, assertions of power by dominant groups as well as assertions of resistance by marginalized groups were both prominent. By analyzing how knowledge claims are generated through political cartoons, we sought insights about how power influenced racial representation depicted in the political cartoons about the historic *Brown v. Board of Education* decsion. These historically situated representations reflect then-contemporary beliefs, ideas, and feelings about race, particularly in regard to integration.

The Evolution of Political Cartoons

The history of cartooning can be traced to Renaissance Italy, where quick and humorous depictions, or *caricaturas,* gained favor as a "counterart" to the formalist portraiture popular during this era. Their usefulness in conveying a particular message was recognized by Martin Luther when he circulated images that contrasted Christ's teachings about humility with contemporary depictions of papal opulence and corruption. Cartoons proved exceptionally effective in gaining the attention of a large population quite literate in visual allegory and symbolic depictions of religious teachings, yet more unfamiliar with written texts. Benjamin Franklin circulated the first political cartoon in the U.S. in the 1750s. Featuring a drawing of a severed snake, in which each segment represented a particular colony, the cartoon included the message, "Join or die" (Backer, n.d., p. 2). The explicit purpose of this cartoon was to forge an intercolonial counterpower to contest British rule.

Over the next century, cartoons evolved considerably in sophistication. Political subjects were blatantly ridiculed or praised in widely circulating newspapers and magazines. As Backer (n.d.) points out, appealing to the person on the street, satiric cartoons capitalized on varied levels of education and recognized the power of common people to enact social change through their collective economic power. In other words, the importance of the general populace in a democracy was not to be underestimated; every viewer of cartoons was a potential voter.[3]

Political Cartoons as Influential Cultural Texts

Berger (1972) notes that previous societies did not contend with the "concentration of images, [and] such a density of visual messages" (p. 129) that rapidly evolved in 20th-century Western life. Within a media-saturated culture, a relentless barrage of images and texts aggressively compete for our attention. One dominant form of media is the newspaper, which circulates on local, regional, and national levels and increasingly in electronic formats. Although most news sources claim at least a certain degree of objectivity, editorial pages are under no such expectation. An integral part of any editorial page, political cartoons are often considered part of the ideology of a particular newspaper. Hence, depictions of issues like desegregation can vary considerably, depending on the assumed readership of a particular newspaper — White or Black, northern or southern.

The contents of any newspaper reflect decisions by editors as well as various writers, cartoonists, and others. In the process of selection, certain positions are favored over others, although rarely are these decisions made explicit. The ideology of those individuals invested with the power to make such choices influences which concepts and ideas make it to final press. Thus, the "circulation" of knowledge is actually determined by those who own the means of production, an observation also made by Marx (1959). Gledhill (1997) elaborates upon this point, writing "dominant classes subject the masses to ideologies, which make the social relations of domination and oppression appear natural and so mystify the 'real' conditions of existence" (p. 348). It could be said that the ideological influence of the media acts as a form of cultural colonization. However, as Gramsci claims, its power lies not in force, but in persuasion: winning consent of particular beliefs, values or practices or competing successfully against alternatives (cited in Gledhill, 1997, p. 348). Thus, a Gramscian conceptualization of power always involves ongoing struggle as dominant (or hegemonic) knowledge claims and normative assumptions are contested, debunked, and/or reformulated. However, the dominant group's ability to persuade others to adopt or internalize their particular version of the truth is far from simple. In other words,

> Hegemony is established and contested in the interaction and negotiation between: (1) industrial production, (2) the semiotic work of the text, and (3) audience reception. Moreover, each stage contains within itself potential tensions and contradictions between the different economic, professional, aesthetic and personal practices and cultural traditions involved. (Gledhill, 1997, p. 353)

Although all knowledge has a particular grounding, there is no assurance that the reader will unquestioningly "take up" the information as intended; meaning is achieved through a complex, interactive process of negotiation. Further, each individual brings cultural, social, and historical forces to the task, influencing how "new" information is received and negotiated. On the border zones of this dynamic interplay between author, text, and individual consciousness, meaning is created (Bakhtin, 1986).

Although we would expect that newspapers would publish cartoons (and select editors) that generally uphold the ideological grounding of the organization and that subscribers would select news sources that matched their own belief systems, another consideration further complicates this picture. Many cartoons are syndicated or republished, often appearing in more than one newspaper. This "borrowing" means that multiple audiences have access to a broader selection of ideologically grounded cartoons. This practice raises many interesting questions: What does it mean when the *New York Times* prints a cartoon from the *Atlanta (Journal and) Constitution,* or *Southern School News* places a cartoon from the *Washington Post* alongside one from the *Chicago Defender?* What are the implications for creating or reading an image of Uncle Sam, for instance, that is depicted in the *New York Times* and then in a southern press? Which cartoons are imported from the mainstream press into the Black press, and vice versa? How does each readership and context change the range of possible meanings of any cartoon or image? What influence does surrounding text have upon the message of a featured cartoon? Obviously, despite the intended meanings of individual cartoonists, or the ideological grounding of a particular press, the open circulation of images creates multiple opportunities for numerous readings and counterreadings by a public influenced by many predictable and unpredictable contextual factors.

Cartoons as a Device for Creating Meaning

How does a cartoon create meaning? Before we can answer this question, it is useful to take stock of the actual format. As a "text," a cartoon has two components: a visual image and a textual component. The writing may be in the form of a caption—a message, quotation, or slogan. Often, supplementary text (typically in the form of labels) may appear instead of, or in addition to, a caption, inscribing particular images with symbolic value. For example, a judge's gavel might be labeled "Supreme Court decision," to clarify how the cartoonist wants the image to be understood. Hamilton (1997) explains that the power of a "telling image" is its ability to catch the attention and engage the interest of spectators (p. 83). The "telling image" is encoded with meaning to which most spectators have access. Garland-Thomson (1997a), for example, discusses familiar tropes of disability in literature and film as "lightening rods" for meaning, guiding the audience to a particular symbolic meaning and calling for a preestablished emotional response (p. 15). Similarly, while open to interpretation, each cartoon draws on familiar imagery to communicate a particular intent that is directed toward a particular audience. With captions and labeling, we the readers are led, often quite didactically, through the image. Thus, Lidchi (1997) suggests that "[a]ll texts involve an economy of meaning: foregrounding certain interpretations and excluding others" in a deliberate attempt to cut a clear route through the potentially ambiguous forest of possible meanings (p. 166).

In some respects, cartoons are similar to advertisements, but instead of promoting products, they promote ideas. Although Barthes (1977) alludes to advertising when he writes, "the caption helps me to choose *the correct level of perception,* permits me to focus not simply my gaze but also my understanding" (p. 39), the same can be said of cartoons. Hall (1997b) concurs that the caption helps to anchor the meaning of the image. In other words, according to Hall, the meaning of a photograph or other visual image "does not lie exclusively in the image but in the conjunction of image and text" (p. 228). Thus, although meanings are rarely fixed once and for all, there remains a *desired* meaning, anchored by words, which the spectator is expected to decode. Once the desired meaning is decoded, however, the spectator then engages in internal negotiations that involve either the acceptance or rejection of the knowledge represented.

To summarize, Hall (1997a) reminds us that meaning is neither inherent nor innate, but rather encoded by individuals (and collectives) situated in a particular time and place, and shaped by culture, society, and history. He explains, "It is we who fix the meaning so firmly that, after a while, it comes to seem natural and inevitable. [Thus,] the meaning is constructed by the system of representation" (p. 21). Meaning, therefore, is not external or "out there," but rather socially constructed. It is not fixed, but created.

Of particular importance to this project is how dominant-group meanings about race and disability come to be taken for granted or "naturalized." Furthermore, because no meaning is neutral, "all representations have social and political consequences" (Garland-Thomson, 2002, p. 75). As Hall (1997a) notes, representations

define what is normal, who belongs—and therefore, who is excluded. They are deeply inscribed in relations of power. Think of how profoundly our lives are shaped, depending upon which meanings of male/female, Black/White, rich/poor, gay/straight, young/old, citizen/alien, are in play in which circumstances. (p. 10)

Despite the fact that the constitution of "normal" is socially fabricated, what is deemed normal also comes to pass as natural. Yet, the notion of "natural" is highly problematic, because it suggests a world independent of human existence or cultural influence. The much-used phrase, "Is it man-made or natural?" captures the binary thinking behind these supposedly opposing concepts, suggesting two worlds, one with and one without human influence. In this binary, the natural world is envisioned as free from human influence; in other words, natural becomes synonymous with neutral. The blurring of normal into natural, and natural into neutral, exerts powerful, albeit unacknowledged, consequences, because many people accept societal notions of normalcy without question. However, an unquestioning acceptance of what has come to mean normal (natural, neutral)—

such as concepts of race—masks the ways certain groups benefit from such categories. Similar to Marx's notion that those who control the means of production therefore control knowledge, those who control the production of normalcy/ naturalness also wield great power.

The Myth of Natural: The Battle to Control Meaning

Barthes (1972) developed a basic premise that what we believe to be natural is actually mythical. He writes, "myth is a language" (p. 11) or "a type of speech" (p. 109) that serves to obscure the dominant-group interests behind it. As Lidchi (1997) explains, myth

> "naturalizes" speech, transmuting what is essentially *cultural* (historical, constructed and motivated) into something which it materializes as *natural* (transhistorical, innocent and factual). Myth's duplicity is therefore located in its ability to "naturalize" and make "innocent" what is profoundly motivated. (pp. 181–182)

In addition to written texts, Barthes believes that photography, cinema, reporting, sports, shows, and publicity are all forms of mythical speech (p. 110). We contend that political cartoons can be added to this list of media as an example of how myth is created, maintained, and also contested.

Barthes traces the creation of myth through a tridimensional system of signs: the signifier, the signified, and the sign. The *signifier* denotes a material reality (in this case, a visual image), the *signified* is a mental representation or abstract concept of that image or object, and the *sign* is the associative total of the image and concept. The cartoonist assumes that this system will be seamless, such that the perceived audience will understand the intended representation. For example, in many cartoons that we analyzed, the image of Uncle Sam (signifier) is used to represent "The United States of America" (signified), conveying particular beliefs and values of the U.S., such as patriotism, self-determinism, and independence (sign). Thus, the image of Uncle Sam stands in for a particular meaning when featured in a political cartoon. However, as previously noted, meaning shifts according to context. Therefore, the same image of Uncle Sam is also used to signify "northern intrusion on state's rights" when featured in a southern White press. Thus, all forms of representation carry the potential for ambiguity, or multiple readings even though an author or artist envisions a desired or intended meaning.

Troubling the "Natural Order" of Race

Barthes (1972) argues that "naturalized" discourse, or myth, is highly visible and accessible to individuals in society. He writes, "However paradoxical it may seem, myth hides nothing; its function is to distort, not make disappear" (p. 121). Race is an example of myth in that it is now understood as primarily a sociocultural construct rather than a biological reality. As a result of European colonization around the globe, the categorization of humans into races became commonplace. The concept of race became solidified by 19th-century scientists (Gilroy, 2000), many of whom were funded by European governmental powers invested in the economic exploitation of the non-European world (Gould, 1996). Race was originally conceived of and classified in terms of "scientific" hierarchies—with Germanic/Nordic/Anglo "races" positioned at the top, and Blacks (sub-Saharan Africans, Native Australians) at the bottom. However, as Haney-Lopez (1996) points out, "Science was not and is not independent of culture and society; science *is* culture and society" (p. 96). The commonly accepted classification system indicates the power of European culture to create and impose its own knowledge of "race."

Recently, critical race theorists have critiqued the very notion of "race," shifting its meaning from a biological phenomenon to an historical, governmental, and legal classification systems. This allows us to understand race in relation to dominant power structures (Haney-Lopez, 1996). Race then becomes foregrounded as a result of social practices based upon ways of thinking, and not as a set of inherent features and qualities. Races therefore are "not objective, inherent, or fixed, they correspond to no biographical or genetic reality; rather, races are categories that society invents, manipulates, or retires when convenient" (Delgado & Stefancic, 2001, pp. 2–3).

The very concept of race requires that physical differences in people stand in for something meaningful. The host of associations are determined, of course, by the dominant culture. Operating in this way, race becomes "naturalized" and taken as fact. Critical race theorists have questioned hierarchies of human value based on race, which have long upheld the superiority of people considered "White" as differentiated from supposedly inferior "people of color" (Haney-Lopez, 1996). Similarly, disability studies scholars have sought to disassociate physical differences (impairments) from the social meanings and consequences of those differences (disability) to highlight how society has created disability and infused it with particular meanings that benefit the dominant (nondisabled) group (Linton, 1998; Oliver, 1996; Garland-Thomson, 1997a).

Using a Discursive Approach to "Racial Difference"

"Concerned with the effects and consequences of representation," a discursive approach focuses on the politics of representation (Hall, 1997a, p. 6). As stated, race is not a "real" distinction, but rather a signifier of difference, of otherness, created by colonizing ideologies of Western culture. As such, race is legitimized through scientific, anthropological, and legal discourses. Ironically, the hierarchical ordering of race and disability says more about the classifying culture than about those who have been classified. Because race is imposed, positionalities are assigned to individuals according to their relative privilege or their lack thereof. Thus, every "race" is placed on a scale of assumed diminishing value from Whiteness that ends

with those who are of African descent (Gould, 1996). Positioned as binary oppo-
sites, Whites and people of color, abled and disabled, each category defines the
other, becoming "an irreducible opposite" of the other (Haug et al., 1987, p. 196).
As with all binaries, the ascendant term is imbued with power, and the descendent
term is contrasted by degrees of deviation and inferiority. Thus, to be White
means *not* being Black/abnormal/a minority. Conversely, to be Black means *not* to
be White/normal/majority.

Images of cultural others in mainstream publications were (and still are) manufactured specifically to emphasize differences. Thus, the body itself is a discursive
site, where differences are oversimplified, reduced, and inscribed into racial categories of White and non-White. As Hall argues, "[t]he representation of 'difference'
through the body became the discursive site through which much of this racialized
[and ableist] knowledge was produced and circulated" (1997b, p. 244).

Hall (1997c) also poses the question, "Does visual language [paintings, draw-
ings, advertisements] reflect a truth about the world which is already there or does
it produce meanings about the world through representing it?" (p. 7). The answer
to his question, in postmodernist terms, is "yes" on both counts. Because there are
no absolutes,[4] truth will always be partially represented, forged by specific ideological forces that are always subject to contestation. However, the very act of asserting a version of "truth" contributes to the circulation of a particularized knowledge claim. Because social structures of a culture (including the categorization of
race and disability) are represented through writing, visuals, photography, sports,
reporting, and so on, their seeming naturalness permeates society. This naturalness, or what Barthes (1972) calls "mythology," obscures the process of subjectification involved in *becoming* "raced"[5] or "disabled." In the words of Haug (1987),
subjectification "can be understood as the process by which individuals work
themselves into social structures they themselves do not consciously determine,
but to which they subordinate themselves" (Haug, p. 59). Furthermore, it is the
willingness of people to conform to preestablished social structures that maintains
and strengthens them. In other words, "It is the fact of our active participation
that gives social structures their solidity" (p. 59).

In a discursive analysis, emphasis is placed on "the historical specificity of a particular form or 'regime' of representation: not on 'language' as a general concern,
but on specific languages or meanings, and how they are deployed at particular
times, in particular places" (Hall, 1997c, p. 6). Because the body is a site where
knowledge and power are constantly accepted and/or contested via discourse, it is
in a state of perpetual subjectification. Foucault (1980) maintained that the disci-
plining effect of power permeates "the very grain of individuals, touches their bodies and inserts itself into their actions and attitudes, their discourses, learning processes and everyday lives" (p. 39). By specifically attending to "race" and the
processes of racialization, of separating individuals into hierarchical structures of
worth, we come to understand how subjectification works. Matsuda et al. (1993)
argue that the impact of racial subjectification permeates all power structures in society. They contend that racism should be considered "not as isolated instances of

conscious bigoted decision making or prejudiced practice, but as [something] larger, systemic, structural, and cultural, as deeply psychologically and socially ingrained" (p. 5).

In an important work on subjectivity, Haug (1999) focused on the way individuals continuously remake society by entering into pregiven structures or categories, thereby reproducing both themselves and society. Gannon (2002), in exploring the legacies of subjectification of gender, concluded that structural exclusions create a sense of inferiority. Conversely, those who have power in a particular discourse exert influence over the lives "others," by controlling knowledge *for* and *about* them. Thus, the majority group defines its own actions

> as laudable, as "correcting" or "saving" another group from its own practices. They may remain oblivious to the fact that their activity is part of a complex system of ensuring that their own discourses and practices prevail as recognizably "superior," that recognized "superiority," facilitating their take-up of powerful positionings within the culture, and ensuring that their own utterances remain hearable as legitimate. (Davies, 2000, p. 20)

Thus, to be racialized as White within a system that prizes Whiteness, or non-disabled in a system that prizes ability, affords one the position of "naturally" subordinating all others. As Barthes's (1972) explanation of myth reveals, multiple forms of representation serve to reinforce and legitimate distortions that serve hegemonic needs of those in power.

Crafting a Theoretical Lens

A primary concern of this project is why certain individuals in society, based on notions of "race" and "disability," have been excluded from mainstream public schooling. Segregation is upheld through dominant understandings of human difference and justified by inherent (or "natural") incompatibility with "normal" students. Thus, to separate individuals based on their perceived differences has become a normalized practice. In our analysis of political cartoons we challenged the notion of inherent differences by carefully examining racial representation. Drawing upon ideas from Barthes (1972), Hall (1997a & b), and Foucault (1980), we focus on the manufactured nature of race, and how it works to uphold the hegemonic beliefs and interests of the dominant group. In our analysis we drew from the following three sets of ideas:

First, we used Barthes's theory of myth as a tool to deconstruct race in the everyday context of political cartoons. In viewing each cartoon, we analyzed the desired meaning—by using the three-pronged system of signifier (what are the images?), signified (what do they stand for?), and sign—(taken together, what do they mean?). This allowed us to consider what Berger (1972) terms "issues of social presence" (p. 33), asking questions such as: What relations of power are evident? What kinds of knowledge do different images help create? How are subjects depicted? How are they positioned in terms of power and knowledge?

Second, we drew from Hall's (1997b) ideas about representation. In viewing images we began with the assumption that meaning is not fixed, but created. This applied to both the production and the encoding of cartoons. By analyzing the visual representations of cartoons, we see how images both reflect and produce understandings of race. As Hall (1997b) stressed, representations are deeply implicated in the operations of power because they are invested with the "power to mark, assign and classify" actions that lead to and justify "ritualized expulsion" (p. 259).

Third, we understood from Foucault (1980) that power is the primary motivation for all human interactions. His theory that the human body is a site of discursive practice focused our attention on the myriad influences exerted upon, and negotiated by, each individual. Foucault's ideas were useful in considering the processes of subjectification, particularly the powerful forces that contribute to the racialization of bodies. This ongoing legacy is inextricably linked with the hierarchical nature of White power.

Fused together, we use these ideas as a theoretical lens to trouble the "nature" of race as it has been traditionally understood and, instead, to analyze race as a discursive construction. By focusing on political cartoons of the *Brown* era, our goal was to deconstruct representations of race and illuminate how these representations served to justify exclusion. In attending to both presences and absences in these images, we highlight the ways in which power is either invested or divested in particular individuals. Challenging "normal" conceptions of race, we locate forces that defended, reinforced, and expanded hegemonic notions of normalcy and upheld the sanctity of racial divisions.

Analysis of Cartoons

In the remaining sections of this chapter we analyze the construction of race by closely reading the juxtaposition of image and words within political cartoons of the *Brown* era.[6] In the following sections we analyze a sample of cartoons selected from both mainstream and independent Black presses. Our selection of cartoons was part calculated and part random. First, our data collection was limited to newspapers published between the years 1952 and 1958, several years before and after the *Brown* decision in 1954. Although there were undoubtedly more cartoons available during this period in selected and nonselected papers, we believe that we collected a fairly representative sample.[7] We collected well over 100 cartoons, but because of space constraints we reduced the number of those that we would analyze to 28, roughly divided among both mainstream and Black presses. The size of our sample allowed for both individual and cross-analysis of images. Finally, although racist depictions of certain animals standing in for race have a long history in the U.S., we include only representations of *human* figures. After eliminating all nonhuman representations, we then took a random sample from the remaining cartoons from each data set (White and Black presses).

Our analysis incorporated two distinct phases. In the first phase we asked the following questions for *each* individual cartoon:

1. What is the image physically depicting?
2. What does the image symbolize?
3. What are the labels used?
4. What do they symbolize?
5. What does the caption say?
6. How does the entire text (image, labels, caption) guide the viewer to an intended meaning?
7. What is the relationship between knowledge and power in terms of "racial" identity?

In the second phase we cross-analyzed each set of cartoons: ones that appeared in the White press and ones that we collected from the Black press. In this stage, we were concerned with themes or bodies of statements that could be said to represent sanctioned knowledge—what is sayable and knowable in each context. By examining each subset of representations as a collective of statements, as opposed to individual or idiosyncratic representations, we were able to see how a concept such as race is constructed and how that construction shifts according to context. We were likewise interested in what had been hidden, covered, or obscured in each context. Our overall goal in this phase was to actively trouble the established notions of *why* things (e.g. in this study, how race and, therefore, desegregation) came to be. Informed by a Foucaultian genealogy, we drew from principles developed by Kendall and Wickham (1999). According to Kendall and Wickham, a genealogy:

1. Describes statements, with an emphasis on power;
2. Introduces power through a history of the present, and is concerned with the unpalatable and disreputable origins and functions of that which is being researched;
3. Describes statements as an ongoing process within webs of discourse;
4. Concentrates on the strategic use of archeology (a discursive approach for looking at a "slice" of history) to answer problems about the present, thereby illuminating a specific historical process.

In summary, our analytic goal was twofold: to more fully understand the social beliefs and practices that constructed race in the slice of history we are calling the *Brown* era; and to consider how these ideas about difference continue to impact contemporary America, particularly in terms of segregated schooling.

Mainstream Press

The following cartoons from the White or mainstream press were published (or reprinted) from May 1952 to July 1957. They were published either in the *New York*

'Oh, Fiddle-de-dee, I'll Put That Off 'Till Tomorrow'

FIGURE 2. *Atlanta Constitution* (1952, May 24), p. 4.

Times, the *Atlanta Constitution* (now *Atlanta Journal and Constitution*), or they were reprinted from other papers in *Southern School News*. If images were reprinted, we note the original source as well as where the image was reprinted. The cartoons span a five-year time frame, before and after *Brown* and each set is presented sequentially.

Atlanta Constitution (1952, May 24), p. 4.
A woman (See Figure 2) stands preening herself in front of a mirror, contemplating the message brought to her by a partially obscured male figure. Her surroundings suggest opulence (mirror, lamps), as does her apparel—a traditional, billowing ensemble of layered lace. In short, the Southern Belle image evokes an ambience

reminiscent of *Gone With the Wind*.[8] The message of "Supreme Court Decision" is held by an undefined figure, possibly a Southern Gentleman or possibly Uncle Sam (top hat) who is nonetheless in the position of servant, usually reserved for Blacks. In saying "Oh, Fiddle-de-dee, I'll put that off 'till tomorrow," the South dismisses the decision as unimportant. As a merged "text" of image and words, the cartoon depicts the South as vain, self-absorbed, and living in a bygone era. The delay tactics used by those who are choosing to disregard the decision of the Supreme Court suggest an unwillingness to address the issue. Living in a time warp, the South appears flippant, powerful, and ignorant. It chooses to look at nothing but itself, and, seeing only its own reflection, has no other gauge by which to measure itself. What it (and the reader) sees represents the character of the South. Personified by the White Southern Belle, mistress of the mansion-plantation, the southern response to integration appears willfully ignorant, decidedly immature, and ultimately self-interested.[9]

Greensboro Daily News, Reprinted in *New York Times* (1954, May 23), p. E5.
Three men (See Figure 3) appear too close for comfort, all exhibiting unhappy faces. The central figure is the Southern Gentleman, old-fashioned in appearance. He is sandwiched between two smaller figures; one is pulling his hair and waving a protest placard, while the other parades in front of him banging on a drum. Both appear to be making a lot of noise ("hysteria") and commotion (sounding "prejudices"). The Southern Gentleman reads a paper titled, "The Problems of Non-Segregation in Public Schools," an ironic twist on the issue at hand. The written text that anchors the intended meaning, reads "Now, if you will all just quiet down. . . ." In the midst of this melee, the South appears composed and dignified, but angry. Placed at the center of the picture, his imposing frame sits amid the circulation of hysteria and inflammatory drum beating of smaller, feminized ("hysterical"), or infantilized (hair-pulling) northern men. The South is being subjected to a pesky nuisance, and is caught in a bind, as the "problem" of desegregation will not go away. The caption conveys a sense of losing control of the situation while realizing the need to regain it. The South assumes that when the hubbub around the emotionally charged issue of desegregation is quelled, its own voice will be heard and "rational" thinking will prevail once more. It is also interesting to contrast the gender stereotypes used. In the previous cartoon the Southern Belle is superficial and self-absorbed, whereas in this cartoon the Southern Gentleman appears eminently reasonable, revealing patriarchal and sexist notions of gender within such depictions.

Richmond Afro American, Reprinted in *New York Times* (1954, May 23), p. E5.
The familiar caricature of the Southern Gentleman (See Figure 4) is driving his car along an inclined country road, framed by flying birds and roadside vegetation evoking a rural setting. Beneath him lies another road looking far more unwelcoming and darkly ominous. The car is labeled "Supreme Court Decision," and the South is currently moving in the direction of "calmness and thought." The alternative route, downhill, is marked by "hysteria and violence" and Blackness obstructs

"Now, if you all will just quiet down . . ."

FIGURE 3. *Greensboro Daily News,* Reprinted in *New York Times* (1954, May 23), p. E5.

a clear view of the road. Taken together, the words and image convey a simple premise: there are two possible routes for dealing with desegregation. Taking the "high road" of calmness and thought will lead to sensible, rational outcomes. The alternative route, by implication the "low road," which appears swamp-like and dangerous, will only lead to anarchy and chaos. Given that an ultimatum is being delivered to the South—requiring an immediate response—the message distinctly urges one route over another. The Southern Gentleman seems unaffected, accepting of the federal ultimatum, and in control of the decision making as it pertains to him. Yet, although the car appears to be chugging along, as evidenced by the exhaust coming out of it, the response is decidedly more thought than action. Thus, while the South ostensibly appears to be making progress, its movement is only toward studying the situation, not implementing desegregation orders.[10]

"Taking the high road."

FIGURE 4. *Richmond Afro American,* Reprinted In *New York Times* (1954, May 23), p. E5.

Clarion Ledger & Jackson Daily, Reprinted in *New York Times* (1957, July 21), p. E5. A well-dressed Southern Gentleman (See Figure 5) waves the Confederate flag toward the U.S. Capitol building. The Capitol looks like a powder keg, poised to explode. In the face of federal legislation, the southerner holds a potent symbol of regional identity positioned high above and larger (or at least closer) than the national institution of power. We, as viewers, are invited to see the nation from the South's point of view. The flag is a visual reminder of the South as a self-identified political entity, holding its own customs, practices, and traditions distinct from nonsouthern states. The same flag was waved in battle against the North in the U.S. Civil War, signifying a region willing to secede from the U.S. rather than end slavery. Desegregation, however, can also be seen as the desire to address social inequalities that were the vestiges of slavery. However, to many Whites in the South depicted in this image, it was viewed as another wave of victor-imposed values on

Howie in The Clarion Ledger & Jackson Daily
"The stars and bars wave again."

FIGURE 5. *Clarion Ledger & Jackson Daily,* Reprinted in *New York Times* (1957, July 21), p. E5.

the vanquished; values that were forced not shared. Thus, the rhetoric emanating from Capitol Hill fills the air with potentially explosive tensions between civil rights for all individuals, the southern way of life, and the sovereign rights of states. The South, in resisting desegregation, claims state sovereignty in issues that the federal government asserts are national interests. Thus, the rhetoric of law obfuscates moral and ethical dimensions associated with racial integration. "State rights" may be more accurately conceptualized as the battle of southern Whites challenging the federal government. Overall, the cartoon depicts the bitter dissension evident within the country. If being American means following desegregation laws, the South does not want to pledge allegiance to that flag, but rather stand by its own.

Chicago Sun Times, Reprinted in *New York Times* (1957, July 21), p. E5.
The cartoon depicts three men (See Figure 6), although the obvious center of the image is a fist-waving southern politician, remarkably close in features to the often-depicted Southern Gentleman. Dressed in traditional "southern" attire, replete

Burck in The Chicago Sun-Times

"Civil wrongs was good enough for mah pappy . . ."

FIGURE 6. *Chicago Sun Times,* Reprinted in *New York Times* (1957, July 21), p. E5.

with goatee, he is animated and demonstrative. The two figures behind him are not identifiably southern, and therefore may represent either a northern or more moderate southern group. They appear disgusted, eyes averted, hands over their ears. The civil rights bill is being discussed, and the southern politician asserts, "Civil wrongs was good enough for mah pappy." His stereotypical diction conveys antiquated and rural mores and hints at the unchanging nature of southern ways. The image and words combined represent the South as a hard-nosed buffoon, intent upon maintaining things the way they were, even if they are "civil wrongs." The politician's assertion is focused on maintaining the way of life of the South, regardless of moral or ethical dimensions, or federal desires. The body language of those who are obliged to listen betrays a sense of hopelessness (and perhaps shame) in the situation. The southern character, despite being ridiculed as comical, is portrayed as formidable because of his inflexibility and stubbornness. In its unwillingness to

"You sure you know what your doing?"

FIGURE 7. *Greensboro Daily News,* Reprinted In *New York Times* (1954, July 18), p. E7.

change, the South exerts a powerful counterforce against desegregation, feeling its quintessential identity is being criticized and its own power usurped.

Greensboro Daily News, Reprinted in *New York Times* (1954, July 18), p. E7.
The figure of Uncle Sam (See Figure 7) leans over a fence appearing concerned about the impending actions of the Southern Gentleman. The latter is positioned with his head on a chopping block. In one hand he wields an enormous axe above his own head. In his other hand he holds a document, "Plans to abolish the public schools." Inscribed upon his backside is a qualifying statement, "some southern states." The "some" signifies that not all states are reacting in this self-destructive manner and the rear-end inscription (whether deliberate or not) associates the states that are with asses. By asking "You sure you know what your [*sic*] doing?" Uncle Sam is positioned as levelheaded, in contrast to the South, which is evidently poised for self-destruction. The question can be seen as an appeal to the South to rethink their current course of action of threatening to abolish public schools. The axe would be better put to use by dismantling the fence between "neighbors." The South, however, has been divested of everything except the power to either destroy itself or listen to northern reasoning. The extreme reaction

FIGURE 8. *Richmond Times Dispatch,* Reprinted in *Southern School News* (1955, July 6), p. 16.

of the South is perceived as an indication of an angry, selfish, unthinking, and ultimately suicidal response. In terms of power, the South, rather than giving the federal government the satisfaction of winning on the issue of desegregation, would rather die by his own hand. To have no public schools rather than integrated schools conveys the desperation and spite of the South.

Richmond Times Dispatch, Reprinted in *Southern School News* (1955, July 6), p. 16. Separated by a huge book that looks like an impenetrable wall (See Figure 8), two figures sit back to back. Each holds a placard demonstrating his point of view on the "public school problem." On one side the Supreme Court Justice looks stern and resolute; on the other side the Southern Gentleman (specifically representing "Virginia") is a mirror image in terms of posture and demeanor. The former is dressed in courtroom robes, and his placard reads "End Segregation 'with All Deliberate Speed.'" The latter clutches his placard featuring the message "Continue Segregation Through the School Year 1955–1956." It is signed, "Governor Findlay and the State Commission on Public Education." The adversarial stance, neither side facing this large "problem" head on, represents a standoff between federal and state authority—portrayed as equal in position and power. However, in one respect this cartoon is unlike many of the other cartoons we looked at, in that it does not appear to favor any particular side. Instead, it seems to reflect the stalemate between the two positions, and the determination of both sides to be unyielding in the face of power exerted by the other. Thus, the two sides are positioned literally as bookends, working in tandem to uphold the "problem" of public schooling. The message of the cartoon is that segregation is propped up by the stalemate between the two sides, not by the cultural and historical roots of Jim Crow. Another interesting aspect of this cartoon is that the agent of change appears as a Supreme Court justice, not Uncle Sam, as in many other depictions. The robed figure is invested with power that the Southern Gentleman resists, but the very courtly presence of the justice and the limited one-year proposal for "continuing segregation" suggests that the southern way of life is not above federal regulation; eventually the Virginia Southern Gentleman will have to face the "problem" and comply.

Nashville Banner, Reprinted in *Southern School News* (1955, September), p. 1.
Uncle Sam smiles as he hears a bell ringing (See Figure 9). A crowd assembles on the horizon, gathered behind a banner reading "1955–56 school year." Musical notes are in the air, emanating from the bell, the crowd, or both. Boldly written on Uncle Sam's lapel is "Public Interest in School Affairs." Directly addressing the viewer, the caption reads "Calling You, Too," referring to *all* Americans. The bell is symbolic of school, and perhaps more important, liberty. Thus, going to an integrated school signifies freedom, but everyone must participate to make desegregation work. The caption evokes a sense of patriotism mildly suggestive of militaristic mobilization. It echoes the famous image of Uncle Sam pointing directly at the spectator, accompanied by the phrase: "Uncle Sam needs you!" Thus, the image serves as an appeal for support of efforts to desegregate the public schools in the upcoming year, as a matter of public and national interest. Altogether, it is an optimistic image, with Uncle Sam's expression of wide-eyed pleasure, calling all readers to join in the effort to bring about integrated public schooling. Of course, because Uncle Sam was typically used to signify the North, southern Whites who opposed desegregation and would not identify with the image of Uncle Sam would also not necessarily share the optimism portrayed in this depiction.

Greensboro Daily News, Reprinted in *Southern School News* (1956, April), p. 1.
Uncle Sam places his hand on the shoulders of the Southern Gentleman (See Figure 10), both standing next to a large cannon. The cannon supports a flag that reads, "Bang!" signifying the empty threat of the southern elite trying to enact a backlash against the Supreme Court decision. Attached to the side of the cannon is

'Calling You, Too'

—Courtesy of Knox. *Nashville Banner*

FIGURE 9. *Nashville Banner,* Reprinted in *Southern School News* (1955, September), p. 1.

a sign reading "Southern Segregation Manifesto."[11] The Southern Gentleman is labeled "Congressional Signers" (presumably of the Manifesto). Standing indignant, the Southern Gentleman holds the torch that lit the cannon, an archaic weapon that invokes nostalgic images of the American Civil War. The Southern Manifesto, despite its strong language, is portrayed as a bluff, "all bang and no buck." Uncle Sam, with his arm around the Southern Gentleman's shoulder, expresses the desire to reconcile through dialogue. By asking paternalistically, "Now can we sit down and discuss the problem?" Uncle Sam acknowledges that the South has demonstrated an angry, impetuous reaction, perhaps stirring deep emotions that have lingered since the Civil War. Although the South is summoning all of its powers, Uncle Sam is confident knowing it will not succeed in resisting the Supreme Court. There is a condescending air to the cartoon, as Uncle Sam humors

FIGURE 10. *Greensboro Daily News,* Reprinted in *Southern School News* (1956, April), p. 1.

the old man, recognizing his dwindling and outdated supply of bluffs and blusters, poised as they are at the edge of a cliff. Just as Uncle Sam prevailed a hundred years earlier, his optimism conveys a sense of inevitability that the resistance, while a nuisance, will not be effective.

Memphis Commercial Appeal, Reprinted in *Southern School News* (1956, April), p. 4
A dapper Southern Gentleman leans against a gravestone (See Figure 11). His pose is confident, his face handsome and determined. Surprising the gravedigger, and looking him straight in the eye, he asks, "You buryin' somebody?" The gravedigger, labeled "federal government," has a far less imposing presence. Undistinguished in dress and smaller in frame, his image is that of a weaker man. Interestingly, the Southern Gentleman is not labeled as such, but as "State Sovereignty," thereby implying the "problem" at hand is not about racial desegregation but state rights. The gravestone reads, "Here lies state sovereignty," recently buried by federal powers. However, as the Southern Gentleman *is* state sovereignty, he appears to the gravedigger as a ghost, or someone who was mistakenly dead. The questioning look and utter surprise of the federal government's face undermines his belief that the matter of state sovereignty is closed. By invoking the rights of states, the South attempts to obfuscate the original "problem" of racial integration. As a power play unfurls, it seems to lose sight of the original intent of the *Brown* legislation. Instead, the power struggle of federal and state governance becomes superimposed upon the historical schism between North and South. It is

'You Buryin' Somebody?'

—*Memphis Commercial Appeal*

FIGURE 11. *Memphis Commercial Appeal,* Reprinted in
Southern School News (1956, April), p. 4

important to note that even though the debate is often framed as a struggle over federal and state jurisdiction, the divide between North and South was always predicated upon the concept of race.

Minneapolis Tribune, Reprinted in *New York Times* (1957, July 21), p. E5.
A clothesline hangs over the globe (See Figure 12). Pinned to it are two items of underclothing, dripping over the "U.S.A." Written on the garments for the entire world to see are "Civil" and "Rights." Sitting nearby is an emaciated old man, Uncle Sam, who covers his nakedness while waiting for his clothes to dry. Portraying civil rights as undergarments connects the surface of outward appearance (democracy) with what lies beneath (lack of civil rights for all). Invoking the common phrase, "Don't air your dirty laundry in public," the image reminds viewers of the importance

"**Embarrassing . . . but necessary.**"

Long in The Minneapolis Tribune

FIGURE 12. *Minneapolis Tribune,* Reprinted in *New York Times* (1957, July 21), p. E5.

of keeping private business private. Yet, the caption seems to imply that despite its embarrassment, the U.S. needs to openly deal with the dirty little secret of racism within its democracy. The cartoon also connects the reader on a personal level with the national identity of the U.S. Thus the image and the caption of "Embarrassing . . . but necessary," guide the reader to think within the framework of the familiar adage, while simultaneously working against it. Uncle Sam is naked, and the world can see his "dirty laundry," and he is obviously embarrassed. The *need* for civil rights is therefore affirmed. It is important to note that the emergence of the U.S. as a super-power after World War I led to an expansion of foreign policy in which its influence exerted support for the growth of "democracy" while suppressing "communism" around the globe. The doctrine of "all men were created equal" differed significantly in theory and practice—and the U.S. was increasingly scrutinized by a world it sought

THE ONLY MAN WHO CAN UNTANGLE IT.

FIGURE 13. *New York Times* (1957, July, 28), p. E9.

to influence. "Airing dirty laundry" meant openly addressing the hypocrisy of a democracy divided by race.

New York Times (1957, July, 28), p. E9.
An old man sits, hunched over, intent upon untying the knots in a length of rope (See Figure 13). He is dressed in sandals and a long cloak, appearing somewhat biblical. Behind him rests a scythe, usually associated with the grim reaper. He is labeled as "Father Time," and his attention is focused on the knotted, convoluted "civil rights snarl." His very presence evokes the issue of time, and may incite the reader to ask, "When will this be resolved?" The caption reads, "The only man who

can untangle it," as if "Only time will tell." Taken together, the image and text create a picture of a sage old figure who has seen many things throughout history and thus appears timeless. By portraying Father Time as the *answer,* the cartoonist ignores the social forces and counterforces continuously exerting themselves in attempts to create or deny change. The image appeals to those wanting to delay or deliberate rather than act. Civil rights are seen as neither universal nor beneficial but rather a "snarl," something that has clouded the picture, made things messy, tangling the straight lines of society. Conveyed as such, civil rights are seen as the *cause* of the current problems, not the answer to preexisting inequities. As a whole, the image brings a sense of abstraction to the process of desegregation, hinting of the apathy that had begun to set in after the first few years of legal and physical wrangling. By implying "Someday . . ." it ignores the agency of the forces involved, and leaves the reader with a mess in mind.

Cross-Analysis

What is most striking about the representation of "race" in these cartoons is that the word race was rarely mentioned. Neither captions nor titles contained the words "race" or "racism," thereby avoiding a literal articulation of race. Moreover, there was a total absence of Black people in these images, and a total presence of White people. Taken together, the sayable and visible representations of Whiteness mask the invisible and unsayable issues of Blackness. Moreover, that a White and a Black person did not appear within the same cartoon indicates the profundity of segregation—as if proximity of the races would lead to undesirable interactions of any nature. Regardless of their ideological grounding either for or against desegregation, all cartoons avoided "mixing" races, leaving them as "Whites only" texts.

This means that the dialogue about desegregation within these cartoons *always* took place between Whites. Thus, the primary source of knowledge about desegregation involved dialogic exchanges, but only between people in the dominant group. In many cartoons the conversation was between Uncle Sam and the Southern Gentleman who were, in essence, two old White men who, apart from attire, are virtually interchangeable. In addition, their advanced age suggests cumulative wisdom. This notion was reinforced by depictions of Father Time, who also resembles Uncle Sam and the Southern Gentleman. Father Time, in turn, by virtue of his claim to the supernatural, calls to mind traditional pictorial depictions of God, enshrined in Western European culture by artists such as Michelangelo and William Blake. Taken together, these representations convey that mature, Whites upper and middle class males represent *all* of humanity, and naturally resemble the physiognomy of God. The lone female figure, the Southern Belle, by contrast, conveys neither godliness nor wisdom. Instead, she is the antithesis of reason.

Uncle Sam and the Southern Gentleman are political characters. Regardless of how innocuous they appear, they represent specific institutions of Anglo American power. As *statements,* cartoons are always located in a particular context.

In southern mainstream newspapers, for example, White southerners were usually positioned as defenders of "state rights," and White northerners as meddlesome enemies who were imposing their will upon the South. By contrast, northern mainstream newspapers usually depicted themselves as law-abiding and "right," while viewing the South as defiant and stubborn. Regardless of who was cast as hero or villain, they dominated the discussion by turns, effectively demonstrating that *Brown* was primarily an argument between forces of White power. This may explain why although cartoons were set in a variety of locations, including the legislature, none were set in schools and none depicted teachers or students.

The most significant institutions featured in these cartoons were those invested with authority. Although the Supreme Court was the ultimate governmental authority, the South in the name of state rights also exerted a cultural and regional claim to authority. The court was sometimes represented by justices wearing robes, but was often used synonymously with Uncle Sam. The *Brown* decision meant that the South would be regulated and monitored for compliance with a decision that was imposed by the North. The South resented this decision, which meant that the regional Jim Crow laws and customs, operating to subjugate and regulate Black citizens, would be abolished. Thus, the "problem" of *Brown*, transformed into a struggle between two forces, both White, who sought either to assert or to maintain power. "Race" was the unseen presence at the center of these institutional interchanges between two factions of the White elite, personified by Uncle Sam and the Southern Gentleman.

The omnipresence of Whiteness and absence of Blackness (and, for the most part, femaleness) symbolizes the system of power operating during this period. White males are depicted as thinking, speaking, acting beings, in charge and in control of everyone else. By implication, Blacks are seen as unnecessary or unworthy of portrayal. Their absence positions Blacks as nonthinking, nonspeaking, and nonacting beings, under the political and social control of Whites. There is no mention of Blacks as organized (the National Association of Colored People [NAACP,] for example), counterassertive, or powerful in any way. This indicates that even the "progressive" or "liberal" newspapers were very conservative in portraying *any* representation of a Black person.

White males constructed their own identities as active, resourceful, powerful, and influential. Simultaneously, White identities were also shaped by the total erasure of Black people. Perceived as unequal, Black people were virtually unrepresented in mainstream press cartoons, even those about desegregation. This point is echoed by Ralph Ellison's (1952) autobiographical *Invisible Man,* a haunting novel about the nonrecognition of Blacks in a White-dominated world. In the absence of a counterimage, the practices that upheld White power (and White supremacy) were ostensibly viewed as normal/natural, serving to reinforce racial difference in social terms. School desegregation, then, was often resisted on the grounds of the inferiority of Black students, thereby creating a circular system that reconstituted and reinforced racial difference.

The Black Press

What is commonly referred to as the Black press includes a wide range of papers (both weekly and daily), beginning with the first publication, the *Freedom's Journal,* in New York City and continuing to this day (Vogel, 2001). By the end of the 19th century as many as 100 Black newspapers were in circulation (Vogel). Other early papers included Frederick Douglass's *North Star,* and rival William Lloyd Garrison's the *Liberator.* Although early papers covered abolition, the cultural work of the Black press was far more wide reaching. As Vogel states, the Black press "redefined [social] class, restaged race and nationhood, and reset the terms of public conversation" (p. 1). The Black press, like all presses, was an inherently social space—prompting dialogic exchange among various constituents. The Black press, however, was also a space of counterdiscourse—helping to create and organize a Black community that crossed geographic and class borders. The unofficial distribution of the Black press, passed from person to person, greatly expanded its readership beyond the number of official subscribers (Vogel, 2001). Moreover, the symbolic importance of the Black press to a people denied literacy and excluded from public schooling is an important context for understanding its evolution and value to the Black community.

Unfortunately, research on the Black press is made more difficult by the failure to preserve many important Black papers.[12] Most of the papers that were available for this study could only be accessed on microfilm and many of these copies were of very poor quality. Some papers are now being digitized and made available on the web or through electronic sources, which should improve access, at least to selected papers. The pioneering *Afro-American* broke new ground by becoming the first established newspaper, White or Black, to go online. Other Black presses followed suit, some offering both electronic and paper subscriptions.

The cartoons from the Black press that we selected to analyze were published or reprinted from September 1953 to September 1954, a fairly condensed time period directly surrounding the *Brown* decision. Although indebted to the many presses that gave us permission to reprint cartoons, we regret not being able to secure permission to reprint any of the images from the *Chicago Defender.*[13] Because the *Defender* is such a significant paper in the history of the Black press, we chose to include our analysis of these images even though we were not able to secure permission to reprint the actual cartoons.

Richmond Afro-American (1953, September 1), p. 4.

Panicking, wobbling, and unable to balance, a scrawny Southern Gentleman (See Figure 14), featured here as a symbol of Jim Crow, balances precariously on a pedestal. Beneath him a Black man, pneumatic drill in hand, works hard to chip away at the foundation upholding the pedestal. Their faces differ considerably. The White man is either sweating or crying, evidenced by the water droplets spraying exaggeratedly from his head; the Black man looks determined, focused intently on

FIGURE 14. *Richmond Afro-American* (1953, September 1), p. 4.

the task at hand. The labels on their clothing suggest that the "NAACP" is undermining the policy of "Jim Crow." The pedestal reads, "1896 Separate but Equal Decision," referring to *Plessy v. Ferguson,* which heretofore had buttressed all aspects of racial segregation in society—thereby reinforcing White supremacy—in places of work, worship, recreation, and education. The caption, "O No! Not That!" expresses the terror of the helpless Jim Crow, who faces the dismantling of his foundations. Without this pedestal, he is no longer self-positioned as superior and thus he is considerably less dignified than images like the Southern Gentleman, typically portrayed in the mainstream press. His identity, inextricably linked to his sense of superiority and power to control, will no longer be guaranteed. In contrast, the Black man (NAACP) is seen as the agent by which the power is dismantled. He represents the strength of political organizing among Blacks and their allies. The "modern" dress of the Black man as well as his power tool sharply contrasts with the outdated attire of Jim Crow, further highlighting a sense of change and progress over outdated policies.

Chicago Defender (1953, September 8), p. 11. (No image)
A beautiful Black woman with a serious expression on her face stands dressed in flowing robes with her arms outstretched, hands open. Behind her float calendar months, conveying the movement of time. In front of her lies an open chest, which is empty. Her appearance is evocative of Lady Liberty in terms of expression and attire, and Christ-like in posture, combined in a steadfast appeal to readers. Labeled as NAACP, she motions to the coffers that read "Funds with which to fight Jim Cro [*sic*] and segregation." The date of October 8th is highlighted in the calendar, noting the date the Supreme Court was scheduled to rehear several segregation cases that would later become *Brown*.[14] The link between mobilization to support these cases and the need for financial power is made explicit. In many ways, this political cartoon functions as a fundraiser, calling upon the conscience of the Black readership of the *Chicago Defender* and their allies. The caption, "Your Help is Needed Now!" conveys urgency, the need to prepare to fight an all-important legal battle. The message reads: commitment of financial support will help influence the outcome in the best interests of the Black community. In short, freedom has a price.

Richmond Afro-American (1953, November 28), p. 4.
A Black man kneels (See Figure 15) at the side of his bed engaging in what is probably a nightly prayer. Representing "All of Us," namely, all people of African descent, he humbly offers gratitude for what he has, and asks for help with what he has not. His words read, "And thank thee for Thurgood Marshall and the NAACP! Help him, O Lord, to show the Supreme Court the truth and light. Amen." These words praise and support Marshall as the great Black hope, and the NAACP as a righteous political organization. He is cautiously but unmistakably optimistic. His prayer equates truth with light, and untruth with dark (reflecting problematic semiotics), in order to invoke the untruths, misrepresentations, and distortions currently upheld

Our Thanksgiving Day Prayer

FIGURE 15. *Richmond Afro-American* (1953, November 28), p. 4.

within the law. Yet, the cartoon also suggests that Blacks can offer light to the nation, reaffirming that resistance to desegregation can be perceived as ungodly. The caption of "Our Thanksgiving Day Prayer" highlights one of the quintessential American traditions, usually portrayed in popular mythology as the coming together of differing cultures (originally Pilgrims and Native Americans). By framing the image and prayer with these words, the *Americanness* of Black citizens is reaffirmed. Perhaps more importantly, the appeal to God aligns the plight of Black Americans with moral, ethical, and spiritual dimensions conspicuously absent from mainstream press.

Richmond Afro-American (1953, December 5), p. 4.
Uncle Sam wrinkles his nose (See Figure 16), looking decidedly displeased at the package he holds at arm's length. Neatly bundled and labeled "School Segregation," the package appears to emit a potent stench. The caption "Isn't it about time to throw it out?" speaks directly to the issue of segregation, which over time has become increasingly repulsive. Portrayed as a commonplace package (even looking like a gift), its inoffensive exterior camouflages the putrid contents inside. Calling forth associations of garbage and rancid waste, the message is that school segregation must be discarded. The text of the cartoon appeals to readers to form an answer, while guiding them to a specific response. In most cartoons Uncle Sam symbolizes the federal government and/or the North, but here it is possible that he may represent the entire country. By encompassing the South within the figure of Uncle Sam, the cartoon does not recognize the South as a separate entity, and therefore negates its claim to independence or sovereignty. Rather, the entire U.S. is burdened with an issue that will continue to putrefy, giving rise to an even worse stench, if it is not disposed of immediately and effectively.

Richmond Afro-American (1953, December 12), p. 4.
A large and imposing female of indeterminate race looks down upon a small and far less significant male figure (See Figure 17). She is clothed in robes reminiscent of biblical imagery; he is clothed in the garments of law. The disparity of size serves to emphasize the presence and importance of the female figure in comparison to the man. It is she who looks down to meet his upward gaze. She is labeled "History" and he represents the "U.S. Supreme Court." The strength of the image lies in its use of the apparatus of the powerful. Roles are reversed, however, and history is positioned as the judge of the courtroom in which the U.S. Supreme Court will stand trial. The image boldly asserts that there are higher powers than the court and no one can escape judgment. Holding a quill in her hand, "History" has crossed out "Slave Trade," "Dred Scott Case," and "Slavery." A question mark lies next to "Segregation" and she is poised, perhaps, to enter the result on that issue. By placing the issue of school segregation alongside slavery and the Dred Scott case, the cartoon highlights both the gravity of the issue before the court, and the historical importance of its decision. The caption succinctly reads, "On trial before the world!" This dramatic depiction reveals past injustices that have been addressed by the court, therefore presenting a cautiously optimistic front. Perhaps

Isn't it about time to throw it out?

FIGURE 16. *Richmond Afro-American* (1953, December 12), p. 4.

more importantly, it reminds the reader that the world will judge the U.S. by how the Supreme Court judges adjudicate the case of *Brown*.

Richmond Afro-American (1954, January 12), p. 4.
The image is startlingly violent. (See Figure 18) The rat stands salivating, paws closed into fists in anticipation of a fight. All eyes are focused upon the rat as three club-wielding men approach. The first man is Uncle Sam, sleeves rolled up, and

On trial before the world!

FIGURE 17. *Richmond Afro-American* (1953, December 12), p. 4.

They've got him cornered at last!

FIGURE 18. *Richmond Afro-American* (1954, January 12), p. 4.

"U.S. Constitution" inscribed on his weapon. The second figure is robed and wears a turban (possibly Arabic or African), sporting a club reading "World Opinion." The third man is a religious figure in cleric's clothes, sporting the club of "Christianity." Together, they symbolize a trinity of domestic, foreign, and spiritual interests, united in the desire to eradicate the despised vermin-like presence of segregation. Shoulder-to-shoulder in collaboration, these forces have "blocked" segregation, confirmed by the caption, "They've got him cornered at last!" By placing World Opinion between the U.S. and Christianity, the image echoes the claim of the previous cartoon, that the eyes of the world are watching. Desegregation is not just about U.S. domestic policy, but also about the image of the U.S. before the world as a self-proclaimed beacon of democracy. The image conveys the notion that "the end is near" for segregation. However, it also serves as a grim reminder that violence will play an inevitable part in the process of change.

Richmond Afro-American (1954, February 6), p. 4.
A book appears as a monument surrounded by a multitude of people (See Figure 19). The crowd stands immobile in anticipation of the knowledge that this text obviously contains. Surrounded by darkness, the knowledge from the book emanates light. Written at the top of the cover is "American History," and beneath it "Containing the Truth About Colored People Thru-out the World." Once again, a religious feeling pervades this image and the imposing book with the word "truth" emblazoned on the cover is reminiscent of the Bible. This book of "truth," however, appears to be the providence of the U.S. The subtitle of the book suggests a necessary *addition* to the established "truths" of American history, which has omitted, distorted, and misrepresented Black people. It asserts that American history has not been truthful to date because it has erased the contributions by, and treatment of, Black people. By centering the word "truth," the image suggests that what has come to be known as history is now being challenged; changes and revisions are inevitable. The caption "The whole world is waiting for this book" suggests that rather than waiting for the U.S. to teach the world its truths, the world already knows a much more complicated history. Thus, what the world is waiting for is for the U.S. to recognize its own mythologies about Black people.

Richmond Afro-American (1954, April 13), p. 4
A Black man climbs a mountain (See Figure 20), bearing a large wooden cross on his shoulder. On his head lies a crown of thorns. Two other crosses appear on the horizon. The imagery is borrowed from the story of Christ's last walk to Calvary. A salivating vulture looks greedily on as the figure struggles past skeletal remnants of an unidentified human. The message is clear: the journey of a Black man is synonymous with Christ's sufferings, and increased faith and determination can be gained through this knowledge. The vulture, though unlabeled, represents all those who will benefit from the fall of the Black man, evidenced in the nearby picked-clean skull. The cross is inscribed with "Segregation" on one cross beam and "Job Discrimination" on the other, reminding readers how various forms of oppression intersect and support one another. The caption "A heavy cross to bear" intensifies the religious parallel, simultaneously conveying the difficulties of being Black in a White-dominated society and suggesting that faith can help alleviate the "burden" of segregation and economic hardships. As a whole, the text is somber, even chilling in its portrayal of powerlessness in the face of seemingly relentless segregation. However, the image can also be seen as a testimony of strength and ultimate redemption,

The whole world is waiting for this book!

FIGURE 19. *Richmond Afro-American* (1954, February 6), p. 4.

A heavy cross to bear

FIGURE 20. *Richmond Afro-American* (1954, April 13), p. 4

More Fuel For The Communists

FIGURE 21. *Richmond Afro-American* (1953, October 23), p. 4.

as the Black man carries his burden in an unwelcoming world, mirroring the earthly experience of suffering and sacrifice by Christ.

Richmond Afro-American (1953, October 23), p. 4.
In the dead of night, a large and powerful Klansman (taking up nearly half of the frame) clutches a thick club (See Figure 21). Beneath him lies a much smaller prostrate Black man, unable to raise himself from the ground. Behind them blazes a burning cross, a symbol of the Ku Klux Klan (KKK). On the club is inscribed "Discriminacion a los negros" ["discrimination of Blacks"]. The visual image stresses the brutality of the "open secret" of the violence of southern "customs." The powerlessness of Blacks at the hands of White institutions such as the KKK is laid bare in this cartoon. The caption, which reads, "More Fuel for the Communists," links the terrorism of the KKK to opportunist communist supporters who further their own political agenda by calling attention to U.S. practices of inequality. Thus, the caption adds another dimension to the image, stressing that the brutal repression of Blacks could serve as a fertile breeding ground for communism, the dread of the American political establishment. While the visual image asks the viewers to empathize with the victim, the caption serves as an appeal to White self-interest. Taken together, the image and caption stress the obviously horrific brutality of discrimination while simultaneously suggesting that discrimination is not just bad for Blacks, but also endangers the nation's ability to withstand communism. It is worth noting that this cartoon was originally published in *The Excelsior* of Mexico City. The caption, which is in English, may have been added later. In many ways, the brutality of this cartoon exceeds most of the imagery found in both mainstream White and independent Black press. It would seem that, although existence of the Klan was common knowledge, it was almost unbearable to openly accept its existence by actual physical depictions.

Chicago Defender (1954, June 12), p. 11. (No image)
The hands of two men, one White and one Black, are seen close up. The Black man has placed his manacled hands across an iron anvil. The White man is in the process of breaking the Black man's chains. Using a mallet labeled "Supreme Court Decision" and a metal chisel, he works to cut through the manacles inscribed with "Segregated Schools." No caption accompanies the image, for none is needed. The stark image represents a history of enslavement, the subjugation of one "race" by another through the exertion of physical, social, cultural, familial, and economic power. The recent decision of the Supreme Court addresses the unfinished, and largely unacknowledged, history of slavery. In other words, by desegregating schools the court is righting past and present injustices. There is a startling directness conveyed in the image: White hands have not yet truly freed Black hands. That chains are still central as an image in Black and White relations evokes a highly emotional response from the reader. With the "problem" of race relations conceptualized by shackles, the cartoon calls for unfinished business of the abolition of slavery to be completed. It is the responsibility of the White establishment to genuinely

"free" Black citizens from the vestigial chains. The image also evokes laborers or workers, perhaps alluding to other forms of exclusion and discrimination, including workplace discrimination and the exclusion of Blacks from labor unions.

Chicago Defender (1954, June, 5), p. 11. (No image)
Uncle Sam sits at the bedside of the Southern Gentleman. Looking serious and doctor-like (spectacles, briefcase), Uncle Sam takes the pulse of the patient, who appears agitated and delusional. The patient is labeled "Rebel South," and appears propped up by a pillow labeled "racism." On his head lies "Supreme Court Decision" like a bag of ice. Ironically, instead of assisting his condition, this "treatment" seems to agitate it. Uncle Sam comments, "Right now he's suffering from shock—but he'll come around alright. Give him time." Positioned as the doctor, Uncle Sam has the power to make a "diagnosis" of an unhealthy South. Appearing compassionate and benevolent, Uncle Sam optimistically predicts that change for the better will occur, and only time is needed for the South to regain its health. The elements of the text combine to convey the message that *Brown* should be equated with health and sanity, whereas resistance is a sickness that must be treated and controlled. The image positions the desegregationist as the staid, stoic, knowing doctor who is empowered to make a diagnosis, and the South as the hysterical patient in need of healing and intervention. In other words, desegregation is a prescription needed by the South for its own good.

Chicago Defender (1954, June 19), p. 11. (No image)
Uncle Sam hands a massive key to a graduating Black student, dressed in traditional cap and gown. They shake hands warmly, as the object is awarded to the student. Between them lies a door, relatively nondescript save for an enormous keyhole. "Supreme Court" is written on the sleeve of Uncle Sam, making the familiar pictorial representation of the U.S. synonymous with decisions made by the Supreme Court. Inscribed on the key is "school decision" referring to the recent *Brown* decision. With this key the young man can unlock the door labeled, "Door to equal opportunity." There is no need for a caption, as the reader has been led to see the desired message: desegregated schools are the key to equal opportunities. Increased education (or access to "socially validated" knowledge) becomes the means by which equality can be achieved. In this image schools are presented as environments in which the amelioration of racial differences (manifested by social, cultural, and economic disparities) will be addressed. The setting of this cartoon is school (or at least the doorway of a school), the site where the impact of *Brown* will be most felt. The picture conveys a sense of hope placed in education by the Black community. It is interesting to note that almost none of the political cartoons in this study that related to *Brown* featured schools, students or teachers.[15]

Chicago Defender (1954, July 3), p. 11. (No image)
In an ironic reversal of roles, a White man chauffeurs a Black man who is riding in the back seat of a convertible. The driver looks either surprised, shocked, or both.

The passenger is dressed in graduation garb, smiling through the chiseled features of youth. In contrast, the driver is a chubby, bald, bespectacled, middle-aged White man. A label indicates that the driver is a "school official," responsible for driving the vehicle of "integration." The "All of Us" inscribed on the graduation gown of the Black rider echoes the "all of us" on the praying man at Thanksgiving (figure 15). The use of "all of us" connects the issue of desegregation to the collective of Black people in America. The positioning of the two figures (White driver and Black rider) and physical contact (rider's hand on the driver's shoulder) contravenes traditional protocol, as does the very direct request of the young man. By saying "Let's put it in high gear!" he conveys both impatience and a mutual responsibility of moving in a particular direction, suggesting the process of integration can be accelerated. The caption, "Sound advice from the back seat," cues the reader to see an assertive young Black man speaking on behalf of the Black population. Although the character depicted addresses the school official driving the car, he also speaks to the readership and their responsibility to expect and even demand greater speed of integration. Once again, this image is unique in that it features a student and a school official. Although the school official seems flustered, the young man personifies the optimism of what lies ahead.

Richmond Afro-American (1954, September 25), p. 4.
The cartoon looks like it belongs to a realist comic strip in which protagonists are in the process of having a conversation (See Figure 22). It is as if one frame has been selected to make a specific point. The two figures are presumably a Black middle-aged couple relaxing in their living room. Their surroundings have many trappings of middle class living—bound books flanked by bookends, flowers, art on the wall, television set, and comfortable sofas. The setting is one of tranquil domesticity in which educated citizens converse about political issues. In many respects, the cartoon features the "ideal" couple, reinforcing a sense of normalcy to counter White perceptions and fears of "difference." They call each other by common "Christian" names. Mary asks, "Why does the Mississippi legislature resolve to abolish the public schools?" John replies, "It hopes to frighten the U.S. Supreme Court into taking a backward step on school desegregation. That bluff won't work." The extreme reaction of Mississippi, threatening to shut down public schools rather than desegregate them, is seen as a desperate move to counter the Supreme Court decision. It is perceived as empty posturing designed to postpone the inevitability of integration. Portrayed as knowledgeable and informed, the Black community, personified by this couple, appears as "ordinary citizens" marked as different only in terms of race.

Chicago Defender (1954, September 18), p. 9. (No image)
A group of six young children, Black and White, hold hands and play together in a circle. All are singing and each one looks happy. In the background, more children play jump rope outside of a school building. Above, the sun smiles as it beams its light, labeled "public education," over the entire scene. The caption, "Let it shine

FIGURE 22. *Richmond Afro-American* (1954, September 25), p. 4.

on all alike," refers to everyone's right to education, an experience to be shared freely in the same manner as sunshine. The joy and happiness of integrated school-ing, the ability of both "sides" to come together both in a formal environment (school) and an informal manner (playground) is openly celebrated. The picture is harmonious, a world in which children play together regardless of race. A power-ful image of idealized race relations, the cartoon is a rare depiction of children at school predicting the changes to be wrought by *Brown*.

Cross-Analysis

In stark contrast to the mainstream press, there are an abundance of images of Black people in the independent Black press. By the diversity of representation, from manual workers to middle class couples, from school children to religious worshippers, Blackness is affirmed as a reflection of human diversity. The presence of Black student-scholars, dignified and proudly smiling in graduation gowns, makes visible the hoped-for outcome of *Brown*. The potential of greater access to education optimistically signifies the chance of economic emancipation from a prescribed array of low-paying jobs. There is also open recognition and support for the NAACP, denoting active participation in organizing, mobilizing, and fi-nancing efforts to dismantle desegregation. As in the White press, the overwhelm-ing majority of images are male. Although there are several portrayals of Black females (wives and children), they mostly stand for abstract ideals such as Liberty or History. Standing in as metaphors or symbols, women are rarely portrayed as serious subjects in either press.

White people are portrayed in similar ways in the Black and mainstream press. Uncle Sam is a prominent figure, usually representing the U.S. government, the constitution, or impending change. The Southern Gentleman, however, appears far less dignified, resembling a sick man in one instance, and personifying a scrawny Jim Crow in another. In addition to these images, Whites are portrayed in more complex and ambivalent terms, blending historical and contemporary refer-ences. In one image a pair of White hands splits the shackles restraining a Black man, whereas in another a Klansman beats a Black man to the ground. Whites are both enslavers and emancipators, for they have the power to do both. It is clear that these images resonate deeply with Black readership and such strong images are noticeably absent in mainstream press.

Another prominent component of Black representation is the connection to re-ligion. Here religious imagery is informed by elements of Black liberation theol-ogy, which links Christianity with liberation from oppression. In several depic-tions, Black men are praying, asking for spiritual guidance, and likening their plight to that of Christ, a figure despised by the authorities of his own time. The spiritual dimension of these images suggests the need for moral strength, but the unwritten subtext reads, "God is on our side." Weighed down by a cross, or im-prisoned by shackles, associations coalesce into the idea that the world, God, and the court of history are all watching. This is visibly reinforced in the cartoon where Uncle Sam, World Opinion and Christianity stand side-by-side wielding clubs to attack segregation. Linking desegregation to slavery and the Dred Scott case, images in the Black press acknowledge the legacy of race-based injustices in the U.S. The book of "Truth" depicted in one cartoon represents the (re)telling of history from a Black perspective. The message suggests that the knowledge of Black people, thus far unarticulated and falsified under the force of White power, will soon be validated now that "our time has come." In contrast, recognition of previous racial injustice is absent from the mainstream press, deliberately ignored or obscured by positing *Brown* as a struggle between state and federal powers.

In the Black press, Black people are portrayed as strong, informed, on the way to becoming victorious, and increasingly impatient with the limitations of Jim Crow practices. The NAACP, an institution largely run by and for Black people, rises in stature and power by being incorporated into these images. An influential organization, the NAACP challenges laws that oppress Black citizens as it demonstrates the abilities, knowledge, and strength of the Black community to exert political pressure through well-calculated maneuverings. These images stress that the Black community did not "wait" for desegregation to arrive, but actively mobilized at the grass-roots level in unprecedented numbers to push for desegregation and civil rights.

The construction of race in the cartoons of the Black press contrasts deeply with the absence of representation of Black people in the mainstream press. Representations of Black people as active, intelligent, achieving, and concerned citizens abound in the Black press. The indignity of distorted or absent images of Black people in the mainstream press (and society in general) are countered in these political cartoons. Here, readers are reminded that the past has yet to be accurately told, the present is imperative for change, and the future holds much promise. In contrast, Whites are not guaranteed central players in these portrayals. Their inclusion reflects a degree of ambivalence: they are framed as originators and upholders of segregation, yet also invested with the power and responsibility to end it.

It is fitting that the last cartoon that we describe in this chapter depicts an interracial group of children playing together as the predicted outcome of *Brown*. One of the few images of school children, this cartoon was published in the Black press. It symbolizes the optimism and promise of *Brown*. For many in the Black community, the Supreme Court decision signaled a change in which they would gain equal access to public schooling, as well as in all public facilities and services. The law calcified the notion that "separate was not equal" and in asserting such a claim, Black became legally equal to White. It was a milestone in upholding the notion of racial equality, informing the population that no race was to be considered legally superior to another.

Conclusion

In exploring the discursive construction of race in editorial cartoons, we gained important insights into dominant ideas about race and integration that were operating in the years surrounding the *Brown* decision. We also captured the radical potential, particularly in the Black press, for challenging racist stereotypes, resituating the terms of the debate, and recasting race as a social and political identity. Thus, in the context of these cartoons, representation becomes an important site of struggle over knowledge and myth making.

Although social, cultural, and historical forces appear to exert influence as separate entities, these lines of power often combine, overlap, and intersect with one another. Governments, for example, use laws, policies, and practices to produce particular kinds of knowledge, which then significantly influences the beliefs and values of its citizenship. Of course, because *forming subjects* is a necessary by-product of hegemonic governmental power, citizens become "raced" in particular ways that privilege the dominant group. Once such knowledge is claimed, it becomes open for counter-assertions by marginalized groups. The cartoons included in this chapter highlight this discursive relationship between power, representation, and race.

Our analytic model was useful for exploring the ways in which governmental practices produce certain sorts of persons—citizens deliberately and consciously encoded into separate categories of race. Social "mixing" was officially restricted by laws (against interracial marriages, for example) and unofficially sanctioned through particular cultural practices (disallowing shared social spaces or interactions). Simultaneously, legal discourses enforced beliefs and values based on "scientific" evidence, and science purported objectivity while actually creating a pseudo-science in order to uphold claims of White supremacy (see chapter 2). The purpose of legal segregation was clear: "to prevent intermixture between peoples of diverse origins so that morphological differences that code as race might be more neatly maintained" (Haney-Lopez, 1996, p. 117). In other words, by maintaining the separation of races, racial beliefs about the superiority of Whiteness could remain unchallenged. The prevention of sexual and social blending of racially categorized individuals was viewed as imperative for the survival of White "race" and all of the privileges that it brought. Still, race did not feature prominently in the White press. By framing the debate over *Brown* as a struggle over state sovereignty, Whites could claim opposition to *Brown* without acknowledging racism.[16]

Race, however, has always been an organizing principle of American governmental policies. Legal discourses have historically sought to exclude Black people from "mainstream" society (West, 1993). The perceived threat to established forms of knowledge (such as White-determined racial hierarchies) by the "otherness" of Blackness motivated the dominant White establishment to continue controlling, regulating, and containing Black people. This containment occurred in almost all aspects of life: economics, housing, employment, and mobility.

All representations of race in popular culture (cinema, television, literature, photography, etc.) are entangled in webs of power. We must remember, however, that just as power is asserted into the very grain of individuals, individuals also have the potential to counteract hegemonic assertions. The goal in attending to counterdiscourse is not, however, to romanticize the resistance of marginalized groups, but to understand "how this resistance clarifies the way power works"

(Vogel, 2001, p. 13). Political cartoons in mainstream press, although a small segment of popular culture, represent the knowledge and belief systems of those in power during this time, as well as their influence in communicating understandings of "race." Conversely, representations within the Black press offer counterassertions about racial identity, U.S. history, and the shaky foundation of White supremacy. By analyzing political cartoons of the *Brown* era—as individual texts in both mainstream White and independent Black newspapers—we can see how the nebulous concept of race reflects exertions of power claimed through particular knowledge claims.

Lessons Learned

In analyzing the cartoons in the chapter, we asked the following questions: Who is represented in the image? How are they represented? What are the implications for "others"? What kinds of knowledge are being generated/obscured in the representation? However, when critically analyzing any form of representation, it is also important to consider not only what is made visible, but also what is erased. What does it mean, for example, that cartoons about *Brown* in the White press were completely absent of images of Black people, students, teachers, or schools? When a cartoon in the White press argues for "rights," whose rights are elided? How do these erasures position the issue of school desegregation as a struggle over particular forms of White power and authority—between nation and state, but not about the civil rights of all children to full educational access and opportunity?

Because we found no political cartoons on inclusion, we can only imagine how disability would be represented and what familiar tropes might emerge. Based on textual examples we can guess that students with disabilities would be presented as dangerous and disordered, lashing out at their unsuspecting classmates and their overloaded teachers. Perhaps cartoonists would take their cues from film, presenting brave, crippled "Tiny Tim" or affable "Forrest Gump," or the angry villain "Captain Hook." They might model them from the plucky yet pitiable poster children from charity campaigns or telethons. Perhaps, instead, like the absence of representation of Black people in the political cartoons about *Brown* in the White press, students with disabilities would simply be erased. One could say that people with disabilities are already erased from the discourse on inclusion. When inclusion is debated in the press or in the professional discourse, whose voices speak the loudest, and whose voices do we rarely hear? Whose voices dominate the discourse for other kinds of educational reforms, such as *No Child Left Behind*? Who has yet to speak on the problem of overrepresentation of students of color in special education?

If a forum existed where children and adults with disabilities could answer back to the dominant ways of thinking about disability, what counterassertions would they offer? Surely people with disabilities would present a different image of disability identity and culture. Although we would not expect a unified point of view or opinion, we would certainly get a more complicated reading of the issues. Like the Black press linking desegregation to slavery, perhaps a disability-centric version of history of education would connect segregated schooling to a long history of exclusion, eradication, and incarceration of people with disabilities. Still, questions remain: How do we make spaces for these kinds of counterdiscourses in education? How do we invite points of view that recognize the intersection of race and disability to disrupt the kind of either/or thinking that has dominated the discussion thus far?

FIGURE 23. Untitled, Jacob Lawrence (1947), Pen And Ink On Paper.

Epilogue: Race in the American Landscape

Figure 23 predates by several years the first political cartoon featured in this chapter. It eerily foreshadows images contained in the "Unfinished Job" (See Figure 1) of racial and religious prejudice. A Black man runs hither and thither, circling, disoriented. Bound by four inescapable planes, he must confront what lies in the distance: a vision of death. The sky lies above, rocks are scattered along the way, and trees stretch on both sides. Despite these organic images, rigid lines are inscribed, superimposed on the landscape. The lines are *visible* social frameworks, forcefully and unnaturally etched by human hand into the scenery, forging the containment of those it seeks to dominate.

5

CHALLENGING NORMALCY: DIS/ABILITY, RACE, AND THE NORMALIZED CLASSROOM

5

CHALLENGING NORMALCY: DIS/ABILITY, RACE, AND THE NORMALIZED CLASSROOM

Introduction: Classrooms as Normalizing Spaces

In the previous chapter, we focused on the constructed nature of race in editorial cartoons following the *Brown* decision. In this chapter we explore the classroom itself as a constructed space, formed in large part by the constant struggle over who is included and excluded. By listening to some of the more resistant and hopeful of voices in the editorial pages covering desegregation and inclusion, we gain insight into what was perceived to be at stake in integrating schools.

In addition to being physical spaces, classrooms are also social spaces where dynamic interactions occur between people in the classroom, as well as among those in the larger sociopolitical context. Schools simultaneously reflect society while actively creating citizens to fit and function within it. As a microcosm of society, classrooms and schools represent the degree to which knowledge and individuals are valued.

Schools are shaped in large part by dominant cultural forces, which define (a) which knowledge is represented in the curriculum and (b) which students gain access to which curriculum. Thus, embedded in their very structure, schools and classrooms teach explicit and implicit lessons about *normalcy*. For example, each time a child with a perceived difference is removed from the classroom for special instruction or isolated from his or her peers within the classroom, the student and all of his or her classmates learn an important lesson about the educational, social, and cultural response to difference. Those who are not removed or given "special" help are assured, at least for the time being, that their status as "normal," "regular," "average," or "mainstream" remains intact. Those who have been removed learn that their difference is the reason they are being separated from the majority of their classmates. Their status in the community is changed forever, and they must learn to manage a stigmatized identity, "spoiled" by their difference from the norm (Goffman, 1963). Consequently, all children come to learn about norms and their own positioning, particularly in relation to others. Thus, classroom walls and more subtle divisions within the classroom act as literal and symbolic borders, assigning students to designated spaces that correspond to their perceived value in society.

Schools have functioned as key sites for the policing of normalcy, creating and maintaining students who look and act in accordance with established norms. The removal or exclusion of students who deviate from these norms has been seen as necessary to maintain the classroom as a normalized space. Thus, American education has an ongoing history of openly excluding and/or segregating students by race and disability. Prior to court-ordered desegregation in the 1950s, for example, American public schools, particularly those in the South, were strictly divided according to race.[1] Therefore, White students attended "mainstream" schools, while Black students in the South, as well as Latino, Native American, and Asian students in other parts of the country, were forced to attend separate, "special" schools. Prior to the late 1980s, "mainstream" American classrooms also excluded students with disabilities. These histories remain with us today as many students with disabilities continue to spend all or most of their school days in segregated classrooms (Lipsky & Gartner, 1997; A. Smith, 2001) and many schools throughout the U.S. continue to be sharply divided by race (Orfield, 2001). Moreover, because students of color are overrepresented in special education and placed in more restrictive placements in underresourced schools, their marginalization and isolation are compounded (Fierros & Conroy, 2002).

On the surface, the term "mainstream" seems innocuous. However, the designation comes into being only in relation to what it excludes, namely, without a "special" education classroom, how does one demarcate a "mainstream" or "regular" classroom? Without an other deemed abnormal, how does one become normal? Although these questions are rarely articulated, they offer an important query into the concept of normalcy. For instance, we might ask, from where does the concept of normalcy come? Who defines what normalcy is and is not? Who benefits and who loses from particular ideas about normalcy? How does the practice of segregated education require a normal/abnormal divide? These questions serve as important paths of inquiry to help us understand the perceived necessity to create regimes for evaluating, classifying, sorting, and placing students in educational settings based on their relationship to the "mainstream" or "normal" population.

Defining Normalcy

The designation of "normal" is typically reserved for people and things that conform to "the common . . . standard, regular, usual" type (L. J. Davis, 1995, p. 24). Despite the ubiquity of the category, the origin of the term is a fairly recent phenomenon. The concepts of normal and normalcy did not emerge in the English language until the mid-19th century (Davis). As stated in chapter 2, the evolution of the concept was contingent upon a constellation of occurrences, including the gradual institutionalization of statistics, which originated in Germany during the preceding century. During the industrial revolution the concept of the "average worker," as defined by industrial expectations, also emerged (Marx, 1959). This conflation of normal/average in Western understanding was therefore cemented by viewing each individual in terms of his or her ability to work. Analogously, in the classroom, students were ranked and sorted not simply by age, but based on their ability to perform on standardized measures in relation to their peers. Thus, schools came to be entrusted with the task of enforcing normalcy (L. J. Davis, 1995) by creating mechanisms for dividing students into normate[2] (Garland-Thomson, 1997a) and nonnormate classifications. Consequently, as Baynton (2001) illustrates, normalcy marks the place where race and disability intersect.

Compulsory Normativity[3]

Schools are places where students are socialized into certain ways of being and thinking. Schooling practices often reinforce inequities in the larger society. As is commonly the case, children of poor families typically attend underfunded schools, while children of wealthy families attend well-resourced schools (Brantlinger, 2003). Glaring inequities also existed in the segregated schools of the South, despite the long-standing promise of *Plessy v. Ferguson* (1896) of separate but equal facilities. Furthermore, education offered in segregated settings has often been cited as inferior to "mainstream" education (Lipsky & Gartner, 1997; Oakes & Lipton, 1999; Wagner & Blackorby, 1996).

   One of the socializing functions of schools is that individuals come to know their place and that of their peers. In this way, schools through their various sorting mechanisms, can be thought of as a colonizing force (Watts & Erevelles, 2004). Students learn the significance of being in (or out of) the "mainstream," "regular," or "general" classroom and whether (or not) they attend a "good" school. Terms such as mainstream or regular, however, obscure any relationship to the concept of normalcy. Yet, students typically know their own approximation to the current construction of normalcy and often reject certain students on the basis of their perceived deviation from the norm. Once separated into different spaces, students are socialized into an us/them binary that reaffirms culturally defined differences or "markings" such as race or disability. Garland-Thomson (1997a) calls attention to the power dynamics of those who mark others, saying "those bodies deemed inferior become spectacles of otherness while the unmarked are sheltered in the neutral space of normalcy" (p. 8). To borrow from de Beauvoir (1952/1989), who stated that woman is made not born, so too is normalcy (and abnormalcy) constructed, imposed on individuals from without, and not inherent.

Ironically, although a very small percentage of people fit the idealized norm (Goffman, 1963), expectations to approximate this ideal are pervasive, and some would argue compulsory. Black and disabled citizens, positioned as the antithesis of the traditional American ideal, are nonetheless defined in relation to—or invariably against—this ideal. Thus, their very existence excludes them from, while simultaneously demanding their conformity to, the ideal.

Striving toward normalcy "against the odds" by "overcoming" obstacles and barriers is an appealing but stereotypical storyline in literature, film, television, and children's stories. Such pervasive cultural scripts reinforce the idea that it is the responsibility of marginalized people to overcome their own (inherent) obstacles and achieve success in spite of their disability or difference. Paul Darke (1998) refers to this trope, which is common in cinematic representations of disability, as a "normality" genre: the individual is valued only when he or she conforms to the expectations determined by the dominant group. Moreover, because barriers are assumed to be inherent within the individual, as opposed to structural or external, the overcoming trope obscures the privilege enjoyed by the dominant group. As this privilege is obscured, the dominant group is positioned as deserving of success, rather than unfairly advantaged by virtue of their social positioning.

Critical race theorists call attention to the ways that power is not "out there," but rather "in the very situations and relationships that shape our lives" (Crenshaw et al., 1995, p. xxiii). Bearing this in mind, we ask: How do the cultural rules of classroom structures and practices influence who becomes "normal" and "abnormal"? How are bodily differences, in terms of physical appearance (race) or physical, cognitive, sensory, emotional, or behavioral characteristics (disability), recast as deficiencies? And, finally, how are individuals stigmatized and devalued in schools through a collective social ostracism and "communal acculturation process" (Garland-Thomson, 1997a, p. 31)?

Social environments such as the classroom create expectations of conformity, and students unable or unwilling to conform to dominant expectations are often relegated to the margins. When normalcy is viewed as static, those who benefit from its current manifestation continue to do so. Conversely, those positioned outside of the mainstream maintain a devalued status, and their removal makes them all but invisible. Inscribed within a purportedly "naturalized" discourse, "normals can remain relatively uncontaminated by intimate contact with the stigmatized, relatively unthreatened in their identity beliefs" (Goffman, 1963, p. 120). By not engaging with those who have been othered, the normate can disregard any reason to change school practices, thereby ensuring the continued socialization of normates and stigmatization of those deemed different. In other words, because the status quo works well for the dominant group, students from nondominant groups experience the imbalance of power and are required to either fit into the existing structures or to risk being relegated to alternative or "special" classrooms or schools.

The Normate Classroom

Just as the constitution of the U.S. reads, "All men [*sic*] are created equal," it follows that American public schools function on a belief that all students are created equal. However, throughout history certain students have been afforded more privilege than others; maintaining separate systems based on race and ability has favored the normate. This has not been lost on those who are positioned outside the classroom's normalized space. Russell (1998), for example, cautions, "implicit in the word 'normal' is a threat to each of us, individually and collectively" (p. 13). As an ideological tool, "'normal' demands political conformity as well as physical conformity, and as such can be used as a tool for social control" (p. 17). Queer theorist Warner (1993) also critiques the usually unarticulated sinister side of normalcy, calling attention to ways in which normalcy becomes entwined in numerous discourses, influencing how people categorize themselves and "others." He believes the entire social realm is "a cultural form, interwoven with the political . . . [due in large part to] normalizing methodologies of social knowledge" (p. xxvii). In other words, social reproduction occurs as a result of the way knowledge is defined and circulated. In the classroom space, socialization and normalization are interconnected. By conforming to normative expectations and acquiring required knowledge and skills (dictated by state and federal authorities), students become socialized, standardized, and normalized. Those who do not or cannot meet these norms are designated as below standard or abnormal.

But what of those who have actively challenged the normate classroom, troubling the standards of the day? In the 1950s Black Americans mobilized in unprecedented numbers to press for legislation that ensured access to integrated public schooling. A few decades later parents and advocates pushed for the right of children with disabilities to be educated alongside nondisabled peers. Because classrooms reflect the larger society, they indicate to what degree change is occurring (or not occurring) in the outside world. Both social movements demanded greater access to opportunities in society at large, but focused primarily on education as a means to more wide-reaching access (financial, social, and political) through integration and inclusion. This suggests that if substantial change is to occur, it is expected to begin first in schools, particularly in "general" education classrooms. By implication, if change does not occur within the public school level, it is less likely to spread in the larger world. However, because both desegregation and inclusion represented a radical challenge to the public education system and in particular its previously accepted exclusionary practices, both were met with much resistance. In the following sections of this chapter we explore the basis of such resistance by probing both the hopes and fears of integrated schooling.

Challenging Normalcy: What Is at Stake?

In this chapter we analyze letters to the editor, op-eds, and editorials written in response to school desegregation and inclusion in the White and Black press.[4] We pay particular attention to moments when the classroom is positioned as a contested or threatened space where various groups struggle over who should or should not be included. In these moments, dominant groups seek to shore up the boundaries between themselves and what they perceive as interloping outsiders. Often we found this discourse took the form of predictions about what would happen *if* schools became more inclusive or integrated. Embedded in these predictions were clues about what was perceived to be at stake by allowing previously excluded groups to participate in a "regular" classroom.

We divide the data into four interrelated sections. In the first section, "predicting the worst," we explore some of the more dire predictions that were made about desegregation and inclusion. In the second section, "opening the floodgates," we examine how integrated education was seen as a gateway to widespread social access. In the third section, "an enemy at the gate," we focus on how previously excluded students were characterized as unwanted interlopers forcing their way into a space that was clearly not theirs to claim. Finally, in "one's gain is another's loss" we attend to ways that integration was perceived as a threat to the dominant group. As discussed in chapter 1, we present the data on desegregation and inclusion as a back-and-forth or call-and-response dialogue, where each set of data is a "sideways glance" of the other (P. Morris, 1994, p. 20). By juxtaposing responses in this way, we aim to highlight the thematic overlapping of these two discourses of exclusion, while keeping each history relatively distinct. Following each grouping, we provide a brief analysis in which we call attention to both their commonalities and differences. We conclude the chapter with several lessons for current practice that we take from this analysis.

Predicting the Worst

Following *Brown* many gloom and doom predictions were made regarding school desegregation. Dire predictions were also made in response to calls for including students with disabilities into general education classrooms.

Many forecasted that integrated schools would bring chaos, destruction, "violence and bloodshed" ("What they say," 1956, June, p. 3).

A Junior College President threatened, "someone is going to get hurt" ("What they say," 1956, February, p. 7).

An editor warned readers to "expect a counter-attack" from opponents and "bloody results" (Hancock, 1954, p. 4).

As Southern governors threatened to close public schools rather than integrate them, one editor wrote, "The day is almost done for our public schools. As we linger in the troubled sunset there shall be time to recall how we cherished them" ("Schley county," 1954, p. 4).

Many opponents predicted that integration would "prove to be fatal to some of the South's vital institutions" (C.P.T., 1955, p. 4).

Others suggested that democracy itself was at risk. A letter to the editor signed by a "Confederate Democrat" (1954) warned, "If the people of the South let them get away with this bald usurpation of power . . . we can kiss the Constitution, liberty, and freedom good-bye" (p. 4).

One prominent Southern governor even predicted the "beginning of the end of civilization in the South as we have known it" (Williams, 1987, p. 34).

Most opponents predicted that inclusion would bring disruption and chaos to general education classrooms (Benning, 1997; Leo, 1994; Lewin, 1997; Reback, 1994).

Students with disabilities would experience cruelty and neglect in an uncaring learning environment (Hunter, 1995) that would be "harmful" to them (Strausberg, 1992, p. 3).

A *New York Times* editorial suggested that school officials calm parents' fears about "a return to the days when [their] disabled children were shunted into corners and ignored" ("Special care," 1996, p. 22).

Others warned that either special education or general education would be "destroy[ed]" (Wilgoren, 1994, p. D1), "dilute[d] or dismantle[d]" (Buckley, 1993, p. A1).

Many warned that students with disabilities would be "left behind" (Reback, 1994, p. A17) or "fall by the wayside" ("Special care," 1996, p. 22).

Several warned that students with disabilities might "lash out in frustration or withdraw in fear"(Maushard, 1994, p. 1B).

They would be "so alienated by . . . inclusion" that it would lead them to "juvenile delinquency, and worse" (Kent, 1998, p. 6).

Predictions of racial integration were often nothing short of apocalyptic. Death, destruction, and rampant violence are all conjured, vividly evoking a picture of societal disintegration. In many respects war is a telling image evoked by supporters of segregation, resurrecting long-standing hostilities between North and South, as if humiliations wrought by the Civil War remained fresh in the South's collective memory. Opponents view the disruption of the existing social and political order as intolerable. Overturning of segregation, in many ways, represents the symbolic death of White supremacy—as well as the last nail in the coffin for the South's liberty, freedom, and autonomy from northern influence.

Although not considered apocalyptic per se, inclusion is characterized by its opponents as chaotic for both general education students and for children with disabilities. Threatening that inclusion would mark a regression to the dark ages before services for students with disabilities, opponents paint a grave picture of dissolution. Notably, no mention is made of going back to the dark ages of institutionalization. Instead, inclusion is seen as a tragic loss of services that would leave students alone, isolated, unsupported, and by all accounts, abandoned. Thus, the disconcerting moral issue of disabled children being discarded and deserted is featured prominently in these examples. Moreover, the mainstream classroom is presented as so inhospitable to students with disabilities that opponents of inclusion predict destruction and violence. In many of these examples, the students themselves are presented as a threat.

Although both desegregation and inclusion provoked predictions of disorder and chaos, they differ in intensity. Desegregated classrooms and schools, for example, are often portrayed as society itself, representing equal access to all aspects of life and full citizenship rights. In terms of inclusion, however, classrooms are viewed literally as contained spaces. Only the tranquility of schools is said to be at stake, with opponents rarely referring to the outside world or society. An assumption in both the dire and the hopeful predictions is the underlying belief that the classroom is a powerful place, capable of shaping students, who in turn shape society.

Because both of these reforms seek to challenge the way classrooms are envisioned and configured, the stakes are perceived to be extremely high. Advocates regard integration and inclusion as watershed reforms that would open the doors to the larger community. To opponents, integration is perceived fundamentally as a loss. Thus, in both debates, the very hopes of equality, access, and broader understandings of human difference held by proponents were mirror images of their opponent's worst fears.

Opening the Floodgates

On both sides of the debate, desegregation is predicted to be the first step to ending all forms of segregation—leading to integrating all public facilities and institutions. In the case of inclusion, the classroom is positioned as having the potential to make or break a student's life chances. A student with a disability might be characterized as a threat waiting to happen or a drain on resources if schools did not provide the proper educational setting. In other words, the worry is not always about the individual student, but on the effect that students might have on the larger classroom or on society. In both debates, the students of color and students with disabilities are characterized as having nothing to offer, siphoning off an unfair share of classroom resources and giving nothing in return.

> *Brown* was seen as a "weapon to attack Jim Crow waiting rooms, travel facilities, parks, playgrounds, hotels, sanitary and health facilities and even housing" ("Prelude to freedom," 1954, p. 11).
>
> Opponents worried that "state parks and recreational areas . . . [as well as] municipally-owned swimming pools" ("Comment on," 1955, p. 16), and even cemeteries (A citizen, 1955, p. 1) would be integrated as a result of *Brown*.
>
> While proponents saw integration as moving the country "toward a more perfect democracy" (Friend, 1954, p. 28), opponents characterized these reforms as an attack on the freedoms of the dominant group, which had already made too many "concession[s]" ("What they say," 1957, February, p. 15).
>
> Thus, public schools were characterized as the "keystone to the foundation of the entire segregation system" ("The decision," 1954, p. 4).

> General education classrooms (often referred to as "normal" or "regular" classes) were characterized as either the entryway to greater access and inclusion and a "more normal lifestyle" (Strausberg, 1991, p. 6) or as "overcrowded" ("Special care," 1996, p. 22) "assembly-line[s]" (Faragoa, 1999, p. 15) with little or no support or patience for diversity or difference.
>
> "Can the rest of the class function. . . . If mainstreaming is slightly better for the disturbed child, but much worse for everyone else," how do we decide what is right? (Baird, 2002, p. 23).
>
> Proponents of inclusion stressed the negative impact of segregated settings on disabled students, who achieved less and suffered "loneliness and lack of choice" in self-contained classrooms (Ruppmann, 1991, p. A16).

> Advocates framed inclusion as more than simply a debate about best practice, but rather about a far more fundamental "human rights issue" (Revell, 2001, p. 6).
>
> While opponents described the general education classroom as drowning under the extra burden of dealing with students, who required a seemingly endless amount of resources and time, advocates perceived inclusion as the key to greater independence (Estrada, 1996), acceptance (Brett, 2002a) and access (Wilgoren, 1994) for individuals with disabilities.

Proponents of the *Brown* decision optimistically view it as the key to the kingdom so long denied. The integrated classroom is seen as opening the door to full access to public places such as parks, cinemas, neighborhoods, beaches, and cemeteries, as well as businesses such as banks, hotels, and restaurants. In brief, all aspects of life, once firmly closed or severely circumscribed would now come into reach. Proponents and opponents of desegregation wrestled over the meaning of democracy, each imbuing the concept with their own ideologies, each claiming theirs was the definitive meaning. The classroom became an explicitly politicized space, a battleground in which opposing claims of democracy were constantly asserted and reasserted. Just as proponents of integration view classrooms as the nucleus for change, opponents recognize the need to claim them as the bedrock of social stability.

Viewed as a dangerous threat, the inclusion of students with disabilities is presented as putting the well-being of mainstream students in danger. Inevitably taking more than they can give, students with disabilities are characterized as a drain on teachers. Proponents, on the other hand, view inclusion as a democratic practice, a responsibility of federal, state, and local governments to support *all* citizens through equal opportunities.

In these examples we see how advocates of inclusion and desegregation characterize these reforms as providing increased opportunity, access, and justice. In both instances proponents assert that increased exposure to diverse classrooms would lead to a better society and ultimately benefit everyone. One proponent of desegregation predicts that a "new era of human relations" (E. O. Jackson, 1954, p. 4) with children brought up "free from prejudice" would result ("We can learn," 1954, p. 11). Similarly, proponents of inclusion suggest that disabled and nondisabled students would benefit by "learn[ing] to respect everyone, despite differences" (Brett, 2002a, p. IJF). In this regard, recognizing and respecting diversity are presented as goals worthy of our best efforts.

Despite the promises of the value of diversity, opponents cast each of these reforms as posing a threat to the dominant group of students, who would supposedly be hindered or held back by less able students. In unpacking the resistance to desegregation and inclusion, we observe the blurring of race and disability as both groups are assumed to not measure up to their peers. Moreover, in voicing resistance, opponents place different groups of students as competing for limited resources—such that every gain by one group is associated with a corresponding loss to another. In this win/lose relationship, students with disabilities and students of color are placed in the position of interloper, aggressively intruding upon the supposed purity of the normative classroom. In seeking to block each of these reforms, opponents often wrote of the need to "protect" the classroom, defending it against dangerous invaders.

An Enemy at the Gate

In the debates over desegregation and inclusion the ideal classroom is often positioned as a kind of Garden of Eden—unsullied by diversity or difference. Students with disabilities and students of color are thus positioned as unwanted and invading forces or as interlopers who are disturbing the "peace" of homogeneity and sameness. Of course, what is in danger here is the normative space of the classroom and the invading force is assumed to be inferior in every respect.

Described as "slow" ("Study made," 1956, p. 12), "retarded" ("School boards," 1956, p. 15), "rowdy" ("Slow learner plan," 1956, p. 6), "lazy" ("First year," 1956, p. 3), as well as aggressive, arrogant, and bad tempered ("Second year of desegregation," 1956, p. 1), Black students were often characterized in the press as unwanted "interlopers" ("Integration," 1954, p. 4) who would negatively "affect the quality of education available to others" ("Second year," p. 1).

Because of their presumed inferiority, Black students are assumed to cause a "lowering of standards" ("Slow learner plan," 1956, p. 6) and present a "menace to the public safety" (Georgia v. U.S., 1954, p. 20).

It was also said that Black students would place an extra burden on White teachers, who would be "drained of vitality due to the strain of managing differences in academic standards, cultural background, behavior patterns, [and] personality" ("Second year of desegregation," 1956, p. 1).

A repetitive phrase to describe desegregation was the mixing of the races. As one person explains, "The basic fear [of Whites in the South] is mongrelization of the races. I just can't visualize a South which is predominantly mulatto" ("What they say," 1957, January, p. 3).

Many suggested the need to protect the public schools from the invading forces of "social equality, intermarriage, and mixing of the races in schools" ("What they say," 1957, January, p. 14).

Because a candidate for Governor of Georgia pledged to "maintain [a] segregated school system," an editor writes, "he will guard our schools and protect our children" ("Hand is their man," 1954, p. 9).

When students with disabilities are included in general education classrooms they are often described as disrupting the otherwise peaceful climate of the classroom and "threaten[ing] . . . people's physical safety" (Reback, 1994, p. A17).

Students with disabilities are also portrayed as causing undue hardship on teachers, who experience "unremitting stress" (Reback, 1994, p. A17) as a result of having to cope with student difference.

Because students with disabilities are believed to require almost constant support they are said to create "a strain on already-scarce [classroom] resources" (Benning, 1997, p. D1) which are "already stretched too thin" (Faragoa, 1999, p. 15).

Parents and teachers describe their experience with inclusion as "a disaster" (Wilgoren, 1994, p. D1) and nondisabled children are said to be "terrified of going to school" because of the dangers posed by unpredictable and violent disabled children (Holladay, 1998, p. A7).

In both debates, students who had been excluded are characterized as disrupting the supposedly homogeneous general education classroom, presenting insurmountable differences that could not be accommodated without a great deal of social upheaval. Black students, for example, were often assumed to be less able than their White peers. In arguing against inclusion, students with behavioral or emotional differences are often the exemplar of choice. These students are presented as "disruptive, abusive, sexually aggressive or violent" (Lewin, 1997, p. 1) and therefore difficult to integrate. The common use of the term "dumping" in referring to the inclusion of students with disabilities leaves little room for doubt of the status of these students, who seek to gain entry into a space that is clearly not their birthright. The difficulty they present is inherent to them alone, not illustrative of any problems in the educational system, which although often characterized as unchanging in its lock-step methods, is assumed to be natural and neutral.

Opponents of desegregation similarly present students of color as invading forces. The fear of miscegenation often was expressed by opponents of desegregation. Thus, students of color are not simply disruptive of the status quo, but actually capable of making White people disappear—their race "swallowed up" (H. J. Johnson, 1954, p. 4). Separation of the races is not simply a matter of state imperative, but supposedly a part of "God's creation and plan" ("What they say," 1957, January, p. 14). Editorial pages in the Black press openly critique the "war cry" of miscegenation, which was "dragged into every issue involving the Negro's progress" (Halliburton, 1955a, p. 4). Many in the Black press question how White people, who claim that even the thought of intimacy or proximity to Black people is so distasteful, would so fear that "mixing" White and Black children in schools would lead to intermarriage (Halliburton, 1955a, p. 4). In other words, those who would claim that Black people are so undesirable are the very people who worry that desegregation would automatically lead to widespread intermarriage. Many in the Black press also wonder why so many White people, who were all but raised by Black caretakers, would find it unsavory for their children to sit next to a Black person in school. Still others suggest that miscegenation was *already* a legacy of slavery, and the rape of Black women by White male slave owners, not integration, was the real cause of "White blood flowing in Negro vein" (Taschereau, 1954, p. 4). Finally, some in the Black press would point to the irony of certain southern governors who, while cautioning their constituents about the "intermarriage" that would supposedly result from integrating the schools, would fail to admit that they themselves fathered children who were "colored on [the] mother's side" (Hughes, 1954, p. 11).

Schools are powerful places that shape students and therefore society (and vice versa). In these excerpts, however, we also see schools, along with the dominant group and its institutions, characterized as highly vulnerable and in need of protection.[5] Here, the institutions of the dominant group are positioned as being under attack and therefore in need of protection to shore up their borders. In response to an outside challenge, dominant groups are able to mobilize and reassert their own privilege and strengthen their hold on power. In the next section we delve deeper into the issue of what is said to be at stake in each of these reforms and ways that integration was presented as a loss rather than a potential gain.

One's Gain Is Another's Loss

In addition to the claims by opponents that integrated schools would lead to chaos, social upheaval and a host of other problems, integration was also associated with either a loss or threat to traditional practice. Resistance to *Brown,* for instance, is not simply about a difference in opinion about educational practice, but about larger cultural imperatives about "rightful" privilege. One of the biggest fears voiced by opponents of inclusion is that it would lead to the destruction or diminishing of special education services (Wilgoren, 1994). Although some voice concerns about the impact of this change on students with disabilities themselves, others seemed more focused on the potential for disruption in the general education classroom and additional demands it would place on general education teachers. What appears to be at stake here, then, is the status quo of the traditional classroom and its structures and mechanisms of sorting students.

Although some voiced worries about school closing or privatization of the schools, for example, opponents claimed that desegregation would upset "domestic tranquility" (Threlkeld, 1954, p. 4) and "centuries of custom" ("Supreme Court reaffirms," 1955, p. 4).

A typical mantra was that integrating the schools would destroy the South's "way of life" (Ponton, 1954, p. 28) including its "heritage and . . . tradition[s]" ("Hand," 1954, p. 9).

Segregation is presented as a normalized and well-established practice, something basic and central to the community and culture of the South and "infinitely stronger than law" (Ponton, 1954, p. 28).

Opponents claimed that desegregating of the schools would set "race relations back nearly a hundred years" (Simpson, 1954, p. 4). Ironically, race relations were often described in the White press as "amicable" until the push for desegregation upset the balance of power. Whether race relations were in fact amicable was, of course, up for debate (Drake, 1956, p. 10E).

Advocates acknowledge that "the traditional classroom, with desks placed in long rows and the teacher writing on the Blackboard" would have to give way to more flexible classroom structures and curriculum (Librach, 1992, p. 1) where children would work in "small groups [and] use a variety of hands-on materials" (Jacobson, 1993, p. J1).

Another states, "taking special education services away from students who need them, in the name of inclusion, may in fact lead to . . . disruptive scenarios" (D. A. Ferri, 2002, p. B8.)

When interviewed, Mark Alter, Chairman of the Department of Teaching and Learning at New York University said, "These kids have academic and/or behavior problems. . . . It's that youngster is to remain in general education, there must be appropriate supports for that kid. Right now, they don't have the resources, the teachers, the support systems to meet the needs of these youngsters" (Belluck, 1996, p. A1).

One parent ironically stresses the need for segregation to support eventual integration, writing "proposed legislative changes would prevent these schools from adding additional classes for children who require one-on-one teaching from specialized educators and therapists to bring them to the point where they can be mainstreamed" (Godfrey, 1999, p. A34).

In the South, desegregation undermined the very foundations of regional culture, and therefore was viewed as beyond the reach of federal law. At the risk of stating the obvious, the more a group of people have to lose, the greater their resistance. The domestic tranquility experienced by Whites is often erroneously ascribed to Blacks, whose enforced servitude and subservience is misconstrued as "amicable" relations. Thus, configurations that blurred racial lines in and out of school are said to disadvantage everyone. Similarly, in terms of inclusion, opponents believe that both disabled and nondisabled students would suffer as a result of inclusion. Conveniently, in these examples, the dominant group often asserts the benefits of segregation for the excluded group. The "educational needs" of Black students and students with disabilities, determined by non-Blacks and nondisabled people, have often been marked by their exclusion rather than inclusion into the mainstream.

What is at stake in both desegregation and inclusion is a challenge to normalizing practices and assumptions. The idea of contesting racially segregated facilities and classrooms "just the way we do things here" is seen as an affront to the customs of the White establishment. In the case of inclusion, the idea that general education classrooms would have to change was, and is, a revolutionary and often unwelcome idea. Although used to the notion that students with disabilities must adapt to the mainstream, either through remediation or normalization, opponents are less enamored with suggestions that the general education classroom must change to accommodate difference. Perhaps this is why we see very little push for inclusion by general educators, even those committed to other kinds of progressive school reform. What is not discussed directly in either of these examples is the redefinition of "student" required of both inclusion and desegregation. Whenever the boundaries around the category of student are challenged to become more inclusive of difference, this supposedly new student type is thought to present difficulties and even dangers. But the danger here, despite paternalistic worries about the impact on marginalized students, was really about the impact on the normative classroom and perhaps to current notions of normalcy itself.

As D. L. Ferguson (1995) writes, the challenge of inclusion requires a transformation of the overriding assumptions that there are two types of students: "regular" and "special" and that only "special" students have "special" needs that only the "special" educator can provide. Thus, because disabilities are perceived as "real" differences between students, justifying their exclusion to specialized settings, inclusion requires a shift in assumptions about ability and difference. If these central assumptions are not questioned, Ferguson argues, then inclusion simply becomes an argument about relocating the place of education for students with disabilities and fails to transform general education.

Conclusion

Both the integration of students of color into classrooms with White students, and the inclusion of students with disabilities into classrooms of nondisabled students, provoked heated debate in the press. Proponents of these movements place the reforms within utopian visions, heralding unprecedented social change and equality of access and opportunity. Opponents, on the other hand, forecasted dire consequences of "mixing" people who were assumed to be too different in the same space. The former upholds the right of individuals to gain access to classrooms that have traditionally excluded them. At the same time, the latter seek to fortify structures that maintain the status quo. The level of resistance to these reforms suggests that much is at stake when those who have been excluded come knocking at the door to demand access.

Inclusion and desegregation call into question many of the assumptions of segregated schooling. For example, both reforms challenge the categories used to divide students into different types. Advocates of desegregation question the educational relevance of racial distinctions and point to the inherent inequality of segregated settings. Likewise, proponents of inclusion question the relevance of special education labels and efficacy of specialized classrooms. While we acknowledge these reforms have yet to fully achieve their original aims, both were radical in that they sought to bring about a reconfiguration of the general education classroom and a shift in its central assumptions.

Lessons Learned

A central lesson of this chapter is that any challenge to the dominant lines of power in the classroom or in society will not be achieved without a struggle—a struggle that often involves a renegotiation of normalcy. Although, as we have discussed, normalcy is a fairly recent concept, it has nonetheless become etched in our minds. Just as opponents of desegregation were incensed at the idea that Black students would dare to stake a claim to their right of access to White schools, detractors questioned the right of disabled children to gain access to general education classrooms. General education classrooms are presented as clearly not designed for students with disabilities. Teachers, who do not see themselves as ready for or capable of teaching children they perceive as fundamentally different, insist on the impossibility of integrating students with disabilities into their classrooms. Tenacious assumptions that "regular" classrooms and teachers were/are for "regular" (i.e., largely White, nondisabled) students, and "special" classrooms and teachers are for other students, have been difficult ideas to challenge. The inherent bias of exclusionary classrooms not representative of true student diversity is rarely questioned.

Because of the difficulty in challenging these basic assumptions, in both cases when previously excluded students did gain entry, the standards and expectations of the general education classroom often did not change—nor did the basic structure of the general education class. After *Brown,* Black students were held to biased assessments and expectations that were firmly rooted in White cultural experiences. Students with disabilities who gain access to general education often find that they are tolerated, but neither welcomed nor accommodated in the everyday workings of the class. It is clear that basic divisions between students often remain intact and access does not always guarantee full integration or transformation of general education.

What must be acknowledged is that the general education classroom does not work well for many students and inclusion is an opportunity to transform education to better meet the needs of all students by blurring the lines of regular and special. Although opponents often refer to inclusion as a loss of supports, when supports are brought into the general education class, there is the potential for a different kind of classroom. Perhaps Italy, a country long recognized as a leader in the field (Sailor, 1991), is a good example for how inclusion can be used to transform the classroom in ways that benefit all students. When the Italian school system adopted a policy of full inclusion nearly 30 years ago, it recognized that general education classrooms could not operate as they always had, and that they, not students with disabilities, were in need of remediation. Remarkably, Italian schools closed all special classes, lowered class sizes to a maximum of 20 students, and adopted a co-teaching model where support teachers and general education teachers work together to serve *all* students in the classroom. When visiting an Italian school, it is difficult to know which teacher is the support teacher (called the *sostagno*). Teachers are proud of their shared responsibility for all students, and it shows. This kind of transformation of regular and special education into something more than a sum of its parts provides an example of how to use inclusion as an opportunity to rethink what is good for all students and to shift supports in flexible ways to enrich the whole classroom.

6

THE POWER OF PERSUASION:
MAKING (NON)SENSE OF EXCLUSION

6

THE POWER OF PERSUASION: MAKING (NON)SENSE OF EXCLUSION

Introduction: Editorial Pages as Multivoiced Texts

Editorial pages occupy a unique place in the newspaper and in popular culture. They are particularly dialogic spaces where the voices of editors, guest editors, and cartoonists commingle with various people who write letters to the editor, including scholars, luminaries of the day, and people from the local community. Letters to the editor are sometimes written in response to a particular editorial or an op-ed, a current event or issue, or to a recently published letter. Although some letters are signed, others are anonymous. Whether the letters that get published are representative of the range of opinion on a particular issue is anyone's guess; these decisions are rarely transparent.

Although the editor's task is to take positions, he or she always writes in anticipation of a response. The common phrase "that's just your opinion" seems to capture the way editorials are taken not as authoritative texts, but rather something open to, and even inviting of, discussion and debate. Thus, while the newspaper reporter writes in a declarative way, typically aiming for some degree of neutrality, the editor aims to encourage conversation and even dissent. Editorial pages may not be balanced, but rarely are they monolithic in tone or opinion. Instead, the editorial page is a carnival of voices and perspectives.

Another important dialogic feature of newspapers involves syndication. It is not uncommon, for example, for newspapers to republish columns, editorials, articles, or even letters from other papers or news sources. Newspapers we researched included columns with titles like, "What they say" (*Southern School News*) or "Pulse of the Public" (*Atlanta Constitution*), which were specifically designed to provide readers with access to opinions from a wider range of sources. Cartoons, in particular, were often syndicated. At least one major paper we researched (*New York Times*) published *only* syndicated or freelance cartoons. This type of borrowing within the editorial page took place among and between both White and Black presses, and crossed geographic and racial borders.

Republication and syndication could be thought of as forms of what Bakhtin might call reported speech (P. Morris, 1994). According to Bakhtin (in Emerson & Holquist, 1986) every utterance is like a fingerprint; it is virtually unrepeatable. When an editorial cartoon is published in multiple newspapers, each subsequent printing changes its context and therefore its intention, intonation, and audience (P. Morris, 1994). Because meaning is shaped by context, the same editorial cartoon takes on very different meanings in the context of a southern White paper and a northern or southern Black paper. Thus, an image of "Uncle Sam," depending on the assumed readership (White/Black; northern/southern) of a particular paper, can easily be double-voiced (Bakhtin, 1986); the same image might be read as signifying democracy in one context or as unwanted northern interference in another. In all discourse, and particularly in reported speech, attending not simply to the image or text, but also the presumed audience and the larger social context, shapes the interpretation. Regardless of authorial intent, the fact that this same image of "Uncle Sam" might be chosen by editors of very different papers and perspectives signals its double-voiced potential and renders its meaning fluid and contextual.

Thus, to study the editorial page is to study a tangle of perspectives and voices, where meaning is rarely decided once and for all. Even if such a thing were possible, we have not attempted to identify any particular editorial point of view for any of the papers we studied. Instead, we chose to use the editorial page as a whole as our unit of analysis. Enacting Bakhtin's idea of a "plurality of equally-valid consciousness" (P. Morris, 1994, p. 93), we place prominent voices, such as Mary McLeod Bethune,[1] Lillian Smith,[2] and Langston Hughes[3] alongside a host of editors, guest editors, and everyday people who wrote letters to the editor. It is not, of course, that hierarchy or power is suspended either in the editorial page or in our analysis, but we purposely decided *not* to give different analytic weight to letters written by anonymous or unknown persons than to those written by renowned editors or writers. Instead, we chose to focus on the patchwork of the editorial page, a place where diverse voices and perspectives provided a snapshot of the range of public opinions on desegregation and inclusion.

In this chapter we attend more closely to the polyphonic nature of editorial pages as we highlight specific rhetorical strategies and language games used to advance arguments either for or against integrated education. We identify specific strategies employed in each debate (desegregation and inclusion) as well as those used across both discourses. In our analysis we also unearth the embedded assumptions about democracy, morality, and citizenship operating within these discourses. In addition to noting the strategies used by dominant groups to maintain the status quo of segregated schooling, we were particularly interested in how marginalized groups used particular language practices and strategies of resistance as powerful tools to enact social change. We drew on the work of Bakhtin to demonstrate how language, particularly within the dialogic space of the editorial page, is a site of ideological struggle infused with webs of power and resistance. We conclude the chapter with the idea that there remains a need for a different kind of discourse, which recognizes both the sociopolitical nature of schooling and the failures of binary thinking to solve complex educational problems.

Bakhtin and the (Inter)Play of Voices

Because of the multivoiced nature of the editorial page, we found the work of M. M. Bakhtin[4] particularly helpful in framing our analysis. A recurring theme in Bakhtin's writings is dialogue, which he saw as infused with multiplicity and conflict. Rather than isolated individuals constructing or owning meaning, or language containing some inherent meaning on its own, Bakhtin saw meaning as a site of ideological struggle and negotiation between the self, the other, and the sign. This struggle, which he termed "heteroglossia," takes place between the stabilizing forces of dominant groups, who seek to close off meaning, and destabilizing forces of marginalized groups, who seek to reclaim or subvert established meanings (Clark & Holquist, 1984; P. Morris, 1994). Thus, although issues are often framed as either pro or con, particularly in editorial pages, these positions are rarely as dichotomous as they seem on the surface. For instance, in our study we found numerous examples of dissent within each community, making it impossible to talk about the Black community or parents of students with disabilities as a unified group with monolithic opinions. Moreover, like Foucault (1990), Bakhtin did not see this kind of struggle as oppositional, but rather as relational and interactive. For Bakhtin, meaning is never fixed, but actively negotiated on the border zones between the self, the other, and language. In other words, meaning is a product of living social interaction and conflict (P. Morris, 1994).

Bakhtin also stressed the idea that individuals acquire words, not from dictionaries, but from the mouths of others, and as a result, all words come peopled with others. Because meaning is always dialogic, the audience is always a reciprocating presence in any text, and therefore, must be considered. Bakhtin (1986) wrote:

> The word (or any general sign) is interindividual. Everything that is said, expressed, is located outside the "soul" of the speaker and does not belong to him. The word cannot be assigned to a single speaker. The author (speaker) has his own inalienable right to the word, but the listener also has his rights, and those whose voices are heard in the word before the author comes upon it also have their rights (after all, there are no words that belong to no one) (pp. 121–122)

Although individuals can never *own* meaning, according to Bakhtin, they can *borrow* it (Clark & Holquist, 1984). As Freeman (1993) explains, even though the self is not sovereign over meaning, it retains the potential to breathe new life into words. Therefore, words like "democracy" or "freedom" can mean very different things depending on speaker, audience, and context. Although we cannot lay claim to a particular word or image, we can infuse it with new meanings. This can be seen in the practice of marginalized groups who reclaim and revalue words like queer, crip, or Black—effectively turning a term of denigration or derision into a symbol of pride.

Returning to the "Uncle Sam" example, utterances (including images as well as text) can be double voiced, creatively speaking to multiple audiences simultaneously. Bakhtin referred to such double-voiced discourse as a "word with a sideways glance" (P. Morris, 1994, p. 20). Like parody, double-voiced discourse can signal intimacy to one's allies at the same time it communicates ridicule to outsiders, functioning as praise and insult simultaneously (Pearce, 1994). Because words are always two-sided acts, meaning is always territory shared (Clark & Holquist, 1984) or half someone else's (P. Morris, 1994). An author, therefore, never acts in isolation or with complete agency, but rather in dialogue with a presumed or imagined other. Again, this becomes quite self-consciously so in the context of the editorial page, where the public interplay of voices renders every contribution polyphonic. Moreover, because every utterance is directed at another or in response to another, agency is always mediated by the existing social order (Pearce, 1994). Thus, although the self maintains the ability to use language as a form of resistance (Pearce), dialogue is always inscribed with power and inequality, which, of course, places constraints on reciprocity and agency.

Thus, in Bakhtin's notion of dialogue, individuals are invested with both agency and constraint, which play out in a constant negotiation with others at the level of discourse. In this chapter we highlight some of the rhetorical strategies used by those seeking to change the status quo of exclusionary practices as well as by those in the dominant group who sought to silence and/or discredit dissenting voices. Our interest, therefore, is not so much on the debate itself, but rather what was going on within the debate—at the level of utterance. As discussed in the introductory chapter, we present our findings in a conversational, back-and-forth format, which we purposely designed to enact Bakhtin's idea of a word with a sideways glance (in P. Morris, 1994, p. 20). By organizing the data this way, we simultaneously allow connections to be made across these two debates without collapsing or ignoring their differences.

Sticks and Stones: Name-Calling as a Discrediting Strategy

During the years leading up to and then following *Brown,* most newspapers featured editorials, op-eds, letters to the editor, and editorial cartoons debating the issue of school desegregation. Conversely, although inclusion has been at the epicenter of much professional debate in recent years, the general public has not taken it up to the same degree. Inclusion, on the whole, appears far less an urgent issue in the public consciousness, more a local concern than a national public debate. It could be said that the editorial coverage of inclusion, like the implementation of inclusion in the schools, has been less than universal.

Of course, the widespread coverage of desegregation is not typical of editorial attention to educational issues. Heated educational debates are generally not found in the pages of major newspapers, but rather in professional journals and at academic conferences. Debates over inclusion within scholarly circles, however, have often taken on a rhetorical style more typical of the editorial page than of professional writing. Moreover, the rhetoric has become increasingly adversarial over time, as the number of scholars challenging some of the foundational assumptions of the field of special education has grown. As Heshusius (2004) explains, "a single voice is not threatening: If necessary it can easily be silenced" (p. 175). According to Danforth (2004), there is within special education a polarization of two interdependent groups: "the orthodox who defend and define a [positivist] belief system . . . and the heretics who put forth a belief system that challenges . . . the orthodoxy" (p. 447). Similarly, Gallagher (2004) describes the field as divided into "opposing camps" (p. viii), positioned in a virtual "standoff . . . with no resolution in sight" (Gallagher, 2001, p. 637). Brantlinger (1997) dubs the two "camps" as traditionalists and inclusionists. What is important in these reviews of scholarly debates within the field of special education is not that these authors are talking about the same group of scholars—although there is certainly a degree of overlap to the various groupings. What *is* relevant to our examination of editorial pages covering desegregation and inclusion, are the similarities in the rhetorical strategies and language games employed in both the editorial coverage and in professional debates. For example, in analyzing editorial coverage of desegregation and inclusion, we were struck by the provocative name-calling we found, particularly by opponents of these reforms. Popular choices included calling advocates of desegregation Communists or traitors, or associating them with evil or insanity. Inclusionists are referred to as religious fanatics, zealots, and even terrorists. The following examples illustrate some of the more striking examples of name-calling. (Note: italics have been added in these excerpts for emphasis.)

Desegregation

"It would be very unfortunate if mixing of the races in schools became such a *fanatic fixation* in the minds of NAACP leaders" ("Fear and obsession," 1955, p. 4).

"sober-minded citizens . . . may be more perturbed at the *rape* of [the] constitution" (Rucker, 1954, p. 4).

"If these *forces of evil* are able to force on South Carolina" ("What they say," 1955, April, p. 13).

"The White people of the South are determined to cut out the *cancerous growth* of the NAACP, which is threatening our traditional way of life" (Volmer, 1955, p. 4).

"It's people like you, the *Jew-led* NAACP and the Communists who are making all the trouble down here" (E. G. Smith, 1955, p. 4).

"[W]ho mistakenly believes that the *lace-cuff, pantywaist,* 'liberal' writers in our magazine represent the people of this great country" (R. H. Davis, 1954, p. 4).

"I am a Republican, but I'm ashamed of it. The Democrats—at least all I know—are part of the same *boot-licking* crew. It's got to the point where we're all afraid. America has become so fat, so rich, so senile, so weak, so stupid—so self-conscious of her importance—that she's like a *doddering old woman* living in fear that she'll offend someone—or break some social custom that must be correct because it originated in some foreign court" (Cornell, 1954, p. 4).

"The federal bench is now composed of *judicial misfits*" ("What they say," 1956, April, p. 14).

"If this *diabolical plan* by the Northern radicals goes through, and we see integration in our schools, we might even see a situation akin to that of A Tower of Babel, when the Lord expressed His displeasure by causing the people to speak in many tongues" (Garrett, 1954, p. 4). [Note: in her letter, this writer refers to the integrationists as a *"rabble-rousing element"* and a *"Northern conspiracy."*]

"In May 1954, that *inept fraternity* of politicians and professors known as the United States Supreme Court . . . *spit* upon the tenth amendment, and rewrote the fundamental law of this land to suit their own *gauzy* concepts of democracy" ("Court order," 1955, p. 9).

"The integrationist . . . bombard[s] the public with a barrage of false *propaganda* designed to *lynch* the character of a fourth of our Nation" ("What they say," 1955, April, p. 13).

Inclusion

> "Social inclusion seems to be the political *flavor of the month*" (Inson, 2000, p. 33).
>
> "Many influential advocacy groups have promoted inclusion with a fervor bordering on *religious fanaticism*" (Barker, 1991, p. A16).
>
> "[I]n their *zeal* for 'full inclusion'" (Rosenberg, 1993, p. A24).
>
> "[T]he gulf between educational 'haves' and 'have-nots' is widening despite the *mantra* of 'inclusion'" (Wharton, 2000, p. 17).
>
> "But a *haphazard* decision to put all disabled children into regular classrooms doesn't advance the education of any child, much less the cause of disability-rights advocates" (Reback, 1994, p. A17).
>
> "[This] storm of mainstreaming . . . *raging* and *washing back onto the beaches* of the public school system without supportive systems they need to negotiate the climate" (Strausberg, 1992, p. 3).
>
> "[It's] a scandal . . . [that] many schools had been left to cope with the influx of pupils brought in by *politically correct* inclusion policies" (Thornton, 2000, p. 6).
>
> "To me, it is a *Utopian ideal*. And that is where I have difficulty with the concept of inclusion" (Brasch-Librach, 1992, p. 1).
>
> "[E]ven before inclusion became *fashionable*" (Hayward & Kane, 2000, p. 18).
>
> "Mainstreaming children with disabilities into public school systems [has been likened] to an act of *terrorism*. . . . And for us to dismantle it is a *terrorist act* against education" (Strausberg, 1992, p. 3).

As these examples illustrate, there are several connections between the various forms of name-calling operating in these discourses. Both desegregationists and inclusionists, for example, are criticized for their so-called fanaticism. Words like fixation, zeal, fervor, and mantra are commonly used to discredit those seeking racial integration or inclusion. Another strategy to discredit opposition is to trivialize either the issue or its advocates. For example, references to desegregationists being subservient ("boot licking") or effeminate ("lace cuff, pantywaist," "gauzy," or like a "doddering old woman") draw on sexist or heterosexist stereotypes in an attempt to undermine or diminish advocates of desegregation. In a similar vein, inclusionists are often characterized as simply going through a phase ("flavor of the month" or "politically correct") or being unrealistic ("Utopian") or trendy ("fashionable"), to call into question the seriousness of the approach or its advocates. Proponents of inclusion and desegregation are presented as villains, terrorists, and rapists, or they are deemed misfits, fanatics, or fools. Whether cunningly evil or pathetically stupid, the portrayals suggest that reformers are not to be trusted with the future of America's children.

Terms of insult can also be strategically redeployed on one's opponents. Often in an attempt to deflect a particular type of name-calling, one side of the debate would ventriloquate the other's insult. For example, while opponents charge that desegregationists are "lace cuff, pantywaist[s]" (R. H. Davis, 1954, p. 4), advocates of desegregation claim that White people are "emasculated by the vagaries of segregation" (Hancock, 1953, p. 4). Advocates of desegregation write that "segregation . . . blinds one's eyes to understanding" ("Out of step," 1954, p. 6), and opponents counter that desegregationists are "blinded by passion" ("What they say," 1956, April, p. 9).

Similarly, both sides of the inclusion debate accuse one another of pushing students into alienating classroom settings. For instance, an opponent of inclusion calls the general classroom "a wilderness of alienation" (Wharton, 2000, p. 17), whereas advocates call special education a "dumping ground," particularly for students of color (Mason, 1994, p. A9). Similarly, advocates of inclusion are described as fanatic zealots, and characterize their opponents as "stubbornly resistant to reform" ("Reforming special education," 1995, p. A26). A common criticism volleyed back and forth in both debates is the charge that the opposition is deluded and not acting rationally. Rationality is often contrasted with disability or disease. Opponents are described as blind, hysterical, lacking in common sense, or riddled with disease. In this language game, however, the stereotypical bias of the insult (sexism, heterosexism, ableism, racism) remains intact even though the object of ridicule shifts. Moreover, deflection fails to shift the meaning of any of the terms. In other words, blindness, regardless of who employed the term, is used as a stand-in for ignorance and lack of insight, maintaining its ableist usage regardless of the context.

Sometimes the name-calling is directed at the students themselves. Opponents claim that the difficulty involved in integration is directly proportional to the numbers of students being integrated. In other words, the make-or-break question becomes, "Exactly how many want in?" The accommodation of diversity is perceived to be easier when it does not threaten the status quo. In one editorial, the governor of Mississippi maintains that the "problem" of integration is more difficult in his state because of the state's large population of Black people. He claims:

This problem is more acute here than in any other state in the nation. It is not something that can be viewed with complacency or ignored, and if you lived in Mississippi and knew the full situation, you would look upon it as we do. ("What they say," 1956, February, p. 15)

The governor assumes that if we understood the "problem" of Mississippi's large population of Black students, we would come around to his way of thinking. Using words like "devouring," "swelling," and "spawning," many similarly portray either special education or inclusion as a stampeding force, or a plague of locusts consuming everything in its path.

At times, the students themselves are the rampaging force. In one particularly racist example, an anonymous educational official from Vermont compares students with significant disabilities to:

Mexicans coming across the border . . . on the one hand you're happy that they're going to get a better quality of life. On the other hand you worry that at some point, if you get too many, it will break the bank and change the nature of what you have. (Lewin, 1997, p. 1)

Obviously the worry is that the dominant group will be threatened if it is no longer the clear majority. Thus, in both examples, the hope is that minority students could be assimilated in such a way as not to change the basic nature of the classroom or the school. In other words, as long as the dominant group is not dislodged from the center—upsetting the whole power structure of majority and minority—then integration is perceived as "tolerable." Of course, the tipping point for "how many is too many" is always defined by the majority—and typically much less than would be dictated by the proportion of students of color or students with disabilities in the state or district. In many instances more than one or two "minority" or "special" students in a class is enough to tip the scales from acceptable to unmanageable.

In the desegregation debate anger is often directed at the NAACP, an organization that was seen by segregationists as an invading force that needed to be curtailed. In a particularly threatening letter written to the editor of the *Richmond Afro-American*, an angry Southerner warns of retribution[5]:

The killing of that preacher in Mississippi is a warning that should be heeded by all you people thinking about joining [the] NAACP. The White people of the South are determined to cut out the cancerous growth of the NAACP, which is threatening our traditional way of life. We are convinced it hasn't spread so far that the judicious use of a little buckshot and a little rope here and there [wouldn't][6] effect a cure. (Volmer, 1955, p. 4)

In contrast, the threat expressed by opponents of inclusion is not a threat of violence from the outside, but rather from the students themselves. Many warn that educating students with disabilities is a high-stakes gamble, arguing that if services for students with disabilities are not provided in the right way, these children will come back to haunt us later. Opponents express concern that if special education classes are dismantled, students with disabilities will be "lost to the streets" (O'Neil, 2002, p. 17) or "lost forever" (Kastens, 1995, p. A15). A typical example of this kind of thinking is evident in the following:

> Long-term costs [of inclusion] will be far greater . . . [if we count] the cost of repeated incarcerations in county jails for petty offences such as loitering, being a public nuisance and the inevitable homelessness that occurs when a parent-caregiver dies. (Souto, 1996, p. A24)

Again, the worry on the surface is about students with disabilities, but also about the potential impact on society if we do not keep students with disabilities segregated. The question we must ask is whether special classes are meant to support students with disabilities or to protect society from them.

As stated earlier, alarmist rhetoric surrounding these two educational reforms has not been confined to the editorial page. Danforth (2004) notes a similar sense of unease and anxiety in scholarly texts by researchers who attempt to suppress diverse opinions. The use of name-calling to discredit colleagues who hold alternative views has been identified by a number of scholars, including Danforth, Heshusius (2004), and Brantlinger (1997). They document how those advocating inclusion, for example, have been referred to as extremists, scam artists, frauds, charlatans, and quacks. Accused of riding on an illusionary bandwagon, their views are dismissed by prominent researchers in the field of special education as dangerous propaganda or meaningless lingo. As Gallagher (1998) writes, critics of special education "have been largely ignored, if not summarily dismissed . . . [and] characterized as rude, ill-founded, aggressive, logically faulty, hostile, unjustified, irrational, and so on" (p. 500).

Scholars who advocate inclusion or other kinds of special education reform are described by those who hold a more traditional view as being out of touch with reality, belonging to a cult, or having sinister motives. As Danforth (2004), Gallagher (2004), and others note, this kind of name-calling does not invite dialogue but rather closes down any possibility for open inquiry or exchange. Those who seek to control the discourse (and the funding) attempt to do so by silencing their opponents. In the bankrupt economy of binary thinking, those holding alternative views are discredited as being on the "wrong" side of false dichotomies like good/evil and reason/emotion. As Ella Shohat (1999) explains, binary thinking is a friend of war, because it refuses complexity and closes down possibilities for dialogue. Perhaps the preponderance of binaries explains why we notice so many analogies to war in these debates.

Call to Arms: School Goes to War

Relying on false binaries between opposing sides of each issue, inclusion and desegregation debates are rife with analogies to war or battle. Although these analogies indicate the importance and seriousness of these educational reforms, they close off rather than invite sustained dialogue. As these examples illustrate, analogies to war or battle leave little room for negotiation or discussion.

Desegregation

"[Governor] Griffin objected . . . on the grounds that it would create a 'Civil Rights Gestapo' with hordes of storm troopers and secret police stalking through the land with the sinister purpose of regulating the individual's business and every action" ("What they say," 1956, April, p. 7).

"Americans who are determined to protect their children from a Black invasion" (O'Brien, 1955, p. 4).

"[Desegregationists] are indirectly helping the Reds to discredit this nation as well as weakening the freedom-loving bloc of democratic countries" (Castro, 1954, p. 4).

". . . the real militancy of the organized Negroes" (Lahey, 1954, p. 23).

"Nothing the Russians have been able to do has thrown this country in as much turmoil as the NAACP" (Kelly, 1955, p. 4).

"Minority groups . . . have mobilized themselves . . . to do battle for equality" (Lehman, 1954, p. 6).

"[Desegregation is part of a] united struggle for peace and freedom, against Jim Crow, colonialism, and the subjugation of peoples and nation by imperialism" (J. W. Ford, 1954, p. 4).

"Discrimination weakens our defense of democracy in our fight against communism" ("Another Negro Father," 1954, p. 4).

"[The] High Court should be congratulated for delivering what will eventually be realized a most damaging blow against communism" (W. Gordon, 1954, p. 4).

"[T]he highest judicial body in the land presents to the world a united front for democratic freedom" ("Editorial excerpts," 1954, p. 20).

"We cannot allow rejoicing over the Supreme Court's anti-segregation decision to lull us into a false sense that the fight is over" (Morrow, 1954, p. 4).

"There will be a resurgence of patriotism unknown since the Colonials were fired and inspired by Patrick Henry's Liberty or Death speech . . . and communism will melt before democracy's advance like frost before the rising sun" (Hancock, 1953, p. 4).

Inclusion

"If everybody's not prepared [for inclusion], then it turns into a battle: Am I going to help the special ed. kid or the regular ed. kid?" (Wilgoren & Pae, 1994, p. B1).

"It has not been demonstrated that regular classrooms, even fortified regular classrooms using the best practices, can accommodate all children all the time" (Lewin, 1997, p. 1).

"[A]t a time when U.S. schools have come under fire to raise standards of elementary and secondary students, inclusion is a misguided policy" (Yatron-Kastens, 1995, p. A15).

"[Inclusion] is what we're fighting for. It's a fight that may benefit other children, too" ("Family's battle," 1993, p. 5).

"Our children and special education have been wed and there cannot be a divorce" (Strausberg, 1992, p. 3).

In these excerpts we see both proponents and opponents of desegregation and inclusion characterizing school reform in terms of war. In the desegregation debate the "war" over integrated schooling is connected to (even conflated with) a battle between democracy and communism. Both sides claim that their position would protect the country from communism and charge the other with the spread of "brainwashing propaganda" (Malcomb, 1954, p. B4). The paranoia associated with the Cold War is also evidenced by a fear of a "Black invasion," which explicitly positioned Blacks as foreigners rather than "real" citizens. Segregationists express fears of being overtaken by an NAACP "Gestapo" or hordes of invading civil rights storm troopers, ironically describing a world closer to the lived experience of Black citizens. Derisive comments imply that integrationists were traitorous pawns succumbing to a Soviet (or enemy) influence and whose sole purpose was to undermine democracy. In response, advocates of desegregation warned that the "eyes of the world" (Hancock, 1953, p. 4; Punshon, 1954, p. 26; Sanders, 1954, p. 4) were watching to see how the U.S. would justify Jim Crow schools and policies within a so-called democracy. Indeed, hypocrisy is a common accusation leveled at segregationists. As Hollowell (1955) writes, "particularly those who teach civics, logic, psychology, history, and religion, do not believe what they teach" (p. 4).

In the inclusion debate the classroom or school became the site of "battle," but mostly over resources, such as teacher attention and taxpayer dollars. In an educational climate where schools are increasingly "under fire" for not performing adequately on standardized tests, inclusion is often viewed as a "misguided" effort—effort better spent on more able students. This mirrors the view of many eugenicists, such as Leta Hollingworth (see chapter 2), who believed educational resources were being wasted on low performing students and would be better spent on the gifted. Classrooms, too, are described as war-torn places where innocent (nondisabled) school children are invaded by a potentially violent (disabled) other or where victimized (disabled) children are portrayed as being "pushed" or "pulled" from one educational setting to another. In both instances when war becomes the metaphor for school reform, the only reasonable response is distinctly adversarial.

Inclusion or Intrusion: Defining Democracy

Analogies to prison, slavery, and other forms of bondage and incarceration are also common in these debates. In the following examples we observe a struggle over what it means to be included or excluded, by those positioned as outsiders and those who feel entitled to maintain their exclusive rights of access.

Desegregation

"[A goal of the decision was] . . . to destroy the three remaining wicked blemishes of slavery—separation, segregation, and discrimination in public schools because of race and color" (Saulter, 1954, p. 4).

"Those who try to ensnare others in a net of injustice sooner or later are caught in a net of their own making" (E. B. Johnson, 1955, p. 4).

"Both human bondage and the psychological slavery of segregation reject the worth and dignity of human life" (Raye, 1955, p. 4).

"The Supreme Court decision is the greatest victory for the Negro people since the Emancipation Proclamation" ("Editorial excerpts," 1954, p. 20).

"[A] fence has two sides and . . . those who have built it jail the jailer as well as the jailed" (Gordon & Roche, 1954, p. E6).

"[S]egregation always restricts the freedom of every person involved in any such system" (Brown, 1955, p. 16).

"Segregation is a hangover from slavery, and its ugliest manifestation has been in the schools" ("Equal education," 1954, p. 14).

"Racial separation was the key pillar in the slave system. It survives today as racial segregation. . . . Segregation is a form of slavery" ("Publisher," 1953, p. 2).

"The magnolia and jasmine tradition of the Old South, with its wise but appropriately humble mammies, along with the happy-go-lucky   banjo-strumming-in-the-slave-quarters-at-night . . . dies hard in certain quarters" (Halliburton, 1955b, p. 4).

"It is true that this decision may, in certain parts of the country, shackle a few politicians. But it frees so many of our children" (L. Smith, 1954, p. E10).

Inclusion

"Children who compare schools with prisons are nearer the truth than they realize: they are the only places where people are obliged to spend time in close proximity with others whose behavior, attitudes, or other attributes may be harmful" (Inson, 2000, p. 33).

"Critics say the special classrooms have been turned into annexes rather than places for education, dead ends for many children" (Goodman, 1996, p. 44).

"[Special education is] like a kid being in prison . . . you are taken out of society" (Richardson, 1994, p. A1).

"Children who compare schools with prisons are nearer the truth than they realize: they are the only places where people are obliged to spend time in close proximity with others whose behavior, attitudes, or other attributes may be harmful" (Inson, 2000, p. 33).

"Critics say the special classrooms have been turned into annexes rather than places for education, dead ends for many children" (Goodman, 1996, p. 44).

"[Special education is] like a kid being in prison . . . you are taken out of society" (Richardson, 1994, p. A1).

"[They] will never put their son in special education again. 'It would be like putting him back to sleep'" (Evans, 1996, p. 4H).

"Why are too many children of color in special education . . . taken off the express train and put on the local? The local never catches up to the express" (Mason, 1994, p. A9).

"His mother tried to wrest him from what she sees as a Kafkaesque cul-de-sac" (Richardson, 1994, p. A1).

"Release the hostages: Full inclusion" (Lewin, 1997, p. 1).

"Would you want your child to be locked away from society, like an embarrassment or would you want him or her to have as normal and happy a life as they possibly could? This is something everyone is entitled to, disabled or not" (Sellitti, 1994, p. 33).

"Sadly, this diverse place is [the] 'stigmatized underbelly' of education categorically known as special education. It is the place nobody wants to have a child" (S. Thomas, 1995, p. A1).

"Many African-American parents regard special education as a not so special reservation for Black youth . . . [a] perceived educational purgatory" (S. Thomas, 1995, p. A1).

"[S]pecial education . . . [employs] an army of psychologists and social workers to administer endless evaluations of marginal worth at tremendous cost" (Mason, 1994, p. A9).

An underlying conflict in these analogies to incarceration is the struggle over the meaning of freedom and democracy. Here, especially, we see the kind of negotiation of meaning that Bakhtin called heteroglossia, where dominant groups seek to shore up meaning of terms like democracy, at the same time that marginalized groups work to keep meaning in flux.

Opponents of desegregation, for example, often speak of preserving the "basic personal freedoms and democratic principles" (Flanders, 1955, p. 4) of White people, of course. They position *Brown* as "taking away the [White] people's civil rights as well as their state rights" (Walker, 1955, p. 4). Similarly, its opponents frame inclusion as *forced* association, where disabled students would be imposed upon general education classrooms and their teachers. In these examples, previously excluded students are positioned as invading the classroom, and White [and nondisabled] children and their teachers are presented as victims (Hollander, 1954, p. 4). In an ironic miswording, one paper even had to print a retraction after mistakenly referring to inclusion as *intrusion* ("Corrections," 1994, p. 2).

Thus, when opponents of desegregation use terms like democracy, they typically only refer to putting the issue to a vote (Cornell, 1954, p. 4; Barrett, 1955, p. 4), where presumably the majority (White people) would prevail. A typical example of this line of reasoning is expressed in this letter to the editor:

> As far as the uses of public institutions are concerned, it would seem that the majority would rule. In this case, the majority happens to be the White citizens of Georgia who say that these institutions should be segregated. If the majority is not to rule, this is certainly not a republic.[7] (Barrett, 1955, p. 4)

Likewise, the democracy implicit in anti-inclusionist rhetoric mirrors the majority versus minority relationship. In this case, the rights of "regular" students who make up the majority are said to be endangered by a resource-grabbing minority. The rhetoric usually focuses on the unfairness of "wasting" resources (teacher time, attention, and money) on so few students. Thus, the meaning of democracy at work in both debates is a direct democracy or majority rule, not the representative form of democracy upon which the U.S. system of government is based. What these examples also demonstrate, albeit indirectly, is how special schools and segregated placements ultimately serve the general education system, even though these programs are supposedly designed for the benefit of marginalized students.

Those celebrating *Brown* as an achievement of democracy, however, are more likely to draw on intangible and underlying principles of democracy, such as equality, individual rights, and community access. Proponents of desegregation, for example, use symbolism such as the "great, White light being beamed from the Statue of Liberty" (Stokes, 1954, p. 4) and "our star-spangled fatherland" (Phillips, 1954, p. 4) to call attention to the relationship between desegregation and the supposedly foundational values of democracy and freedom of the U.S. Here democracy is about access and equality and the charge is for the U.S. to live up to its ideals.

Advocates of inclusion also stress the right of all students to gain access to the general education classroom and a "normal life" (I. Clarke, 2001, p. A7). They focus on "full participation" (Brasch-Librach, 1992, p. 1) and equal opportunity. Often advocates draw on the *Brown* decision to argue that segregating students with disabilities represents inherently unequal treatment ("Students speak out," 1989). Conversely, opponents typically assert the right of students with disabilities to "special" services. They generally argue that the only way to ensure equality for students with disabilities is to sometimes "treat them differently" (Hartz, 2000, p. 13). The idea that special education services are tied to a particular place is rarely questioned. In other words, the assumptions that everyone in a general education classroom must be treated the same and that special education services must be provided in a separate setting remain unchallenged. Again, the underlying message is that reform cannot change the status quo without a heated and sustained battle.

In addition to democracy, words like freedom are also a site of struggle in both debates. Opponents of desegregation stress the "freedom" to associate with one's own "kind" and therefore to exclude others, whereas advocates often stress "principles of equal justice" for all (G. Jackson, 1956, p. 9). Words like noble, wisdom, fairness, justice, equality, and liberty abound in the discourse of those supporting integrated education. In these examples, advocates point to the incongruity of claiming freedom if that freedom diminishes the freedom of others. Thus, inclusion and access represent the letter and spirit of the constitution and exclusion is positioned as the "cancerous growth" that must be excised for democracy to flourish (Volmer, 1995, p. 4). Advocates of inclusion stress the entitlement of every child to "a sense of belonging" (Brasch-Librach, 1992, p. 1), acceptance, and tolerance (Perricone, 1994). They challenge opponents of desegregation and inclusion to justify the hypocrisy of exclusion within a democracy.

Claiming the Moral High Ground

A final struggle in both desegregation and inclusion debates is the claim by each side that they are on the "right" side of morality. This is especially true of the desegregation debate where both sides argue that religion is on their side.

Desegregation

> "As I read my Bible, God was the first segregationist" ("A Texas citizen," 1955, p. 1).
>
> "I consider segregation a part of God's plan" ("From Kinston, Tennessee," 1955, p. 1).

"There is nothing in the Bible as far as I know (and I have studied it for 40 years) that can be legitimately used today to show that Negroes should keep their children in separate schools" (Strong, 1954, p. 4).

"Jesus is against it [segregation] and wants us to fight it" ("Out of step," 1954, p. 6).

"[Desegregation] is in harmony with the Christian principles of equal justice and love for all men" (G. Jackson, 1956, p. 9).

"The segregationists are not only doing a terrible thing, but they are doing a dangerous thing to put White supremacy above the Ten Commandments" (Hancock, 1954, p. 4).

"Each act of segregation, and accompanying humiliation, must hurt Him more than each nail that pierced his flesh. Certainly . . . [segregation] is . . . so evil as to be a mockery of His teachings, and even of Christ Himself" (Steinberg, 1954, p. 28).

Inclusion

"This year, I just want to get down on my knees and beg for forgiveness of my regular education parents" (Baird, 2002, p. 23).

"This [inclusion] would have seemed, and still does, like a cruel thing to do to any handicapped person" (Hunter, 1995, p. A22).

"This [inclusion] is terribly disturbing, frustrating, and cruel to these children and their families" (Kremen, 1997, p. A20).

"Few people today question the moral imperative of integration—that is, except when it comes to children with disabilities" (Head et al., 1996, p. C8).

"Exclusion of any kind somehow means we value certain students more or less than others. Since that position is intolerable, we put them all together to show that every child is of equal moral worth. But . . . some children's needs are better served in a non-inclusion classroom" (Hartz, 2000, p. 13).

"To the opponents who say inclusion takes away from other students, I say don't sell the other students short. . . . They are learning a lesson in desire and persistence from the experts, a lesson not found in any book" (Shore, 1994, p. A13).

"We must never forget that exceptional children deserve our attention, support, guidance, love and any other help we can give them" ("Kudos," 1987, p. 17).

In these excerpts the struggle is over which position in debate can claim that ethics, morality, religion—and, indeed God—are on their side. Claiming that God is a segregationist and Jesus a desegregationist, each side calls upon the Bible as an authoritative cultural text (at least for Christian people). Desegregationists stress the morality of equal justice and caution against placing White supremacy above religious law. They sometimes evoke the crucifixion of Christ as symbolically equivalent to the segregation of Black people at the hand of White oppressors. Segregationists claim that "racial" differences among people are "proof" that God was against racial amalgamation of any kind.

Christianity is also evoked, although in a more implicit way, in the rhetoric of inclusion. A teacher, for instance, positions herself as a supplicant, begging forgiveness, for the "sin" of attending too much to the disabled students placed in her class. Although some parents characterize segregation as inflicting cruel treatment on children with disabilities, others affirm the charitable basis of segregated placements in protecting disabled children from cruel treatment they would receive in general education classrooms. Religious allusions undergird both claims about the moral imperative of maintaining separate settings, and the insistence on the moral worth of every child to be included. Although religion is usually thought of as a form of what Bakhtin would call an authoritative discourse (P. Morris, 1994), its meanings are negotiated and renegotiated as multiple sides of each debate attempt to lay claim to the morality of their position. The prevalence of religious iconography and imagery illustrate the power and influence of religious ideology, but also how religious meanings shift as they became "peopled" by others (Bakhtin, 1986).

Regardless of position, those on all sides of the inclusion debate struggle to position themselves as acting in the best interest of students with disabilities. In their arguments, however, the general education classroom takes on many different meanings. At times general education is characterized as a "wilderness of alienation" (Wharton, 2000, p. 17) where disabled students would be verbally "mocked and taunted" (Revell, 2002, p. 6), or physically taken advantage of (Miller, 2002, p. B23). At other times the "regular" classroom is the "key to unlocking a world of opportunities" for students with disabilities (Evans, 1996, p. 4H). Others claim that removing students with disabilities is the only appropriate response to unwelcoming and abusive general education classrooms or practices. The inhospitality of this classroom space is not seen as the locus of the problem—it is taken simply as fact.

Conclusion: The Difficulties of Dialogue

When we first discussed writing this chapter, our goal was to highlight the many powerful uses of language we saw in our data sets. Although much of the rhetoric is humorous, some of it is maddening or frightening, and some is even inspiring. In focusing on the overlaps between discursive strategies in both debates, however, our goal was to explore how individuals use language in persuasive ways to enact or refuse social change. Unfortunately, although there *were* exceptions, many of the language practices in these two debates effectively close down rather than invite dialogue. Certainly discourse informed by binary thinking and name-calling only leads to the kind of war mentality that Patton (2004) and others have criticized. This kind of discourse, although provocative, seems least likely to lead to the kind of open and engaged dialogue or discussion that Danforth (2004), Heshusius (2004), Mariage et al. (2004), and others hope to see.

Discourses, offering the most potential to invite dialogue, are not without struggle or conflict, however. We see the most promising examples of dialogue in the instances where individuals struggle to define terms like "democracy" and "freedom." This is also where we observe the most evidence of Bakhtin's notion of heteroglossia, in which dominant groups seek to close down meaning and marginalized groups seek to keep meaning open and in play. In these examples we observe dominant groups defining democracy in very limited ways—fitting a model of direct democracy in which the majority rules. Those advocating inclusion and desegregation actively work to expand this narrow definition by focusing on democracy's underlying values, such as full participation and a sense of belonging. Similarly, freedom is a site of negotiation between those who claim the freedom to exclude, while others demand that freedom requires equality for all. In these exchanges we believe there is much potential to begin to remake education in the spirit of an expanded notion of democracy and freedom. We are led to ask: What forms would services for students with disabilities take if, instead of advocating a medical-based model of disability, we engaged in a model of disability informed by democracy and freedom? If our debates over inclusion could start from this framework, a completely different model might emerge—one where every child would be guaranteed access to a supportive learning environment and access to more than one equally good option would be the minimum requirement for choice.

Bakhtin's ideas about the fluidity of language and meaning are important to consider in all of our efforts at school reform. Because we can only borrow meanings, when we use a term like "inclusion", for example, what exactly do we mean? How might a similar acknowledgment that terms such as "research based" and "empirically sound" are highly contextual, subjective, and perpetually in flux yield a more informed and nuanced debate about best practices?

We also agree with Patton (2004) who calls for different "scriptwriters," who can enact new forms of knowing informed by their own experience as cultural outsiders. It is striking that so very little of the debate over inclusion or desegregation has engaged students themselves. While professionals, scholars, administrators, writers, and even families debate these issues, how do actual students make sense of their lived experience of inclusion/exclusion, or desegregation/segregation? How might their situated knowledge inform our thinking about these and other educational issues? We, like Gallagher (2004), find informed and genuine dialogue seriously lacking in these debates.

Lessons Learned

The lesson we take from this chapter is the importance and difficulty of dialoging across difference. Along with Patton's (2004) call for the need for different scriptwriters in the field of special education, we also see the need for a different kind of script. The well-worn genre of opposing sides going off to war has not served the field well and has limited our ability to learn from our differences. These limits have left the field entrenched in a time warp and resistant to change—whereas the rest of the academy has already embraced different and multiple ways of knowing as equally valid. Limiting our discussion to a model informed by debate, as opposed to dialogue, has also stifled innovation and experimentation. It has limited scholars to circumscribed roles and dualistic perspectives. As Danforth (2004) explains, when an oppositional relationship forms between an orthodoxy and heresy, available responses are limited to either conformity or competition. Neither of these options embraces the dynamic interplay of ideas that Bakhtin envisioned in the tangled and tension-filled promise of dialogue.

7

SHARED LEGACIES: *BROWN* AND THE COUNTERPULL OF INCLUSION

7

SHARED LEGACIES: *BROWN* AND THE COUNTERPULL OF INCLUSION

Introduction

In the previous chapters, we highlight how shifts from race to ability in the wake of *Brown* contributed to the growth of special education and the maintenance of racially segregated education. In this chapter we turn our attention to some of the specific *technologies* (or ways in which knowledge is used) associated with special education and how they have served as mechanisms of containment, particularly for students of color. We argue, for instance, that the continual redefinition of standards and norms, as well as testing, labeling, and tracking (re)produce students within a discourse of disability and thereby validate their removal from "general" education. We note how the expansion of certain disability categories, particularly the "soft" labels of mental retardation, emotional disturbance, and learning disability, have been particularly effective mechanisms of containment for students of color.

In the second part of the chapter, we argue that the least restrictive environment (LRE) clause of the *Individuals with Disabilities Education Act* (*IDEA*) has inadvertently sustained the widespread *exclusion* rather than inclusion of students with disabilities. We then draw a brief history of the inclusion movement, noting its important function as a counterpull of resistance to segregated schooling for students with disabilities and students of color. Although critical of easy analogies between *IDEA* and *Brown,* we argue that inclusion marks a necessary next wave of social integration that began with *Brown's* push for racially integrated schools.

"The Emperor's New Clothes": Maintaining Segregation

In many respects, our society's dilemma of placing inordinate numbers of students of color in special education classes is like the children's story written by Hans Christian Andersen, The Emperor's New Clothes.[1] To paraphrase the tale:

> There once existed a king who desired the finest clothes on earth. Two conniving tailors asked him for gold to spin into cloth, inspiring them to produce garments so fine that no one could actually see them. Yet, fearful of being thought stupid and foolish, no one admitted they could not see the garments. At last the day came for the emperor to parade himself to an admiring public, who dutifully "oohed" and "aahed" in awe of his "fine" clothes. Spectators complied with expectations of flattery, and everyone went through the motions of the occasion, until, in the crowd, a small boy whispered, "The king has got no clothes on." As word circulated through the gathering, echoing the boy's observation, the king overheard that he was naked. But, instead of stopping the procession, he held himself stiffer than ever, and continued to walk in front of his officers who carried the invisible train.

Like the king, nobles, and crowd, we too have come to believe many myths. We like to believe, for instance, in a "democratic" system of education to which all students have equal access and a fair chance. As Brantlinger (2003) writes, "We like to 'believe' that schools are fair and enable social mobility, [that] they are meritocracies" (p. 3). As special educators, we also want to believe there is something inherently "special" about what we do and that special education is, despite its flaws, a benevolent and effective practice. Yet, in order to believe these things we must remain willfully ignorant of the vast inequities in education. We must explain away the overrepresentation of students of color in special education—believing, like the teachers after *Brown*, that academic differences are attributable to *anything* but race, racial inequities, discrimination, or bias. Like the emperor's clothes, if the current system is made transparent, we all see what we already know, but are unwilling to admit to each other and perhaps to ourselves. In many ways, what we believe about education is often simply untruths that we have accepted, illusions upheld by consensus. Like the little boy in the crowd, research on overrepresentation of students of color *should* serve to clarify our vision and dispel any doubt that racism and ableism circulate within the daily practices of our education systems.

For instance, while the 1990s could be remembered as the decade when the U.S. schools became more diverse, it could also be remembered as the decade when the nation's schools became increasingly racially segregated (Orfield, 2001). Most recent discussions about school segregation focus primarily on the racial composition in large urban districts. Yet, as previously discussed, White students continue to be the most racially segregated of all student groups. Orfield finds that "the vast majority . . . [of White students attend] schools with few or no students of any other race" (in Irons, 2002, p. 292). In the 1990s, despite the fact that segregation was increasing to levels not seen since *Brown*, the Supreme Court began relinquishing its oversight of school desegregation (Irons, 2002). The impact of the court's retreat was compounded by funding formulas that fostered "glaring disparities between . . . poorly funded, low achieving" urban districts attended by mostly African American and Latino students and "lavishly funded, high-achieving suburban districts" attended almost exclusively by White students (Martin, 1998, p. 232). Thus, in failing to develop a policy to address segregation in large metropolitan areas, the court showed a lack of resolve. In reneging on its commitment to school desegregation, the court effectively put the brakes on desegregation efforts (Clotfelter, 2004), leading some to conclude that "school integration . . . failed, or—put more honestly—was never seriously tried" (Irons, 2002, p. 339).

Because of the overrepresentation of students of color in several disability categories, the field of special education has come under increased scrutiny from the U.S. Office of Civil Rights (Losen & Orfield, 2002). Recent studies show how the label of disability triggers disparate outcomes for White students and students of color. For more privileged White students, special education eligibility is likely to guarantee access to extra support services, maintenance in general education classrooms, and accommodation for high-status examinations (Parrish, 2002). For students of color, however, being labeled as disabled can result in decreased access to general education and poorer transition outcomes (Oswald et al., 2002; Parrish, 2002; Fierros & Conroy, 2002; Osher et al., 2002; Artiles et al., 2002). These different consequences related to special education placement are particularly problematic given the disproportionate number of Black and Latino students who are identified as disabled and placed in highly segregated settings (Losen & Orfield, 2002).

As stated in the introductory chapter, students of color continue to be overrepresented in special education programs (Arnold & Lassmann, 2003; Hosp & Reschly, 2004; MacMillan & Reschly, 1998; Salend et al., 2002). The most recent studies have shown that Black males are more than twice as likely as Whites to be labeled mentally retarded in 38 states, emotionally disturbed in 29 states, and learning disabled in 8 states (Parrish, 2002). The labels of emotional disturbance (ED) and mental retardation (MR) continue to be disproportionately ascribed to students of color—assigned to Black and Latino males several times more often than any other group of students (Losen & Orfield, 2002; Osher et al., 2002). Furthermore, students of color who are given the labels of MR, ED, and learning disability (LD), are more likely to be removed from regular classrooms than White students with the same labels (Fierros & Conroy, 2002). In analyzing nationwide data collected by the U.S. Office of Civil Rights, Parrish (2002) concludes that White students are generally "only placed in more restrictive self-contained classes when they need intensive services. Students of color, however, may be more likely to be placed in the restrictive settings whether they require intensive services or not" (p. 26).

It is increasingly clear that special education labels and placements serve to perpetuate the marginalization of students with disabilities, especially students of color. Because of the excellent work done by Losen and Orfield (2002) and others, we now have real facts about racial inequities and overrepresentation in special education. In the previous chapters of this book we have also untangled some of the shared histories of segregated education for students with disabilities and students of color. Both kinds of documentation are critically important. Now that the facts are out and the histories have been told, we can no longer claim ignorance—we can no longer remain in denial. Knowing these facts, however, we must now ask, what current practices in special education continue to allow such inequities to exist and what can we do to disrupt this pattern of inequality? In the following sections of this chapter we begin to unpack some foundational assumptions and everyday practices by turning to the discourse and technologies of special education to examine their role in maintaining such exclusionary practices.

Technologies of Exclusion Within Special Education Discourse

A Foucaultian analysis helps us to view the field of special education as a set of discursive practices operating within education. By discourse, "Foucault meant a group of statements which provides a language for talking about—a way of representing knowledge about a particular topic at a particular historical moment" (Hall, 1997a, p. 44). These statements form the assumed, unquestioned bureaucracies, practices, methodologies, terminologies, and histories that form the everyday landscape of special education. Together, these statements coalesce into a powerful regime of truth that privileges certain kinds of knowledge and ignores, dismisses, or suppresses others.

In stressing how knowledge is inextricably linked with power, Foucault (1982) draws our attention to the way people become subjects within discourse. Foucault writes,

> this form of power applies itself to immediate everyday life which categorizes the individual, marks him by his own individuality, attaches him to his own identity, and imposes a law of truth on him which he must recognize and which others have to recognize in him. It is a form of power, which makes individuals subjects. (p. 212)

Foucault claims that discourse actually *produces* the very people about which they speak through technologies of power. Thus, the act of labeling a student "disabled," for instance, sets particular discourses in motion, actively producing a new kind of student subject. Although Foucault (1995) writes that technologies of "hierarchical observation" (p. 170), "normalizing judgment" (p. 177), and "the examination" (p. 184) operate in all discourses, these mechanisms are quite reified in the field of special education.

For instance, within the process of assessment, or what Foucault would call "the examination"—in itself, a quintessential panoptic event—students are given the label of disability. In exploring contingencies that lead to the pathologizing of prisoners, Foucault (1995) writes, "A whole set of assessing, diagnostic, prognostic, normative judgments concerning the criminal have become lodged in the framework of penal judgment" (p. 19). If we substitute "struggling learner" for "criminal" and "educational judgment" instead of "penal judgment," the sentence would read: "A whole set of assessing, diagnostic, prognostic, normative judgments concerning the struggling learner have become lodged in the framework of educational judgment." Moreover, the very foundation of special education has been built upon "examinations" performed by professionals wielding the specialized tools of assessment—tools "scientifically" validated and assumed to be objective and therefore neutral. Testing is also a necessary precondition for the general concept of normalcy and the notion of fixed intelligences measured by IQ scores. These, in turn, signal the need for categories to demarcate individuals who deviate from established norms. These categories or labels then help to rationalize specialized placements and exclusive practices designed for identified students. This dividing practice transforms particular students into "docile bodies" (Foucault, 1995, p. 135), or compliant and subordinate subjects (re)defined within school structures. Nonetheless, an overreliance on diagnostic testing continues to be a staple feature of special education, despite the questionable validity or efficacy of such practices.

Because special education discourse is predicated upon medical model perspectives, medical/clinical perspectives influence how educational professionals "naturally" view students. Hence, when students struggle academically, they are "referred" to a team of "clinicians" who then "examine," "diagnose," and "prescribe" an educational "treatment." Because this highly ritualized normalizing gaze is considered standard practice (Baker, 2002), professionals in the field are trained to perform tasks, but are not encouraged to question the knowledge base that informs them.

Groups of professionals typically gather at interdisciplinary team meetings to discuss results of a particular educational evaluation, psychological profile, and social history. In this role, as "the master[s] of truth," they are invested with much power and authority (Foucault, 1994, p. 115). Professionals (evaluators, clinicians, psychologists, social workers, etc.) are positioned as gatekeepers, determining whether or not to label a child disabled. They are an integral part of the apparatus that maintains the hegemony of the medicalized and institutionalized discourse of special education. As Varenne and McDermott (1998) write, "the only tasks professionals may, indeed must, perform as professionals given specific authority by the State is to document what is wrong. . . . This is their job and responsibility" (p. 38). Moreover, the cadre of specialists "can find in almost anyone's behavior evidence of the kinds of problems they know how to look for and record in ways that still others can use" (p. 29).

These technologies of power maintain the status quo of the dominant group and position people with disabilities, not as members of a minority group, but in a subordinate role as "client" or "patient" (Biklen, 1988, p. 37). Because they operate within a medical model paradigm, what clinicians find "wrong" is nearly always located within the individual child that they assess, not within the social or political structures of the classroom, school, or society. Of course, because authoritative discourses are meant to be accepted whole and unquestioned, professionals typically operate without consciousness of the discourses in which they are engaged

(P. Morris, 1994). Furthermore, the discourse is so effective that individuals themselves internalize it, making it their own, becoming "willing agents in their own discipline" (Allan, 1999, p. 24). In other words, these discourses become so ingrained in our consciousness and ways of knowing that even as everyday people we no longer require professionals to diagnose ourselves, or each other—we become the arbiter of our own normalcy.

Ligget points out that as a field we need to become conscious of "the institutional practices in . . . which disability is constituted" (cited in Allan, 1999, p. 18). By characterizing special education practices as discursive, we seek to trouble the notion of disability as inherent or the placement of "disabled" students in segregated settings as natural. Schools typically function in ways that uphold and reinforce the dominant beliefs of society. As such, they are often dynamic examples of racism and ableism in practice, although they are rarely portrayed in this way. Their purported neutrality, however, masks their power. Foucault (1990) underscored how technologies of power are accepted "only as a condition that it masks a substantial part of itself. Its success is proportional to its ability to hide its own mechanisms" (p. 86). Because the asymmetrical positioning of students of color and/or children with disabilities in schools is indicative of their status in the larger society, their exclusion seems natural and is taken for granted as inevitable. As Biklen (1988) contends, "the more severe the disability, the greater likelihood that the person will be regarded . . . as a 'patient'" than as someone who experiences discrimination (p. 128).

Technologies of exclusion, including ability testing, tracking, labeling, and special education have all played a major part in resegregating schools after *Brown*. In previous chapters we engaged critically with how desegregation and inclusion are framed in these different but connected histories. Connecting these two histories, we gain deeper understanding of both the resistance to integrated schooling for all students and the unchanging nature of public education. As racial segregation fell from official favor, we see, for example, how it reemerged as segregation based on disability. In the remaining sections of this chapter, we examine particular discursive practices *within* special education that contributed to this problematic history of exclusion and segregation.

The Expansion of "Disability": Problematizing the "Soft" Labels

Given that one of the tasks of disability studies is to trouble assumptions about *all* categories of disability, it can be argued for the purpose of exploring the nexus of race and disability that certain categories may be considered more problematic than others. Mandell et al. (2002), for example, find racial disparities in the age of diagnosis of autism in White and Black students, even when other factors are controlled. Similarly, since the early 1970s the U.S. Office of Civil Rights has reported a persistence of overrepresentation of minority children in categories requiring specialized clinical judgment. As stated in chapter 1, racial disparities are most highly pronounced in the specific categories of MR, ED, and LD (Salend et al., 2002). Thus, "invisible" disabilities of a cognitive and/or social nature (i.e., pertaining to academic development or behavior) are disproportionately ascribed to students from racial and linguistic minorities. In contrast, less subjective categories such as blindness and deafness are proportional to the overall population. This indicates that overrepresentation is much more pronounced for more subjective disability labels than in diagnoses that are more obvious or objectively determined.

The most recent government reports find that while Blacks constitute 14.8 percent of the population, they represent 20.2 percent of all students in special education (National Alliance of Black School Educators, 2002). In fact, Black students remain the most overrepresented of all student groups nationwide (National Alliance of Black School Educators). In looking at the top three categories, Black students remain three times as likely to be labeled as MR as White students, two times as likely to be labeled ED, as well as almost one and a half times as likely to be labeled LD (Parrish, 2002). Although not overrepresented to the degree that Black students are, data on Latino students are complicated to analyze because these students tend to be *under*identified in elementary school, but *over*identified in high school. Moreover, students who are English language learners (ELL) or labeled limited in English proficiency (LEP) are more likely to be overrepresented in special education, especially in the upper grades (Artiles et al., 2002). Additionally, for Black children, as well as children from other racial/linguistic minority groups, the likelihood of being overrepresented in these three categories is markedly higher in states where "the minority group constitutes a relatively large proportion of the state's population" (Parrish, 2002, p. 21). For instance, Latino children are three times as likely to be identified as MR, ED, or LD in states that have a high Latino population compared with states with a low proportion of Latino students (Parrish). Parrish also finds that similar patterns emerge for other racial/linguistic minority students, such as children of Asian/Pacific Island origin in Hawaii and American Indian children in Alaska. For Black students the risk of being labeled MR, for instance, is twice as high in states with large numbers of Black students than in states that are predominantly White. Black students in racially integrated schools are also more likely to be placed in lower tracks (Ferguson & Mehta, 2004). An exception to overrepresentation of minorities is the underrepresentation of Asian American students in special education programs. Stereotyped as the "model minority," and often academically outperforming White students, Asian students are far less likely to be labeled in the subjective categories of MR, ED, or LD than any other minority group.[2] Clearly, overrepresentation of racial/linguistic minorities in each of these "soft" disability classifications warrants further attention.

Mental Retardation

Among official categories, MR remains most likely to be assigned to Black (particularly Black male) students. Oswald et al. (2002) concur that while "increased poverty is associated with increased risk of disability" (p. 7), there is still a systematic bias which results in Black males being identified as MR, while Whites with a similar ability profile receive the (arguably) less stigmatizing label of LD. Racial bias is also reflected in national statistics that show the likelihood of a Black student being labeled MR to be between four and five times that of Whites in Connecticut, Mississippi, North and South Carolina, and Nebraska (Parrish, 2002). Furthermore, Black students who attend school in wealthier communities are *more* likely to be labeled MR and assigned to segregated classes than those attending predominantly Black, low-income schools. This finding contradicts the assumption that overrepresentation can be explained by factors associated with socioeconomic class. In a study by Parrish and Hikido (1998) examining the relationship between poverty, minority representation, and state funding, the authors conclude that there is "a much stronger relationship between special education and race than between special education and poverty" (p. 33).

Emotional Disturbance

As is often the case in special education, terms such as "delinquent" (Franklin, 1987) and "culturally deprived" (Carrier, 1986) are discarded in favor of other, more clinical-sounding labels, such as emotionally disturbed or behavior disordered. As stated, second to MR, Black students are labeled ED with over twice the frequency of White students. However, while discussions about cultural differences in behavior and general interactions are featured prominently in multicultural literature (Banks & Banks, 1997; Delpit, 1995), they are downplayed in traditional special education journals. Failure to explore different behaviors, vocabulary, understandings, and expectations, customarily posit students labeled ED as lacking in relation to unstated and unquestioned cultural and behavioral norms of White, middle class culture. Thus, any cultural mismatch between student and teacher or student and test is factored out of the assessment process, as well as zero tolerance policies. These findings are disturbing and suggest that classification rates for ED—over twice the rate for White students in 29 states (Osher et al., 2002)—may account for the disenfranchisement of Black youth in schools, as well as their poor transition outcomes and graduation rates.

Learning Disability

In addition to MR and ED, the category of LD, which emerged as a label during the 1960s, is deeply implicated in issues of race and social class. Students with LD are described as having average or above average intelligence, specific rather than generalized deficits, and a cultural/familial background that is not connected to the academic difficulties the child is experiencing in school. Spurred on by advocacy of middle class White parents, the category was initially dominated by White students. This meant that even when students had similar levels of academic achievement, they were given different labels depending on their racial, ethnic, gender, and class backgrounds (C. E. Sleeter, 1987). In the first ten years after the emergence of the category (1963–1973), the vast majority of students labeled LD were White, middle class males (Sleeter). Similar to the way tracking was used to resegregate students by race and social class in general education (Mickelson, 2001; Oakes, 1985), the category of LD allowed special education to become racially segregated by disability category. Thus, White students are overrepresented in the LD and gifted categories, and Black students are overrepresented in the MR and ED categories and underrepresented in gifted classes—even when they achieve test scores comparable to Whites (Losen & Orfield, 2002). Over the years, White students continue to be overrepresented in classes for the gifted and talented, but the demographics of LD programs have shifted from predominantly White students to students of color, particularly those residing in urban areas (Fierros & Conroy, 2002; Parrish, 2002).

Facilitating Containment: Disability Labels, Race, and Segregated Placements

As previously mentioned, there is a marked correlation between the type of disability label and the restrictiveness of placement. Furthermore, the disability categories most associated with overrepresentation of students of color (MR, ED, and LD) are also the classifications that require the most clinical judgment because they are the least obvious to diagnose. These disability classifications are nonetheless associated with surprisingly restrictive placements. In other words, even students who are labeled with "mild" disabilities spend a surprising amount of time removed from the general education classroom. Drawing from recent data from the U.S. Department of Education, for example, Fierros and Conroy (2002) report that 82 percent of students labeled MR, 70 percent of students labeled ED, and 56 percent of students labeled LD spend more than 21 percent of their school time outside of regular education classrooms. In analyzing these data more closely, Fierros and Conroy (2002) note that minority students found eligible for special education who attend high minority urban school districts are "at a very high risk of being placed in a restrictive educational setting" compared with their peers in suburban schools (p. 58). This research, along with previous studies (Conroy, 1999; Harry, 1992) suggests that the amount of time a student with disabilities is removed from the general education classroom is directly related not only to the so-called "severity" of the disability classification, but also to his or her race. Moreover, of all the factors related to overrepresentation of students of color in special education, achievement is the weakest predictor (Hosp & Reschly, 2004).

Available research suggests a strong relationship between overrepresentation and restrictiveness of placement for students of color, which, we argue, has undermined the promise of desegregated schooling set forth in *Brown.* Yet, how are we to interpret or explain the restrictiveness of educational setting experienced by students of color? Parrish (2002) implicates financial incentives, which encourage schools to overidentify students with disabilities and place them in more rather than less restrictive settings. He argues that such incentives may lead to labeling students who have "fewer advocates to protect them" (p. 32). This could certainly account for White suburban students being placed in less restrictive settings compared with minority and urban students. In keeping with our interest in discourse, however, we decided to focus our analysis on the phrase that seems to most embody *IDEA*'s promise of integrated education for students with disabilities: the least restrictive environment (LRE) clause. What LRE represents, how it is interpreted and used, all determine the placement decision for a particular child. Like *Brown*'s contentious phrase, "all deliberate speed," for implementing desegregation orders, the LRE clause has invited more than its share of litigation. In the next section of this chapter we trace a brief history of the embattled LRE clause.

The Bone of Contention: Interpreting the Least Restrictive Environment

The *Brown* decision drew from the 14th Amendment of the U.S. Constitution: "No state shall make or enforce any law which shall . . . deny to any person within its jurisdiction the equal protection of the laws" (United States Constitution, n.d., ¶1) In other words, the court determined, "If states have undertaken to provide an education to its citizenry, then they must do so for all its citizens" (Yell et al., 1998). This sharply contrasted with educational policies at the time regarding students with disabilities, since "laws in most states allowed school districts to refuse to enroll any student they considered 'uneducable,' a term generally defined by local school administrators" (Martin et al., 1996). Parents and advocates of children with disabilities saw the wider implications of *Brown*—namely, the need to extend educational rights to disabled students as a matter of law. In 1975, their combined efforts resulted in Congress passing the hallmark legislation of P.L. 94-142 (*Education of All Handicapped Children Act*), which mandated a free and appropriate public education for all children with disabilities. Even though it took 20 years longer, to many disability advocates this legislation is every bit as powerful as the historic *Brown* decision. The law upheld that *all* students regardless of disability were entitled to a public education that heretofore had not been guaranteed by federal law.

The original legislation of the *Education of All Handicapped Children Act* required that an educational evaluation be conducted to determine eligibility for services and to decide what would constitute an appropriate educational plan for any child deemed eligible for special education services. As stated, the law required that the educational plan be provided in the LRE. LRE allowed schools to determine the appropriate placement for each student, including the *option* of a placement located separate from their nondisabled peers. Thus, as doors finally opened for students with moderate and severe disabilities, schools were also invested with the power to determine which students would be eligible under the new act. If a disability was confirmed, the evaluating team was charged with considering the LRE[3] in which the child could be educated. Thus, the placement of students has always been based on a continuum of services, which includes general education at one end and separate schools or facilities on the other. Although P.L. 94-142 afforded students with disabilities access to public education, we argue that the preponderance of decisions, which place students in more rather than less restrictive settings, contributed to a largely segregated system.

According to Taylor (1988) the principle of LRE is characterized by a number of "serious conceptual and philosophical flaws" (p. 45). For example, according to Taylor, the LRE legitimizes restrictive placements in the guise of presenting a range of choices. By equating the intensity of services a child can receive with the physical setting, it has led many to assume that special education is a place rather than a set of specialized practices or services. Indeed, the whole discussion over LRE has tended to focus more on physical settings than on services. For many disability rights advocates (Lipsky & Gartner, 1997) and activists (Linton, 1998), LRE is a loophole that allows educational institutions to maintain the segregation of people with disabilities in schools and, by extension, in society. To other scholars (Kauffman & Hallahan, 1995a) and some parents (Carr, 1993), LRE is a necessary protection that ensures flexibility and individualization of placement for students who might otherwise be overlooked and/or overwhelmed in general education. What cannot be argued, however, is that students with disabilities continue to be placed in classes that segregate them from their nondisabled peers (Gartner & Lipsky, 1987). A recent report on the LRE, for example, shows that "In New York City, the majority of children receiving special education services spend most of their school day in segregated placements, where they are often poorly prepared for educational success and integration into their communities" (Kamin & Berger, 2001, p. 2). Thus, it would seem that the determination of "least" restrictive assumes that a certain level of restrictiveness is necessary. Given the history of institutionalization of people with disabilities, LRE does little to debunk the notion that individuals with disabilities must be contained and should not be trusted to mingle with the general public. As a result there remains "a persistent tension between the requirements of appropriate education and the least restrictive environment" (Martin et al., 1996, p. 35).

Moreover, because disproportionate numbers of students of color continue to be identified for special education services and placed in the *most* restrictive of placements (Artiles et al., 2002; Fierros & Conroy, 2002; Lipsky & Gartner, 1996; Osher et al., 2002), it is clear that special education, despite being designed to meet the needs of individual learners, has nonetheless been used to create and perpetuate the marginalization of students based on the interconnected discourses of race and ability. Thus, in maintaining borders that keep out the unwanted by labeling them deficient, these practices run counter to the very democratic ideals often attributed to the U.S. educational system[4] (Lipsky & Gartner, 1997; Skrtic, 1991b).

It is important to note that many scholars in the field of special education immediately criticized placement options outlined in P.L. 94-142. Reynolds and

Birch (1977), for example, viewed them as *too restrictive* and counterproductive to the intent of the law. Semmel et al., (1979) were also quick to state that there was no "conclusive body of evidence which confirms that special education services appreciably enhance the academic and/or social accomplishments of handicapped children beyond what can be expected without special education" (cited in Reynolds, 1989, p. 7). On a similar note, Stainback and Stainback (1984) asserted "the instructional needs of students do not warrant the operation of a dual system" (p. 102). Challenging the notion of two "types" of students, they called for a merger of general education and special education into one system that would support all students. By the mid-1980s, Wang et al., (1986) and others became increasingly concerned about the growing enrollment of minority students in special education and "the continuation of segregation of many students in disjointed programs" (p. 26).

It was around this time that proposals like the Regular Education Initiative (REI) were formulated. Developed by Madeline Will, Assistant Secretary to the U.S. Department of Education in charge of special education and rehabilitation programs, the REI called for more collaboration between general and special education. A primary goal of the initiative was to include more students with mild to moderate disabilities in general education and to counteract how schools were "unwittingly, [creating] barriers to their successful education" (Will, 1986, p. 412). Among the "myriad faults" in the special education system, Gartner and Lipsky (1987) criticized the financial incentives given to local education authorities to place and maintain students in more restrictive environments. Although these financial incentives counteracted the spirit of the original legislation, they help to explain why so many special education students continue to be placed in pullout or self-contained settings (Gartner & Lipsky, 1987; Kamin & Berger, 2001). Moreover, as Sapon-Shevin (1987) suggests, there continues to be a lack of data on students with disabilities placed in segregated settings, which seems to imply that some children are simply not worth "officially" counting.

As a result of these and other problems, REI had only limited success. From the outset, it was perceived as a special education initiative designed without general education input. Lieberman (1985) describes this *faux pas* as tantamount to hosting "a wedding in which we, as special educators, have forgotten to invite the bride" (p. 515). Viewed by critics as nonspecific, illogical, and flawed (Kauffman, 1989), it was even seen as harmful to the needs of students with disabilities (Fuchs & Fuchs, 1995). Yet, the REI obviously hit a nerve. In many ways it heralded the beginning of significant change in special education for supporters and detractors alike.

In 1990, for instance, Vermont passed extensive legislation to ensure that to the maximum extent possible students with disabilities would be placed and supported in general education (Lipsky & Gartner, 1997). This legislation underscores the responsibility of schools to *all* students (Schattman & Benay, 1992). Other states such Kentucky, Colorado, and Pennsylvania made similar changes at state and local levels. This changing climate for students with disabilities led Reynolds (1989) to write, "The history of special education delivery systems can be summarized in two words: progressive inclusion" (p. 7). Of course, as we illustrated in chapter 3, gradualism has proven to be an ineffective strategy for instituting real, substantive change.

Following the debate over REI, the discussion about where to best educate students with disabilities intensified. The provision of mainstreaming had been practiced since 1975, but was only "applicable to those students who were considered to be most like normal" (Lipsky & Gartner, 1997, p. 77). In other words, mainstreaming assumes a readiness model (Taylor, 1988) in which only students who can cope independently with the academic and social demands of a general education classroom are included. In contrast, inclusionists argue that *all* students with disabilities could benefit academically and socially from the general education classroom, even if their goals were different from those of other students. Although mainstreaming and inclusion are often used interchangeably, they differ significantly in terms of definition and philosophy. Nonetheless, each of these reforms (REI, mainstreaming, and inclusion) was designed to increase the levels of cooperation between general education and special education. Ultimately, they paved the way for an all-out push for the full inclusion of students with disabilities in general education.

Waves of Integration

Responding to the criticisms of overrepresentation of minority students and lack of demonstrated efficacy of special education, advocates in the late 1980s and early 1990s began to push harder for more inclusive placements for all students with disabilities. As a result of increased awareness about the disproportionate placement of students of color in special education, the Reauthorization of *IDEA* (1997) required school districts and state departments of education to determine whether problems of overrepresentation and underrepresentation existed and to develop procedures to address both problems (Salend, 2001, p. 19). Many within the disability rights movement argued that exclusionary schooling practices reflect patterns of society at large, which continue to resist inclusion of people with disabilities in schools and society (Fleisher & Zames, 2001). However, like school desegregation, the inclusion movement elicited strong opposition in the press and inclusion proponents were similarly vilified. (See chapter 6.)

The Reauthorization of P.L. 94–142 (as P.L. 101–476), renamed the *Individuals with Disabilities Education Act* (*IDEA*) in 1990, furthered the general public's awareness of people with disabilities and their right to increased access to all aspects of society. Although the REI stressed inclusion for *some* students with disabilities, full inclusion was now the ultimate goal. Sailor (1991) characterizes full inclusion as a zero-reject (no exceptions) policy in which all students with disabilities attend their neighborhood schools, where a "natural proportion" of disabled and nondisabled students learn together in age-appropriate placements. There are no self-contained classes and, instead, special education supports are provided in integrated learning environments. Often proponents of inclusion draw on the language of social justice to help explain their resistance to segregated placements for students with disabilities. Villa and Thousand (1995), for instance, suggest that inclusion goes beyond the issue of where services should be provided to encompass "a way of life, a way of living together . . . a belief that each individual is valued and does belong" (p. 11). As Gabel (2002) writes, this shift to a more libratory model of social justice requires that people with diverse abilities are included at the level of theory as well as practice.

In response to the increased controversy over inclusion, most professional organizations and child advocacy groups issued official position statements on the practice. These positions varied widely. The Learning Disabilities Association (LDA) stated that "the placement of ALL children with disabilities in the regular classroom is as great a violation of *IDEA* as is the placement of ALL children in separate classrooms on the basis or type of their disability" (1993). The National Joint Committee on Learning Disabilities agreed that full inclusion "violates the rights of parents and students with disabilities as mandated by *IDEA*" (1993). Several organizations supported a moderate stance of fully supported inclusion for most children (National Parent Network on Disabilities, 1993), but many others weighed in on the side of maintaining the current continuum of services (Council for Exceptional Children, 1993; Council for Learning Disabilities, 1993). Several organizations did, however, support full inclusion (Association for Persons with Severe Handicaps, 1993; United Cerebral Palsy Association, 1993; American Association of Mental Retardation and Association of Retarded Citizens, 2002).

Following a national report on the transition outcomes of students with disabilities after high school (Wagner, 1991), concern began to surface in the national media about the poor academic and social outcomes for students in the special education system. An article in *U.S. News & World Report* expressed concern about the overrepresentation of minority students in special education classes, commenting "nearly 40 years after *Brown v. Board of Education,* the U.S. Supreme Court's landmark school desegregation ruling, Americans continue to pay for and send their children to classrooms that are often separate and unequal" (Shapiro et al., 1993, p. 46). On television, the Merrow Report asked "What's So Special About Special Education?" (Stacey & Tulenko, 1996). Critics talked about special education as "welfare annexes" and "dead ends for many children." And, the film, *Educating Peter* (Wurtzburg, 1992), which chronicled the trials and ultimate triumph of an "included" 10-year-old boy with Down syndrome, won an Academy Award for Best Achievement in Documentary Short Subjects.

In educational circles, inclusion was increasingly defined from a social justice framework (Gerrard, 1996; Christensen & Rizvi, 1996), and became virtually synonymous with special education reform. Not surprisingly, scholars and educators who were satisfied with the existing model of special education felt that the foundation on which they stood was under attack. Fuchs and Fuchs (1995) wrote "the reformist impulse has been radicalized" (p. 216) and "the field's rhetoric has become increasingly strident and its perspective increasingly insular and disassociated with general education concerns" (p. 215). They charged supporters of inclusion as possessing "unjustified optimism," and they expressed "doubt that most teachers will tolerate students more difficult to teach than they currently have" (Dorn et al., 1996, p. 16). In the *Illusion of Full Inclusion,* scholars Kauffman and Hallahan (1995b) edited a series of essays that offered a systematic critique of inclusive practices and the professionals who supported them. Citing the success of segregated programs for students who are deaf (Bina, 1995) and blind (Lane, 1995), the editors forcefully maintained that a continuation of current practices, admittedly in need of refinement, was the more appropriate course of action. In response, Brantlinger (1997) analyzed the debates, charging that "while marking inclusionists as ideological, traditionalists assume—or attempt to create the impression that their work is non-ideological" (p. 436). She claimed the denial of ideological positioning was responsible for "reifying disability and naturalizing special services" (p. 440).

Coinciding with the Reauthorization of *IDEA* (1997), which stressed increased access to the general education curriculum, Lipsky and Gartner's *Inclusion and School Reform* (1997) offered a comprehensive overview of inclusion in relation to shifting policies and practices of education. The field of gifted education soon became implicated in the debate, as proponents claimed that all students could and should benefit from instructional enrichment traditionally reserved for "gifted" students (Sapon-Shevin, 1996). It was also argued that integration of gifted students would no longer "perpetuate, even exacerbate inequities in our society" (Borland, 1996, p. 132). In a commentary on the field of special education, Kauffman (1999) stated, "Inclusion has become virtually meaningless, a catch-word used to give a patina of legitimacy to whatever program people are trying to sell or defend" (p. 246).

It became apparent that the field of special education had grown divided, even polarized, on the issue of inclusion. Andrews, et al. (2000) succinctly outlined two broad and conflicting positions in an article titled *Bridging the Special Education Divide.* Traditionalists, who favored a policy of incremental improvement, believed that the current model of special education was sound and that disability was best conceptualized within a medical or deficit-based model. They advocated the enhancing of academic and social performance by tying curriculum to postschool adaptive functioning and introducing more scientific rigor to teacher preparation programs. Conversely, reconceptualists argued that special education was a flawed system and that notions of disability should be recast in a social model. They argued that current structures were limiting because they denied access for people with disabilities. Reconceptualists also articulated the need to rethink the entire education system to place more emphasis on human diversity and an ethic of care, and less emphasis on labels and categories. Obviously the groups were operating from paradigmatically conflicting stances (Paul & Ward, 1996). Although Andrews et al. (2000) express an optimistic message, each ideological position is so differently structured that it is hard to imagine the possibility of reconciliation.

Conclusion

In this book we challenge the assumption that *IDEA* was simply an outgrowth of *Brown*. Although we acknowledge the enormous role *IDEA* has played in realizing basic citizenship rights for disabled people, we are compelled also to call attention to its complicities and failures, which have resulted in the overrepresentation of students of color and the continued segregation of students with disabilities. We argue that the everyday technologies of education (tracking, "gifted" classes, etc.) and special education (testing, labeling, segregated placements, etc.) have contributed to the problem of producing and excluding "disabled" students and to the maintaining of White middle class privilege. In this chapter we consider how the proliferation of mild or "soft" categories of disability allowed disability labeling to grow in unprecedented ways, disproportionately affecting students of color. We also consider the paradox of the LRE. Seemingly designed to ensure integrated educational placements, we contend that the LRE clause has actually been used as a mechanism to thwart the integration of students with disabilities, particularly those of color. Thus, despite a widely held claim that the primary intent of special education is to serve students with disabilities, we contend that through its everyday mechanisms special education has also served the agendas of both segregationists and anti-inclusionists.

To counteract exclusionary impulses in general and special education, the inclusion movement, intent upon the integration of all students with disabilities, steadily gained momentum since the late 1980s. As with *Brown*, we have yet to see the full realization of the promise of inclusion—and, like *Brown*, inclusion has faced its share of resistance. Indeed, the field of special education remains divided over inclusion. But regardless of one's positioning, if we focus only on the positives of special education, like the emperor with no clothes, we remain in denial of the ways that race and disability have been used to deny equal access to educational opportunities for all students. We also fail to envision new possibilities that might through a combined and intersectional effort bring about real educational transformation.

Lessons Learned

Technologies of power manifest themselves in many forms. In special education they include excessive testing, biased norms, segregated placements, and stigmatized labels. Taken together and accepted without question, these technologies of difference construct and fortify inequitable relations of power, uphold existing modes of exclusion, and foster new forms of containment. To each of these technologies we in the field must ask, why is this necessary? Who does this practice empower and disempower? How does this practice get us closer to or farther away from our ideals about democracy and freedom?

To counteract such acts of power and exclusion, marginalized groups offer counterassertions and demands for access and inclusion. In response, dominant groups seek to shore up their privileged position. While the ebb and flow of power and resistance can seem endless and cyclic, each wave can be seen as providing the necessary energy for the next. Thus, while *Brown* is often seen as a distinct and landmark decision, it was really just one event in an ongoing struggle for access to educational opportunity[5]. And, as history shows us, access is rarely met without resistance. Inclusion, too, could simply be seen as another wave of resistance to the exclusion of people with disabilities that began with *IDEA*.

What we have come to see is that we are always already a part of these struggles, whether we acknowledge it or not. We believe that the task remains to face squarely both our successes and failures and to recognize that the struggles of others are connected to our own. What we can no longer ignore is that we in special education share in the failure of *Brown*, and therefore we have a responsibility to work toward achieving its promise. To work toward desegregation without acknowledging how ableism and racism interdepend has proven ineffective. To achieve inclusion without addressing racial inequities remains a hollow and incomplete endeavor. To work toward an education that is inclusive, integrated, and supportive of all learners will require the collective forces of all of our best efforts.

8

LEARNING FROM *BROWN:* THE FUTURE
OF DEMOCRATIC SCHOOLING

8

LEARNING FROM *BROWN:* THE FUTURE OF DEMOCRATIC SCHOOLING

Introduction

This book has largely been about remembering. Poring over pages and pages of archival newspapers, we hoped to be able to return to the years of *Brown* and bring back lessons about how people make sense of excluding others. We remain haunted by some of the words and images that we encountered as well as by those we failed to adequately address.[1] We remember federal troops, school and church bombings, mobs of angry faces, and riots. And, we remember crisply dressed Black children "walking gauntlets of jeering White adults" and "enduring spitting and spiteful assaults" (O. L. Davis, 2004, p. 96). We remember White politicians standing, physically and figuratively, in doorways, blocking any threat to White supremacy. So, too, we remember the awful legacy of eugenics and its aftermath, as well as the cruel realities of institutionalization, sterilization, and euthanasia. But it is not enough simply to remember. We must also find ways to act (O. L. Davis, 2004).

In this final chapter we explore the need to reimagine educational practice in ways that enact a coalitional and intersectional approach to desegregation and inclusion. We are indebted to many ideas first articulated in Black feminist scholarly traditions; for example, we draw on some of the "core themes" of a Black feminist standpoint outlined by Collins (1991, 2000). Central to Black feminism is the accounting of how various kinds of oppression, such as racism, sexism, heterosexism, classism (and, we would add, ableism) intersect. According to Collins (2000), "oppression cannot be reduced to one fundamental type, and . . . oppressions work together in producing injustice" (p. 18). Certainly the history of overrepresentation of students of color in special education is an example of a *"matrix of domination"* (Collins, p. 18) at work. Another idea central to Black feminist thought is the importance of attending to the situated understandings, sometimes called an oppositional standpoint, of individuals who are collectively positioned at the margins. From this idea we note the importance of attending to the insider perspectives of students of color who have been labeled as disabled. How might they see the intersectional discourses of racism and ableism operating in schools? Moreover, if education and learning are fundamentally political, how can we as educators enact a counterhegemonic "pedagogy of resistance" rooted in an antiracist (hooks, 1994, p. 2) and antiableist struggle? In this chapter we also draw on the idea that thought and action are interdependent. In other words, one must deconstruct the false binary between scholarship and activism, connecting "what one does and how one thinks" (Collins, 2000, p. 24). How should our practice, as informed by such understandings, change? Finally, we conclude the chapter with the importance of dialogue and the necessity of enacting coalitional politics to address the interworkings of power in our schools.

We begin this chapter by revisiting lessons learned from our analysis of editorial coverage of desegregation and inclusion in order to reaffirm the continued need for change. We follow this by contemplating the purpose of schools, particularly the paradoxical role of educational institutions to uphold traditional practices of racism and ableism, while professing democracy and individual freedom. Given that we have analyzed the past in relation to the present, we now must consider possibilities for change in the future. Bearing this in mind, we pose four questions: (1) Given the lessons of desegregation and inclusion, what shape should classrooms take? (2) What curricular changes are needed? (3) How should teacher preparation shift? (4) What current practices require rethinking? These questions symbolize our desire to challenge many existing practices, and to encourage different ways of thinking about *what* and *how* to educate teachers, who, in turn, influence *what* and *how* to teach the youngest citizens in our democracy. Given the breadth of issues raised, and obvious restraints in terms of the length of this book, we acknowledge that our responses are brief and somewhat provisional. However, our intention is to offer them as starting points for deeper conversations, further research, and the development of practical ways to create and maintain change to improve the quality of education, and lives in general, of all citizens.

Revisiting Lessons Learned

In each chapter of this book we conclude with a particular lesson that we take away from analyzing discourses of exclusion in debates about racial desegregation and the inclusion of students with disabilities in general education classrooms. In chapter 2 we trouble the near-exclusive claims of knowledge about disability and race within the field of science. We critique how the pervasiveness of scientific notions of disability and race have been maintained by cultural practices masquerading as objective thought. The framing of race and disability by the scientific establishment throughout history contributes to lowered expectation for, and oppressive practices toward, students with disabilities and children of color. In chapter 3 we explore how various stakeholders have advocated a particular pace and scope of change, arguing either for gradual implementation or more immediate and widespread reform. We find that given more time or more resources, those who are resistant to change find ways to maintain the status quo. We maintain a degree of skepticism about reform that is instituted incrementally. We also see how, because of the intersectional nature of power, single-issue solutions fail to enact truly transformative reform. In other words, because legislation typically focuses only on either race *or* disability, it fails to prevent the ways that racism and ableism work together to marginalize students of color in special education.

In chapter 4 we examine the significance of representations as a window into how systems of power operate. We also learn the importance of creating and maintaining discourses that challenge or talk back to dominant ways of knowing about human difference. Although racial representation in political cartoons from the Black press offered important alternative constructions of race, we could not help but notice the relative absence of images of disability. Instead, the meaning of disability remains the exclusive domain of medical and clinical discourses. Such popular and everyday counterassertions and alternative claims of knowledge about human difference and disability remain an unfinished task of disability studies.

In chapter 5 we argue that resistance to integrated schooling has always been inextricably bound to contemporary notions of what constitutes "normal." Inflexible norms and rigid expectations often prevail in general education. These exclusionary norms seek to homogenize students, actively negating the naturalness and value of human difference. We conclude this chapter with the need to learn from other countries, like Italy, who have reconfigured their education systems to accommodate all students.

In chapter 6 we highlight barriers that inhibit our ability to dialogue across our differences and disrupt binary thinking. When dominant groups seek to silence the opinions, values, and understandings of those advocating change, this leads to an impasse that ultimately stifles any potential for growth. The lesson we take from this chapter is the need for all parties to be open and engage in dialogue across differences.

In chapter 7 we chart special education's growth as well as the counterpull of inclusion. We take a critical look at educational structures and practices that value sameness over diversity. We conclude by stressing the interconnectedness between racism and ableism as concepts used to justify exclusion, and the need to work toward educating all students together. Although we find much to learn that is relevant in each of these chapters, in order to change exclusionary practices we must put these lessons into action. We begin first by analyzing our beliefs about the purpose and function of public schools.

The Purpose and Function of Public Schools

Everyone has some degree of familiarity with public schools. The vast majority of Americans have been educated in the pubic school system, and those who have not have sought out private schools, often in reaction to the perceived inadequacy of public schools. From their very inception, the purpose and practices of public schools have always been contested. Tyack (2001) writes, "When citizens deliberate about the education of the young, they are also debating the shape of the future for the whole nation" (p. 2). It is clear that schools are considered not merely as places in which children are taught useful skills, but rather are complex institutions that shape both individual and national character.

American public schools have a long, rich, complicated history of struggle, both in terms of who is to be educated and where, but also what is to be taught in terms of curriculum. In other words, various reforms have sought to influence which forms of knowledge should be valued over others. The impact of these decisions cannot be underestimated, as curriculum actively shapes self-understanding as well as perceptions of the larger world (Kliebard, 1995). Gaining access to the mainstream curriculum, and receiving an equitable education for *all citizens* has been, and still is, a key educational issue. Unfortunately, as Prendergast (2002) asserts, inequity in education should be thought of as an "American tradition rather than an aberration" (p. 207). Nonetheless, grassroots organizing by or on behalf of previously excluded groups have led to legislative changes, which has led to improvements in education for working class and poor children, females, students of racial or linguistic minority groups, immigrants, children of migrant workers, English language learners, and children with disabilities. Each of these movements has pushed the boundaries of who has the *right* to be educated in the public schools (Mondale & Patton, 2001). Yet, the right to a public school education has not guaranteed equality (Crenshaw, 1998; Darling-Hammond 2003; Prendergast 2002) or integrated classrooms or programs within schools. As Katsiyannis et al, (2001) suggest, the primary issue at stake in *IDEA* (and we would add *Brown*) was simply access, but the next wave of reforms must be about excellence and equality for all students.

Scholars argue that because of housing patterns, gerrymandered school district attendance zones, and the repeal of bussing, it is virtually impossible to create integrated public schools that are representative of the local population in terms of race and ethnicity (Kelebay, 1992; O'Keefe, 1994; Wrong, 2000). Others concur that effectively supporting students with disabilities in mainstream settings is also an unachievable goal (Kaufman & Hallahan, 1995a; Fuchs & Fuchs, 1995). However, in the following section, we assert the need for educators to rethink what might be done and what can be done. As Tyack (2001) suggests, the time is overdue to revisit current practices in public schools and to envision new alternatives for ensuring that a quality education is truly accessible to all students.

America and the Pursuit of Liberty

"Liberty for all," is a popular and enduring American mantra, in theory if not in practice. In 1944, a now infamous study called *An American Dilemma,* sponsored by the Carnegie Corporation, was considered the most comprehensive study of race relations to date. A Swedish economist, Gunnar Myrdal, highlighted the contradiction between America's democratic ideals and its pervasive institutionalized racism, concluding "most Americans had internalized American Creed values such as equality and justice, and that a dilemma was created for Americans because of the gap between their ideals and realities" (in J. A. Banks, 2002, p. 13). Myrdal's frank response angered and embarrassed the Carnegie Foundation, which subsequently curtailed its support for research on race relations until the 1960s.

Racism, sexism, and homophobia are "particular manifestations of the same disease" according to Lorde (1984), who asked, "Can anyone here . . . still afford to believe that the pursuit of liberation can be the sole and particular province of any one race, or sex, or age, or religion, or sexuality, or class?" (p. 140). Lorde's comments highlight the need to recognize that diverse forms of discrimination have the same roots of intolerance, which, if allowed to grow, collectively stifle how other forms of domination are experienced. We must add "disability" to the list generated by Lorde, because, as we have seen, it is perhaps the most overlooked category of oppression. Fleischer and Zames (2001) emphasize that disability is an all-inclusive category because nondisabled people often acquire disabilities, particularly as they age, and because people with disabilities constitute the largest minority of American citizens (approximately 54 million). The authors position the disability rights movement at the forefront of the struggle for human rights. Experiencing limited access to the mainstream world, oppressive stereotyped portrayals, lowered expectations, and threats to full citizenship, people with disabilities personify the struggle for liberty.

Bearing in mind that our central focus has been the need to change educational practices to include students of color and students with disabilities, we now explore several possibilities for restructuring schools. First, we contemplate how classrooms could be restructured. Second, we examine issues of curricular inclusion and transformation. Third, we consider the teaching force and the role of teacher preparation. Fourth, we conclude with a look at common educational practices that inhibit change, and discuss the need to reevaluate what is done in schools.

1. What Shape Would Classrooms Take?

The Acceptance of Diversity

A classroom in which uniformity is prized in terms of student expectations is antithetical to diversity and inclusion. When teachers claim that certain students "don't fit," or "don't belong," we need to critically examine the assumptions behind such assessments. As educators we must ask: On what grounds don't they fit? What makes them not belong?

If there are students who "cannot do the work" (a common reason cited for exclusion), this should be a signal that there is something wrong with the access to instruction, not with the student. In diverse classrooms, work must be differentiated to meet students at the juncture of what they can and cannot do. Several strategies for differentiating instruction in diverse, creative ways have been developed by educational scholar-practitioners (Gregory & Chapman, 2002; Kluth et al., 2003; Tomlinson, 2001; Udvari-Solnar, 1996; Udvari-Solnar et al., 2002). Moreover, many of the progressive and constructivist practices, such as cooperative learning, are well suited to inclusive classrooms and improve the educational experiences for all students (Thousand et al., 2002). As Garland-Thomson (1997a) has noted, "Disability, perhaps more than other differences, demands a reckoning with messiness of bodily variety with literal individuation run amok" (p. 24). In other words, by their very existence, students with disabilities challenge the hegemony of uniformity, normalcy, and standardization that are seemingly ingrained in school practices. Those who consider themselves uniform or "normal" often perceive disability as something "missing" or "wrong" within the person, but it should instead signal to us that something is wrong with our practice. Unfortunately, disabled students continue to be positioned as lacking in a particular quality or function, therefore justifying their relegation to separate classrooms.

Sapon-Shevin (2000) argues that to value diversity we must relinquish our desires to create and maintain homogeneous classes. She writes, "Educators need to transcend discussions of diversity as a classroom *problem* [italics added] and regard it as a natural, desirable, and inevitable occurrence that enriches educational experiences for both teachers and students" (p. 34). Her sentiment is echoed by J. A. Banks (1999), who claims diversity means focusing on those who have traditionally been excluded, with an aim to "bring people and groups that are now on the margins of society into the center" (p. 8). It is interesting to note that despite much progress, many students continue to experience marginalization and exclusion. In a study to determine which groups of students would have the hardest time fitting into a small, rural Southern college campus, for instance, Globetti et al. (1993) found that students believed that gay and lesbian students would have the hardest time fitting in (79.6 percent), followed by international students (57.1 percent), disabled students (42.8 percent), and African American students (30.5 percent). Their findings suggest that different hierarchies of tolerance may exist in any school population and that efforts toward inclusion must take a multipronged approach.

Taking a Stance in Promoting Integration

Teaching in a society that discriminates against individuals on the basis of their race, ethnicity, national origin, disability, gender, sexuality, or other social markers is a demanding and complex task. Throughout history some teachers have shied away from challenging the status quo, while others have embraced issues of social justice as a part of the practice of teaching. hooks (1994) writes that one positive aspect of her experiences in her "beloved" Black schools was the opportunity to learn from Black teachers who understood education as the "practice of freedom" (p. 3), who saw learning as a "counter-hegemonic act," and teaching as a "pedagogy of resistance" (p. 2). For hooks, these were teachers who knew that education was fundamentally a political act. She remembers, "My teachers were on a mission" (p. 2). Similarly, many in the special education community worry about the loss of potential for nurturing disability community in inclusive schools. It can be particularly important for students with disabilities, who like many gay/ lesbian children and some adopted children, grow up in families that may not share their difference(s). What rarely comes up in the inclusion and integration debates, which typically take the form of pro/con arguments, are more nuanced calls for what we might call "strategic" segregation. Therefore, in our efforts toward instituting inclusion and integration, we would be wise to consider ways to retain the positive and political possibilities of community while defining community in more fluid and provisional ways. In other words, how might schools foster communities based on neighborhood, interests, aspirations, in addition to the more traditional identity groups based on race, ethnicity, gender, class, sexuality, or dis/ability?

Whether acknowledged or not, the classroom is a space in which manifestations of prejudice surface daily. Rather than brushing such instances aside, teaching against prejudice should be central to everyday classroom life. Educators with a strong sense of social justice address intolerance, discrimination, stereotyping, and exclusion. Sharing the responsibility for all students in the classroom can be an important first step. Yet, as Sapon-Shevin et al. (1998) note, simply being physically included does not guarantee meaningful integration into the life of the classroom. Many students with disabilities and students from other marginalized groups remain isolated in so-called inclusive classrooms. To counter this, teachers must be concerned with promoting meaningful integration, by creating opportunities for students to learn from each other and unlearn stereotypical attitudes, beliefs, and social practices that have misshaped their understanding of "others."

2. How Would Curricula Change?

Transforming Knowledge

Like our classroom structures, much of our current curriculum must be critically examined. We must ask: Who is represented? How are they represented? Who is representing whom? For what purpose are they being represented? Who and what has been omitted or erased? In what ways is reality more complicated than this particular representation implies? Garland-Thomson (1997b) maintains that one way to challenge our assumptions is to focus on the knowledge of groups who have previously been relegated to the margins. The concept of transformative knowledge, informed by ethnic studies and multicultural education movements and the U.S. civil rights movement of the 1960s and 1970s, offers much potential for challenging oppression (J. A. Banks, 2002) and transforming curriculum.

Transforming the Mainstream

Advocates of multiculturalism and inclusion have sought to transform mainstream beliefs and practices to be more accepting and valuing of human difference. Valles (1998), for example, calls for more bilingual and multicultural courses in teacher education programs to help curb inappropriate referrals to special education. This would also lead to better instruction and more culturally relevant curriculum. J. A. Banks (1994) describes a five-dimensional framework for implementing multiculturalism in the classroom. His framework can be adapted to all classroom contexts, but it requires that: (1) diverse curricula are inclusive and respectful of difference and integrated in a meaningful manner; (2) all knowledge is understood as constructed and located within a particular cultural context and history; (3) educators are equally respectful toward all cultures and subcultures to actively reduce prejudice by helping students to develop positive attitudes about different groups; (4) educators incorporate a variety of pedagogical approaches that allow students to interact and respond in ways that are not at odds with cultural norms and expectations; and (5) support for multiculturalism is not confined to the classroom, but upheld and sustained by an empowering school culture and social structures, which acknowledge and celebrate the strength and benefits of diversity.

Because additive approaches allow mainstream knowledge and values to remain centrally positioned and largely unquestioned, diversity cannot be considered an *add-on* to the curriculum. Furthermore, many multiculturalists argue that curriculum should be broad and inclusive of diverse local, national, as well as global perspectives. Wax (1993) believes, for instance, that school curricula should reflect the population of the school. Yet, we would argue that it is important to decenter dominant perspectives and ideologies regardless of the population of the school. As we noted in the introduction, White suburban students have some of the most insular school experiences, so we have a particular responsibility to expose those students to nondominant understandings and perspectives. At the heart of both a local and a more global approach is the desire for education to incorporate multiple perspectives and vantage points.

As an example, history is a discipline in which the "official story" is often delivered without variation or question. M. Morris (2001) argues, however, that "teaching history as a single story with pure endings is inadequate and in fact, does violence to the text of historical memory" (p. 2). Traditional approaches where history is taught with defined beginnings and endings and cause/effect relations that imply the inevitability of certain notions of "progress" are particularly problematic and exclusionary.

Instead, by seeking the complicated, conflicting, and messy entanglement of issues, students actively learn the complexities and contradictions of history.

Teaching Race

A concept that is increasingly explored in college courses but rarely in K–12 classroom settings, is race. The concept of race as biologically determined has increasingly given way to an understanding of race as a social construction that benefits one group over another. J. A. Banks (1995), for instance, explains, "Race is a human invention constructed by groups to differentiate themselves from other groups, to create ideas about the 'Other,' to formulate their identities, and to defend the disproportionate distribution of rewards and opportunities within society" (p. 22). Whiteness, therefore, is a historical concept largely formulated through colonial expansion, and reinforced by equating nationalism with skin color. In the history of the United States, for example, "various White ethnic groups were perceived as different races, some inferior to others" (J. A. Banks, 1995, p. 20). The various incarnations of who constituted White and who did not, according to the vagaries of written legislation, has been chronicled by Haney-Lopez (1996) and Guglielmo and Salerno (2003). Teaching "Whiteness" or "Blackness" or any other racial label as a construction pertinent to a particular time, place, and history, exposes "students [to] the ways in which knowledge is invented and reinvented through time" (J. A. Banks, 1995, p. 22). Furthermore, a critical understanding of race opens the possibility for students to gain important insights into the operations of power between dominant and nondominant groups. Goffman (1963) argues that unless critically examined, normalcy is allowed to remain "relatively uncontaminated by intimate contact with the stigmatized," and those occupying the normal category remain "relatively unthreatened in their identity beliefs" (p. 120). Thus, by exposing students to how Whiteness is taken to mean normal, we expose them to the workings of power inherent in such constructions.

Teaching Dis/ability

Just as the concept of "race" should be examined, explored, and critiqued, so should disability and ability. Through disability studies teachers gain new and critical ways to present the concepts of disability and normalcy throughout the curriculum.[2] Such understandings dislodge the dominant medical model discourse, which positions disability as deficit or lack. Moreover, a disability studies model encourages teaching disability in a manner that reflects the lived experiences of people with disabilities over the perceptions and beliefs of the nondisabled. As J. Morris (1991) explains,

> The general culture invalidates me both by ignoring me and by its particular representations of disability. Disabled people are missing from mainstream culture. When we do appear, it is in specialized forms—from charity telethons to plays about an individual

struck down by tragedy—which impose the non-disabled world's definitions on us and our experience. (cited in Barnes et al., 1999 p. 191)

Beginning to counter such marginalization in our curriculum and our practice creates the possibility of transforming knowledge of dis/ability.

P. M. Ferguson (2001) has developed a tentative set of guidelines to facilitate the fusion of disability studies into the general curriculum. He suggests a range of activities, such as having students: (1) talk with adults with disabilities about their lives; (2) conduct accessibility surveys in their schools and community environments; (3) write about people with disabilities; (4) discuss stories that have disability themes; (5) conduct interviews with individuals with disabilities; (6) write essays on stereotypes; (7) watch documentaries about eugenics; (8) write biographies of noted individuals with disabilities; (9) learn ASL (American Sign Language); (10) learn the alphabet in Braille; (11) go to museums to look for representations of disability; (12) prepare photo essays; (13) learn about different brain functions; (14) design assistive devices; (15) conduct Web-based research on disability resources; and (16) design a new graphic symbol to signify disability.

Of course, these are simply a beginning point for involving students in alternative ways of knowing about disability. Each curricular area brings up a multitude of possibilities for infusing disability studies into the curriculum. For example, science offers the opportunity to discuss disability in relation to the history of eugenics and to current scientific work such as the Human Genome Project. In history classes, eugenics, immigration, and sterilization laws can be taught as troubling precursors to the Holocaust and the disability rights movement can be taught as an important civil rights struggle. In government classes, the experiences of people with significant disabilities would inform various citizenship debates thoughout history. Literature, art, and film abound with representations of disabilities, as does popular culture, which can all be interrogated from a critical perspective. Contemporary debates about the "right" to die, euthanasia, and legal cases related to disability can be infused into discussions about current events. Autobiographies of individuals with disabilities can offer important counternarratives to the medical and deficit-oriented perspectives of disability. Finally, as anyone who interacts with young people knows, students' (and sometimes colleagues') everyday discourse is peppered with disability analogies. When words like insane, lame, and retarded crop up in classroom talk, they beg to be interrogated as examples of ablesim. As these examples show, inclusion must not be simply about who is in the classroom, but also how we teach and what we learn.

Citizenship in a Democracy

J. A. Banks (1994) argues that multicultural education is closely connected to issues of citizenship. Thus, education in a pluralistic, democratic society should help "students acquire the knowledge, skills, and attitudes needed to actualize American democratic ideals" (Banks & Banks, 1997, p. 191). This model of transformative knowledge requires not just thought, but action. It requires "teachers to move beyond teaching passive knowledge and to connect the curriculum to the lives of students and to their location in the political, economic, and social institutions of society" (Banks & Banks, p. 187). A curriculum predominantly structured around social history is "based on the notion that many people contributed to making the nation—not just presidents, generals, and 'heroes,'" (Singer, 1992, p. 84). Furthermore, curriculum should not be limited to national history, issues, and concerns, but linked to the world at large, cultivating connections and helping students to "acquire a delicate balance of cultural, national, and global identifications" (J. A. Banks, 2001, p. 9). Moreover, because disability figures so prominently, it must be central to any discussion of citizenship (Baynton, 2001) or even humanness (Baker, 2002). In other words, because individuals marked by race, class, and disability are "constructed . . . as inferior, dangerous, and of little value" there is a need to "address systemic structural social inequalities" within democracy from an intersectional framework (Watts & Erevelles, 2004, pp. 292–293).

3. How Would Teacher Preparation Change?

Diversifying the Teaching Force

Of great concern is the disparity between "race" and ethnicity of teachers and that of the student population. As Gordon (1990) notes, "Realistically speaking, most children of color who attend American public schools in the foreseeable future will be taught by Anglo teachers" (p. 89). Ideally, the teaching force should be representative of the overall population in terms of race, ethnicity, disability, and gender. Instead, the teaching force has been (and continues to be) overwhelmingly White, nondisabled, and female. Moreover, colleges of education are similarly White and nondisabled. The impact of a racialized *and* feminized *and* nondisabled teaching force has not yet been sufficiently explored in educational research. We do not believe, however, that having more teachers "of color" and educators who are male or disabled would automatically produce equitable education, free from prejudice. As we have seen, inequality is multifaceted and intersectional. However, we do contend that the shaping of an increasingly diverse American population in classrooms largely taught by White, nondisabled females is a concern and must be acknowledged. Moreover, because a disproportionate number of students of color are identified as disabled, we must openly question how much of this trend reflects bias. As Dyer (2002) writes, power because it is seen as normal "reproduces itself regardless of intention, power differences and goodwill" (p. 13). When educators fail to examine and reflect on their own privileged position and the power that a dominant identity affords them, they risk holding all students to White, middle class, and ableist norms of academic performance, social interactions, and classroom behavior.

Radical Shift in Teaching and Researching Race and Disability

As a result of an imbalanced teaching force, there remains a need to cultivate an awareness of how White and nondisabled teacher expectations of students of color influence school practices. Solorzano and Yosso (2001) and others remind us how "tracking, teacher expectations, and intelligence testing, have historically been used to subordinate of color" (p. 4). The same mechanisms have also been used to relegate students with disabilities to special education classrooms. How, then, can potential or experienced teachers use their role as mediators of knowledge to begin to transform school and societal practices that continue to marginalize students of color, students with disabilities, and particularly students of color with disabilities?

What we are advocating is for educators to shift their thinking about how the phenomena of race and disability are conceptualized. Just as critical race theorists have recast race as a social, rather than a biological construct (Haney-Lopez, 1996), disability studies scholars have similarly recast ability and disability. As Garland-Thomson (1997a) explains,

> disability is a representation, a cultural interpretation of physical transformation or configuration, and a comparison of bodies that structures social relations and institutions. Disability, then, is the attribution of corporeal deviance—not so much a property of bodies as a product of cultural rules about what bodies should be or do. (p. 6)

By shifting away from the medical and deficit models of disability, disability scholars emphasize the social expectations or cultural norms that govern understandings of and ascribe significance to disability. Viewing disability as primarily a social experience forces all individuals to examine and reflect upon their complicity in upholding or challenging perceptions of and interactions with people signified as abled and those signified as disabled.

Many scholars in disability studies have been working to conceptualize disability in more intersectional ways. Kudlick (2003), for example, argues for the need for disability to be more widely understood as a marker of identity, joining race, ethnicity, gender, and sexual orientation. Moreover, because of the intersectional nature of experience, markers such as "race" and "disability" cannot be viewed as independent elements of an individual's identity. As Delgado-Bernal (2002) insists, "one's identity is not based on the social construction of race [or any social marker] but rather is multidimensional and intersects with various experiences" (p. 118). Certainly beginning with the experiences of students of color who are overrepresented in special education programs can serve as a crucial starting point for analyzing the intersection of race and disability in education. Yet, despite the long-standing problem of overrepresentation, there remains a dearth of special education research examining how disability is "influenced by sociocultural and contextual factors" (K. M. Collins, 2003, p. 1). As a result of the acontextual and asocial view of disability, we "continue to fail to interrupt the processes that result in the overrepresentation of students of color and those from low-income and poor households in special education programs" (K. M. Collins, p. 2). Similarly, there remains a lack of critical attention to issues of race, class, ethnicity, and nation in disability studies research. Perhaps it is time for disability studies and critical race theorists to work together to interrogate systemic, structural, ideological, and social inequalities at the "intersections of race, class, and disability in educational, social, and legal contexts" (Watts & Erevelles, 2004, p. 293).

4. What Current Practices Would Require Rethinking?

Countering the Lack of Diversity

Banks and Banks (1997) note that current school reform efforts pay insufficient attention to diversity. Moreover, the focus on standardization, high-stakes testing, zero-tolerance policies, and student performance indicators marginalize both the multicultural and inclusive movements. The uniformity of state curricula, as mandated by the federal government, appears far more concerned about student performance of discrete skills than on exploring and appreciating the diversity of human experience through multiculturalism or inclusion. Moreover, in the current school efforts put in place during the second Bush administration, we have actually lost ground in terms of minority graduation rates, the achievement gap, and post-secondary attainment (Orfield, 2000). We have also seen a return to larger class sizes, which were reduced during the Clinton administration (Orfield, 2000). The current "reforms" narrow the scope of curricula and are seemingly indifferent to the value of pluralism or diversity or the problem of concentrated poverty in our society. In contrast, Wax (1993) describes a student in his class, who defines multiculturalism as "a marvelous worldly flea market exhibiting a diverse breadth and depth of ideas, beliefs, behaviors, languages, stories, images and so on. The opposite of this I see as the company store" (p. 107). This astute observation begs the question: Can the transformative knowledge of multicultural and inclusive education change the "company store"?

Another way to view this analogy is in terms of conformity or individualism. Although the company store example suggests safety in uniformity, the flea market conjures many more options and possibilities. The analogy also calls into question contradictory beliefs, deeply rooted in the collective American psyche, about the value of uniformity and individualism. Garland-Thomson (1997a), noting this dilemma, writes "If the principle of equality encourages uniformity while the principle of freedom invites distinction, American selfhood is balanced on the tension between the desire for sameness and the longing for uniqueness" (p. 130). As such, multiculturalism and inclusion both underscore the tension between identity and community and should be seen as central to exploring this aspect of American culture and schooling.

Questioning the Value of Special Education for "Students of Color"

Special education is typically thought of as a human service or a helping profession. Barnes et al. (1999) argue, however, that the whole focus of disability in the human services is about "changing disabled people to make them more like 'normal' people rather than challenging the ideal of 'normality'" (p. 74). This is why many scholars have come to view special education as primarily a sorting mechanism (Brantlinger, 1997; Lipsky & Gartner, 1997; Skrtic, 1991a &b; Varenne & McDermott, 1998). Fierros and Conroy (2002) concur, stating that special education, particularly for those labeled mildly retarded, has been "one device to screen out minority students" (p. 39). To make matters worse, the academic success of children of color in comparison to White students is further jeopardized by their disproportionate placement in special education. Thus, students of color in special education face a "double jeopardy" in terms of being denied educational opportunity, "first on account of racial discrimination and again on account of their disability status" (Losen & Welner, 2002, p. 171). Although oppression is intersectional in nature, it is clear that being a student of color *and* labeled disabled dramatically increases the chances of school failure (Losen & Orfield, 2002). As Losen and Orfield note,

> many schools today still operate under a deficit model, where school authorities regard students with disabilities as the embodiments of their particular disability and ask only what the special educators are required to do in order to accommodate the student's problem. (p. xxix)

Thus, special education becomes a place to send students who confound the standards and norms of the dominant group. It is no surprise, then, that students of color face a greater risk of being relegated to the margins of our educational system. Yet, because disability is assumed to be a medical or clinical phenomena, independent of race or culture, the idea that disability can be understood differently, and often *is* understood differently in various cultural contexts, is ignored.

Labeling Disability and Race

The conferring of labels in schools is a commonplace practice. Students are officially placed into categories such as "gifted," "learning disabled," "emotionally disturbed," or "mentally retarded." Despite the widespread use of labeling, rarely do we draw "attention to unequal power relations between the labeled and the labeler, not only in possessing the authority to 'attach' the label in the first place, but through continual interventions which attempt to reinforce, stabilize and amplify it" (Thomas & Loxley, 2001, p. 86). Nonetheless, to receive a special education label is to be subjected to an imposed definition, a definition that obscures other aspects of identity and carries stigma. Students who receive labels are subjected to further technologies of scrutiny and surveillance within special education, including perpetual reevaluations and reassessments (Baker, 2002). Thomas and Loxley (2001) remind us that policy is never neutral, but rather reflects existing power relations. Thus, scholars in the inclusion movement confront segregation and increased monitoring of students labeled disabled as particular manifestations of ablesim.

Moreover, by linking ableism with more familiar forms of oppression, scholars in disability studies claim all forms of oppression share a common ground, namely the experience of being marginalized by the dominant group because of one's perceived difference. As Campbell and Oliver (1996) argue,

> Like racism, sexism, heterosexism, and all other forms of human oppression, it [ableism] is a human creation. It is impossible, therefore, to confront one type of oppression without confronting them all and, of course, the cultural values that created and sustain[s] them. (p. xii)

The negative repercussions of such "markings" are commonplace in terms of both race and disability. Greene (1992), for instance, critiques the restrictive and misleading use of labels such as "Asian American." She writes,

> To view a person as being in the same sense "representative" of Asian American culture (too frequently grouping together human beings as diverse as Japanese, Korean, Chinese, and Vietnamese Americans) or Hispanic culture or Afro-American culture is to presume an objective reality called "culture" as a homogenous and fixed presence that can be adequately represented by existing subjects. (p. 256)

On a similar note, "European American" is a relatively little used phrase, and hardly represents the diversity of Iceland, Spain, Greece, Ireland, France, England, and Poland. It does serve in a rough manner, however, to equate itself with "White," in similar ways as "Black" is equated with people of African descent. These labels serve no other purpose than to divide people based on arbitrary geographical and national boundaries, largely etched by former colonial and imperialist governments. As we have discussed, the one who assigns the label maintains the power to define. Yet, those subjected to such labels often take them up, reify the definitions, and in effect *become* racialized (Black, Latino, Asian, White, etc.) and/or disabled (LD, ED, speech impaired, etc.).

Yet, issues of race and disability are often considered taboo subjects for classroom discussions. So, although race and disability remain a ubiquitous presence in all aspects of schooling, they remain a submerged aspect of the curriculum. In particular there appears very little room for honest conversations about race and disability as they relate to power. Why is this? Are schools institutions that support a democratic populace, or are they examples of governmental power that perpetrate inequalities? In practice, we would have to admit that "schools often reflect rather than transform inequality" (Orfield, 2000, p. 401). Yet, schools are places in which the dynamics of being raced, dis/abled, classed, and gendered, co-exist and interact with each other. As Losen & Orfield (2002) contend, such differences are maintained by

> many complex and interacting factors, including unconscious racial bias on the part of school authorities, large resource inequalities that run along lines of race and class,

unjustifiable reliance on IQ and other evaluation tools, educators' inappropriate responses to the pressures of high stakes testing, and power differentials between minority parents and school officials. (p. xviii)

Disability and race, therefore, pose a challenge to the fundamental operations of school to standardize the population.

Standardization

Bigelow (1999) contends that standardized curricula and tests run against the grain of multiculturalism and, we would add, inclusion. He writes, "whereas standardization tends to paper over" difference, a critical multiculturalism welcomes opportunities to examine contradictions in curriculum and practice (p. 37). He argues for the need to problematize phrases such as "the common good," because they fail to acknowledge *whose* common good. Moreover, because history is layered, complex, and contradictory, great benefits can be gained by exploring issues and events from various perspectives. For example, the suffrage movement was largely White and middle class. Thus, in their position of privilege, "White women ignore[d] other important issues, such as treaty rights of Mexican women, sexual abuse of enslaved African-Americans, and workplace exploitation of poor White women" (Bigelow, 1999, p. 39), as well as eugenics and sterilization laws. Black feminists similarly question the erasure of gender in critical race movements (P. H. Collins, 1998; hooks, 1981). By failing to attend to the complex nature of power and privilege, the curriculum and classroom structures are neutralized, homogenized, and ultimately sanitized.

Conversely, frameworks within teacher education that focus on acknowledging and celebrating the diversity of student affinities, abilities, and preferences, offer great opportunities to cultivate classrooms in which all students can be included and succeed to the best of their abilities (Gardner, 1983; Levine & Reed, 1999). J. A. Banks (1999) notes that students come to school with many stereotypic attitudes about race, ethnicity, and other social groups. Optimistically, he claims, "the use of multicultural textbooks, other teaching materials and cooperative teaching strategies can help students develop more positive racial attitudes and perceptions" (J. A. Banks, p. 9). Yet, by incorporating flexibility in terms of materials, teaching methods, as well as a positive attitude toward diversity, teachers wield enormous influence in maintaining or changing student perceptions of race and ability.

Teaching Capitalism

Economics is intertwined with race, ethnicity, and dis/ability. Torres (1998), therefore, urges educators to look at "contradictions among education, citizenship, and democracy" (p. 446). By exploring both race and disability in relation to capitalism, we can begin to see clear relationships between the economically oppressed and the competition and demands of the workplace. By troubling contemporary democracy as synonymous with unfettered capitalism, we see how the former is used by those with political acumen to defend the practices that maintain other people at subsistence levels of living. As Torres notes,

> We need a theory of multicultural democratic citizenship that will take seriously the need to develop a theory of democracy that will help to ameliorate, if not eliminate altogether, the social differences, inequality, and inequity pervasive in capitalist societies and a theory of democracy able to address the draconian tensions between democracy and capitalism, on the one hand, and among social, political, and economic democratic forms, on the other. (p. 423)

By exploring how capitalism allows, perhaps even depends upon, a large contingency of working class and poor people working for relatively little pay and often overspending their means, we underscore connections between race, class, and ability in relation to economic mobility through education. The discrepancy in performance according to race is hardly predicated on genetic inferiority, as claimed by Herrnstein and Murray (1994), but rather linked to social factors (Losen & Orfield, 2002). Oswald et al., (1999) write that "too many African American children do not have the same learning opportunities as their peers, and they are identified as disabled in a disproportionate fashion as compared to those peers" (p. 204). It is clear that when students of color and disabled students are included in mainstream classes, they increase their likelihood of competing for coveted jobs or professions. Integration and inclusion therefore bring long overdue access into the mainstream classroom and mainstream American society.

Conclusion

The questions posed in the previous section may be useful in beginning to reframe the long-standing issues of race, disability, and special education in American schooling. If this project has taught us anything, it is the importance of looking at the world through a multifaceted lens—one that is critical of all kinds of exclusions and demands meaningful integration of diversity in all aspects of schooling. By imagining classrooms that we desire, rather than accepting the way they are currently configured, we can strive to create schools that bring those desires to fruition. In thinking about curriculum, we must challenge concepts used to devalue and marginalize certain groups of students by stressing an underlying tenet of American citizenship—equality. In teacher education, we must encourage educators to take up the task of addressing and mitigating social injustice in their everyday practice. Finally, if we are to be reflective educators, we must confront all educational practices that maintain injustice.

Unfortunately, questions often beget questions. In asking and responding to questions, we are inevitably faced with new ones. For example: How can we disrupt the concept of normalcy as it applies to children (and teachers) in schools?

How can we think in ways that disrupt margins and centers—and the tension between them? How much, and in what ways, do schooling practices influence the processes of socialization? If classrooms reflect society, what are our responsibilities in terms of changing the society, and how does an educator start in his or her own classroom? How have policies at different times during the history of schooling promoted conformity or individualism, and what can be learned from them? Can special education, as it is currently configured, be remediated—or should we create alternative structures informed by other ways of understanding disability? How do we work against the omnipresence of race when even the words we use, such as "students of color," reify it? Similarly, how do we work against reifying disability or race without denying diversity, difference, community, and culture? How do we continue to disrupt the hegemony of the medical paradigm in understanding the concept of disability and the institution of special education?

While we do not profess to know these answers, we do declare an ongoing interest in pondering how these and other questions can lead us in furthering our thinking to create better public school systems, reflective of the full range of diversity in this country. We close with a thought from J. A. Banks (1995), who asserts, "Schools should be model communities that mirror the kind of democratic society we envision" (p. 8). We have journeyed but so far in the promise of equal schooling, and must be reconciled that we have a long way to go. Let us take up this challenge, and keep our eyes firmly on the prize.[3]

NOTES

Chapter 1

1. New York University hosted its 50th Anniversary Conference titled "Brown Plus Fifty: A Renewed Agenda For Social Justice" between May 17–19, 2004. Similar conferences were held at universities across the country, including Syracuse University, where Linda Brown and Cheryl Brown Henderson spoke about their experiences as "daughters" of Brown.
2. The label TMI (Trainable Mental Impairment) was used to describe students with moderate cognitive disabilities. The label was given to students with "mental impairments," considered to be more significant than those who were deemed "educable" or EMI. Of course, the idea that some students are educable and others merely trainable is both inaccurate and demeaning.
3. The art program had been cut in order to pay for the new class, which was not a popular decision among teachers or parents.
4. The diversity I encountered in school as a result of bussing did not include disability, however. Every day I sat next to a student whom I never saw in school. Instead, she rode the bus to school only to be picked up by another bus that took her to a sheltered workshop. She would tell me on the way home each afternoon how many pens she had assembled that day. I remember telling her, when I found out how little she was being paid for her work, that she needed a labor union!
5. The report, *Status of the American Public School Teacher, 2000–2001,* has been compiled by the NEA (National Education Association) every five years since 1961. The most recent data show that White teachers now make up 90 percent of the teaching force in America. African American teachers, who made up 8 percent of the teaching force

in 1991, represented only 6 percent of the teaching force in 2001. Latinos are even more poorly represented in the teaching force. Although the report lists race, marital status, sex, age, and even political affiliations and philosophies of teachers and the employment status of spouses, it does not include any data on the number of teachers with disabilities. Again, disability is not thought of as an aspect of diversity in this report, nor is there any concern that the teaching force may be lacking in terms of disabled teachers. This omission most likely reflects an unstated assumption that while some students may be disabled, teachers are nondisabled.

6. Of course, this does not account for how these identities intersect or overlap.

7. *New York Times* has been in continuous circulation since 1851, when it was called *New York Daily Times*.

8. The *Atlanta Constitution,* regarded as the "voice of the new south," began circulation in 1868 and later merged with its rival, *Atlanta Journal,* which had been in circulation since 1883. The two papers were jointly owned from 1950, but did not officially merge until 2001.

9. The *Washington Post* has been in continuous circulation since 1877.

10. The *Atlanta Daily World* was founded in 1928, by 26-year-old William Alexander Scott II. It was the first successful Black paper in the U.S., widely circulated throughout the South. In 1932 it became a daily, setting it apart from other Black papers, which were published weekly. When Scott was shot and killed in 1934, his brother, Cornelius Adolphus Scott, took over the paper and remained its editor, publisher, and general manager for 63 years until he retired at age 89. In 1997, Scott's grandniece, Alexis Scott Reeves, was named publisher of the paper.

11. The *Afro-American* has been in circulation since 1892, when former slave, John Henry Murphy, Sr. founded the paper. The paper was circulated in Baltimore, with regional editions published in Washington, D.C., Philadelphia, Richmond, and Newark. In 1938 the *Afro-American* bought out the historic *Richmond Planet* (the oldest Black weekly) and published the first edition of the *Afro-American and Richmond Planet*. By 1939, the paper would simply be called the *Richmond Afro-American,* joining the *Afro-American* line of newspapers. Although the *Afro-American* continues to be published (both in Baltimore and Washington, D.C. editions), the Richmond edition is no longer in circulation. The *Richmond Free Press,* which began circulation in 1992, continues to be published weekly.

12. The *Philadelphia Tribune* is the oldest of the Black daily newspapers, beginning circulation in 1884.

13. The *Chicago Defender* began circulation in 1905. Calling itself "the world's greatest weekly," the paper was widely read throughout the south and was the first Black paper to have a circulation over 100,000. Passed from person to person and smuggled across the Mason Dixon line, it is estimated that each paper was read by at least four or five people, making its circulation much higher than the official numbers. In 1965 the *Defender* became the *Chicago Daily Defender,* the largest Black-owned daily in the world. The *Defender* was notable in that it did not use the terms Negro or Black, referring instead to African Americans as "the Race" or as "Race men" and "Race women." Columnists included Walter White and Langston Hughes. Early poems by the Pulitzer Prize–winning poet, Gwendolyn Brooks, were also published in the *Defender*.

14. Historically newspapers have been divided into Black and White presses; however, this does not account for the blending of readership among these papers. For an excellent book of historical and literary essays on the Black press, see Vogel (2001).

Chapter 2

1. We borrow this description from a talk given by Ellen Brantlinger at the 2004 *Common Solutions: Inclusion and Diversity at the Center* conference at Syracuse University, in which she discursively analyzed a range of introductory special education textbooks by the major presses. Her work illustrates how special education introductory textbooks form an identifiable (and in many ways problematic) genre of writing about disability in education.

2. For a more detailed history of disability and the Holocaust, see Mostert (2002) and Proctor (1995). See also an excellent video produced by Mitchell and Snyder (2001), *A World without Bodies* (Brace Yourself productions) and the disability history timeline at the Disability Social History Project Website at http://www.disabilityhistory.org/ [last visited November 2004].

3. An excellent resource for archival material from the eugenics movement is available on the Web from the Dolan DNA Learning Center & Cold Spring Harbor Lab at the *Image Archive on the American Eugenics Movement* at http://www.eugenicsarchive.org [last visited August 2004].

4. For example, *The Black Stork* (1917) and *Tomorrow's Children* (1934).

5. Eugenic posters and exhibits were displayed at state fairs and expositions in Oklahoma, New York, Kansas, Arkansas, Massachusetts, Michigan, Georgia, Pennsylvania, and Texas.

6. The Alpha and Beta tests, which were co-authored by Goddard (founder of the Vineland Training School for Feebleminded Boys and Girls), Terman (author of the famous gifted studies), and Yerkes (known for his primate studies) were first used to assess military recruits and then to screen out undesirable immigrants (Selden, 1999). They are widely considered the direct precursors to contemporary intelligence tests, such as the Binet, which was also translated and normed by Goddard.

7. A wide range of scholars from across the globe and in various disciplinary locations align with a "social model" of disability. Despite their different approaches, all share skepticism about medical model understandings of disability and advocate for more sociopolitical, cultural, critical, and/or discursive approaches to conceptualizing both disability and ability.

Chapter 3

1. *Brown v. Board of Education*, which was decided on May 17, 1954, is often referred to as the "most important civil rights case of the 20th century" (Williams, 1987, p. 35). This Supreme Court decision, which overthrew *Plessy v. Ferguson*, was delivered by Justice Earl Warren. The unanimous decision concluded that separate educational facilities were inherently unequal. Despite this ruling, only three school districts in the South began integrating their schools that year (Williams, 1987). Throughout the rest of the southern states, not one classroom was integrated. *Brown II*, which was delivered a year later on May 31, 1955, was to set the implementation plans for *Brown*. Rather than a firm deadline for compliance, *Brown II* required states to proceed with integration "with all deliberate speed," a phrase like "least restrictive environment" that would be debated for years to follow.

2. According to national statistics, Black males are more than twice as likely as White students to be identified as mentally retarded in 38 states, emotionally disturbed in 29 states, and learning disabled in 8 states. In analyzing these data, Parrish (2002) concludes that "Whites are generally only placed in more restrictive self-contained classes when they need intensive services. Minority students, however, may be more likely to be placed in the restrictive settings whether they require intensive services or not" (p. 26).

3. The 1992 OCR (Office of Civil Rights) report documents the underrepresentation of racial minorities in gifted programs in the U.S. In analyzing these data, Ford (1998) finds that in 1992, for example, Black students represented 21 percent of the school age population, but only 12 percent of students identified as gifted—an underrepresentation of 41 percent. Similarly Latino students were underrepresented by 42 percent, whereas White students were overrepresented in gifted placements by 17 percent (Ford, p. 6).

4. In editorial pages the opinions or stances expressed often take the form of either strongly pro or strongly con on whatever particular issue is being debated. This particular aspect of the genre points to a limitation of using editorial pages; that is, the middle ground position is most likely less represented than opinions that are more firmly positioned on either side of a debate. We wish to acknowledge Susan Gabel for pointing out this limitation.

Chapter 4

1. This image also evokes the 1940's antilynching anthem, "Strange Fruit." The lyrics, written by a Jewish schoolteacher from the Bronx, were made famous by singer Billie Holiday in 1939: "Southern trees bear a strange fruit/Blood on the leaves and blood at the root/ Black body swinging in the southern breeze/Strange fruit hanging from poplar trees." This image was also borrowed by author Lillian Smith for her controversial novel by the same name, published in 1944.

2. Mainstream presses from which we selected images included *New York Times, Atlanta (Journal &) Constitution,* and *Washington Post.* Images from the independent Black presses included *Chicago Defender* and *Richmond Afro-American.* We also used images reprinted in *Southern School News* from *Greensboro Daily News, Nashville Banner, Memphis Commercial Appeal, Richmond Times Dispatch,* and *Minneapolis Tribune.*

3. Although African Americans were theoretically given the right to vote in 1868 with the passage of the 14th Amendment, that right was neither encouraged nor ensured until the *Voting Rights Act* of 1965. In addition, women did not have the right to vote until 1920.

4. Admittedly, to assert that there are no absolutes is a postmodernist paradox. The very act of asserting that there are no absolutes is itself an absolutism.

5. See Guglielmo and Salerno's (2003) edited text, *Are Italians White: How Race is Made in America,* which explores how Italian immigrants negotiated available racial hierarchies in order to assert and claim Whiteness.

6. We had hoped to do a similar reading of editorial cartoons depicting inclusion, but we were not able to find any such cartoons in the newspaper sources we researched. Instead, we use these images as a means to help understand the possible connection between representations of disability and justifications for segregated schooling in the "Lesson Learned" section of this chapter.

7. Particularly in the beginning of our data collection we may have missed some cartoons because we were focusing more on editorials and letters to the editor. Because we could not find any parallel cartoons on inclusion, initially we planned to use only a few cartoons as chapter heads or to illustrate some of the major themes of the book. After collecting a few dozen of these images, however, we decided that they warranted their own analysis and began a more careful search of cartoons.

8. The historic 1939 film, based on the novel by Margaret Mitchell, was set on a cotton plantation in North Georgia during the Civil War era through Reconstruction.

9. Of course, this symbolism also relies on sexist notions of femininity, such that we do not have to be told to read this woman as ignorant, immature, and vain.

10. This reading is consistent with the many proposals by southern communities to form groups to "study" the situation after the *Brown* decision. Often what was being studied was not how to best implement desegregation orders, but rather how to delay or avoid those orders. The fact that this cartoon was reprinted from a Black newspaper invites a more critical reading of the images.

11. The "Southern Segregation Manifesto" is a reference to "The Southern Manifesto," a document written in March of 1956 in response to *Brown* (reprinted in Martin, 1998). Senators Strom Thurmond (South Carolina) and Harry Byrd (Virginia) are credited with writing and disseminating the document, which was signed by 96 other members of the U.S. Congress. The manifesto, which called for the use of "all lawful means" to reverse *Brown* helped to "fuel the White racist counterinsurgency against the evolving southern Black civil rights" movement (Martin, 1998, p. 219).

12. We would like to thank reference librarians and interlibrary loan staff at the following libraries: the New York Public Library, the Schomburg Center for Research on Black Culture, Teachers College Millbank Library, Columbia University Butler Library, and Syracuse University Main Library. There are a limited number of indexes for the Black press, but we consulted the Black Newspaper Index, as well as the Ernest D. Kaiser Index to Black Resources (available at the Schomburg) to locate articles about inclusion in the Black press. Because the coverage of *Brown* was so widespread, our search related to *Brown* was much more straightforward, involving simply a manual search of each paper on microfiche or microfilm.

13. Although we had hoped to reprint all of the images we describe, the permission fees for the *Chicago Defender* were exorbitant (ten times higher than fees charged by other papers), which made these images inaccessible to us. We regret not being able to include these images and hope that the *Defender* will change its policy in the future.

14. Several desegregation cases came before the Supreme Court in 1952 and were later combined to form *Brown*. The court delayed ruling on what was sure to be a volatile decision and scheduled a date of October 1953 to rehear the cases. The justices instructed the attorneys to come prepared to answer several questions, including the intent of the framers of the 14th Amendment to the Constitution, particularly with regard to schools. The date was then changed to December 7, 1953.

15. Several cartoons (both in the Black and White press) featured books. Perhaps the idea that schools were social spaces was more threatening than conceiving schools as places where knowledge was imparted. Even in this image the student is presented as a lone graduate, not a member of an integrated graduating class.

16. This is reminiscent of school officials (see chapter 3) whose opposition to integration was often framed as not having anything to do with race or racial differences between students.

Chapter 5

1. Because of the various delay tactics employed after schools were ordered to desegregate, many schools remained segregated long after *Brown* was passed in 1954. Moreover, many schools outside of the South were also segregated and resegregated due to housing patterns, gerrymandered school district boundaries, and the failure of schools to institute bussing across district lines in large metropolitan areas.
2. In using the term *normate,* Garland-Thomson (1997a) denaturalizes the "unmarked" category of normalcy and signals its constructed nature (p. 8).
3. We borrow this idea from Adrienne Rich (1980) who first introduced the idea of compulsory heterosexuality to interrogate the "naturalness" of heterosexuality.
4. We collected editorial pages from the following papers: *New York Times, Atlanta Journal & Constitution, Washington Post, Atlanta Daily World, Richmond Afro-American, Philadelphia Tribune, Chicago Defender,* and *Southern School News.* This range of papers represents both White and Black independent presses from both the North and South. Data on desegregation were collected between the years 1953–1956, and data on inclusion ranged from 1987–2002. In total our data set included over 1000 photocopied pages and over 100 editorial cartoons. For a more detailed explanation of our data collection and analysis procedures, please see the introduction.
5. Ironically, as we were writing this chapter, the U.S. Senate was voting on a proposal to amend the constitution to protect the institution of marriage from gay and lesbian couples, which would allegedly weaken the bonds between heterosexual couples. Here, too, the institution of marriage is characterized as vulnerable to an attack by those who are excluded.

Chapter 6

1. Mary McLeod Bethune (1875–1955), daughter of former slaves, was an influential educator. She founded a college for African American girls in Florida called the Daytona Normal and Industrial Institute for Negro Girls, which later became Bethune-Cookman College. She was a leader in the Black women's club movement and served as the president of the National Association of Colored Women and the vice president of the NAACP. As the director of the Division of Negro Affairs, she became the first Black woman to head a federal agency. She also wrote a column in the *Chicago Defender* from 1948 to 1955.
2. Lillian Smith (1897–1966), born in Florida, was a frequent contributor to the *New York Times, Nation, Life, Saturday Review* and *New Republic,* as well as *Chicago Defender.* She used her fiction and nonfiction writing as a platform to decry the damaging consequences of segregation and White supremacy. In 1944, she wrote the controversial novel, *Strange Fruit,* which chronicled an interracial love affair and the resulting lynching of a Black man in a small Southern town. The novel sold over three million copies and was translated into 14 languages. Smith also published a series of essays in *Killers of the Dream,* and a quarterly magazine with her lifelong companion, Paula Snelling.
3. Langston Hughes (1902–1967) was born into an abolitionist family in Missouri. He attended Columbia University and graduated from Lincoln University in 1929. Hughes published his first book in 1926 and proceeded to publish 16 books of poems, two nov-

els, three collections of short stories, 20 plays, among his many other publications. Early in his career he traveled widely, but returned to Harlem and became an important voice in the *Harlem Renaissance*. He wrote a humorous column in the *Chicago Defender* as well as a series of books based on a character he called Jess B. Simple.

4. M. M. Bakhtin was born near Moscow in 1895 and came of age during the turbulent political and cultural upheavals in Russia during the first two decades of the 20th century. Bakhtin's adult life spanned the Russian Revolution and Civil War, the rise of Stalinism, the German invasion into the Soviet Union, the Cold War, and the years of Khrushchev and Brezhnev. Several of his most widely read works were written while in political exile and could not be published until the 1960s. Bakhtin's writing spans literary genres as well as philosophical, textual, and social analyses. Despite the proliferation and influence of his writing, Bakhtin spent most of his life without an academic position in the Russian academy or any source of steady income until after the Second World War. Bakhtin lived with osteomyelitus (an inflammatory disease of the bones) and had his right leg amputated as a result. Among Bakhtin's publications are three disputed texts that were authored by Voloshinov and Medvedev, associates of Bakhtin and members of the "Bakhtin circle." When authorship of these texts came into question by scholars who contended that the texts were actually written by Bakhtin, he refused to settle the matter, and scholars continue to debate the authorship of these texts. As Bakhtin was a scholar most known for dialogue, it is somewhat ironic that so much attention has been paid to attributing these texts to a solitary author.

5. This letter is particularly troubling coming so close to the brutal lynching of Emmett Till that same summer (August 28, 1955) in Money, Mississippi. The fact that a letter as threatening as this is signed by its author is also instructive: the author is completely secure in his cloak of White supremacy, perhaps even proud to have this letter attributable to him. Moreover, as the subsequent trial of Emmett Till would demonstrate, he has nothing to worry about in terms of legal retribution even if he makes good on his threat.

6. Although the meaning of the sentence is clear, this particular word was illegible in our photocopy.

7. Of course, a republican form of government is *not* a direct democracy in which everyone directly votes and a majority rules. A republic, instead, is a system of government like the U.S. where individuals elect representatives who then vote on their behalf.

Chapter 7

1. After writing this chapter we came across an essay by Sleeter, Gutierrez, New and Takata (1995) that also drew an analogy to "The Emperor's New Clothes." (In J. L.Kincheloe, & S. R. Steinberg (Eds.). *Thirteen questions: Reframing education's conversation* (pp. 181–190). New York: Peter Lang.

2. The data are not sufficiently disaggregated to determine if there are within-group differences among Asian students based on social class, immigrant status, etc. We also do not know what impact ESL (English as a Second Language) class participation has on referral rates.

3. "Least restrictive environment" refers to the placement of students with disabilities in special or separate schools or classrooms only when the nature or the severity of the

disability is such that even with the use of supplementary aids and services, the general education setting cannot satisfactorily meet the child's needs. The obvious goal of LRE is to educate children to the maximum extent possible with nondisabled children, while still providing all of the necessary aids and services that the child is entitled to receive. The idea that schools are responsible for determining the appropriate placement for students with disabilities parallels the pupil placement boards that were instituted after the *Brown* decision. In effect, pupil placement boards were designed to maintain segregation, not to implement desegregation.

4. Karagiannis (2000) calls attention to the correlation between the number of students labeled as disabled and the rates of imprisonment. He charges that schools are serving as "places of pre incarceration for disadvantaged students" (p. 115). Although some may find his characterization of schools as pipelines to prisons harsh, his sentiments do strike a chord. In an interview, Reid Lyons revealed that some states even use third grade reading scores to estimate spending for prison buildings (Sicker, 2002).

5. Although we know it as *Brown,* it was really a collective of five different cases, bringing together plaintiffs from Prince Edward County, Virginia, the District of Columbia, Wilmington, Delaware, and Topeka, Kansas.

Chapter 8

1. For example, similar battles were waged by Chinese Americans 30 years before *Brown,* and by Mexican Americans in California in the 1940s (Patton & Mondale, 2001).

2. For an excellent Web-based resource for teachers who want to include Disability Studies in the curriculum, see *Disability Studies for Teachers* at http://www.disabilitystudies-forteachers.org/. The Website includes lesson plans, links to educational resources and materials, and essays on differentiated instruction and disability studies. The project is sponsored by the Center on Human Policy at Syracuse University.

3. The phrase "Eyes on the Prize" is taken from the PBS series of the same name, documenting America's civil rights years, 1954–1965. See also the companion volume, *Eyes on the Prize: America's civil rights years, 1954–1965,* edited by Juan Williams (1987).

REFERENCES

A citizen from Louisiana. (1955, January). [Letter to the editor]. *Southern School News*, p. 1.

A Texas citizen. (1955, January 6). *Southern School News*, p. 1.

All of our children are 'gifted.' (1995, June 12). *Atlanta Constitution*, p. 8A.

Allan, J. (1999). *Actively seeking inclusion: Pupils with special needs in mainstream schools*. Philadelphia: Falmer Press.

American Association of Mental Retardation/Association of Retarded Citizens (2002). Policy Statement on Inclusion. Washington DC: Author.

Andrews, J. E., Carnine, D. W., Couthino, M. J., Edgar, E. B., Forness, S. R., Fuchs, L. S., Jordan, D., Kauffman, J. M., Patton, J. M., Paul, J., Rosell, J., Rueda, R., Schiller, E., Skrtic, T., & Wong, J. (2000). Perspective: Bridging the special education divide. *Remedial and Special Education*, 21 (5), 258–260.

Another Negro father. (1954, May 22). [Letter to the editor]. *Atlanta Constitution*, p. 4.

Arkansas Gazette [excerpt]. (1955, June). *Southern School News*, p. 8.

Arnold, M. & Lassmann, M. E. (2003). Overrepresentation of minority students in special education. *Education*, 124 (2), 230–236.

Artiles, A. J., Rueda, R., Salazar, J. J., & Higareda, I. (2002). English-language learner representation in special education in California urban school districts. In D. J. Losen & G. Orfield (Eds.), *Racial inequity in special education* (pp. 117–136). Cambridge, MA: Harvard Education Press.

Association for Persons with Severe Handicaps. (1993). *Resolution on inclusive education*. Baltimore: Author.

Ayres, W. C. (2004, April). Developing communities of practice for social justice: Infusion, inquiry, chismes and praxis (Discussant). American Educational Research Association, San Diego, California.

Backer, D. (n.d.). A brief history of political cartoons. Retrieved May 22, 2003 from http://xcroads.virginia.edu/~MA96/PUCK/part1.html.

Baker, B. (2002). The hunt for disability: The new eugenics and the normalization of school children. *Teachers College Record, 104* (4), 663–703.

Bakhtin, M. M. (1936/1984). *Rabelais and his world*. Bloomington: Indiana University Press.

Bakhtin, M. M. (1986). The problem of speech genres. In C. Emerson & M. Holquist (Eds.), *Speech genres and other late essays* (pp. 60–102). Austin: University of Texas Press.

Baird, D. (2002, February 9). Integrating disabled students. *Los Angeles Times,* p. 23.

Banks, C. M., & Banks, J. A. (1997). Reforming schools in a democratic pluralistic society. *Educational Policy, 11* (2), 183–193.

Banks, J. A. (1994). Transforming the mainstream curriculum. *Educational Leadership, 51* (8), 4–8.

Banks, J. A. (1995). The historical reconstruction of knowledge about race: Implications for transformative teaching. *Educational Researcher, 24* (2), 15–25.

Banks, J. A. (1999). Multicultural education in the new century. *School Administrator, 56* (6), 8–10.

Banks, J. A. (2001). Citizenship education and diversity: Implications for teacher education. *Journal of Teacher Education, 52* (1), 5–16.

Banks, J. A. (2002). Race, knowledge construction, and education in the USA: Lessons from history. *Race, Ethnicity, and Education, 5* (1), 7–27.

Barker, J. (1991, November 27). Where the disabled do best [Letter to the editor]. *Washington Post,* p. A16.

Barnes, C., Mercer, G., & Shakespeare, T. (1999). *Exploring disability: A sociological introduction*. Malden, MA: Polity.

Barrett, J. D. (1955 December 2). Segregation helps Negro in Business. *Atlanta Constitution*, p.4.

Barthes, R. (1972). *Mythologies*. New York: Hill & Wang.

Barthes, R. (1977). *Image, music, text*. New York: Hill & Wang.

Battle over special education. (2001, December 12). *New York Times,* p. A30.

Bauman, H. D. L. (1997). Toward a poetics of vision, space, and the body. In L. Davis (Ed.), *The disability studies reader* (pp. 315–331). New York: Routledge.

Baynton, D. C. (2001). Disability and the justification of inequality in American history. In P. K. Longmore & L. Umansky (Eds.). *The new disability history: American perspectives* (pp. 33–57). New York: New York University Press.

Bell, D. A., Jr. (1992). *Faces at the bottom of the well: The permanence of racism*. New York: Basic Books.

Belluck, P. (1996, November 6). A plan to revamp special education. *New York Times,* p. A1.

Benning, V. (1997, July 10). Court backs decision to remove autistic boy from regular class; Suit against Loudon schools is thrown out on appeal. *Washington Post,* p. D1.

Berger, J. (1972). *Ways of seeing*. London: British Broadcast Corporation and Penguin Books.

Bethune, M. M. (1955, March 19). Ignorance, root of prejudice, is serious foe of democratic living. *The Chicago Defender,* p. 9.

Bigelow, B. (1999). Why standardized tests threaten multiculturalism. *Educational Leadership, 56* (7), 37–40.

Biklen, D. P. (1988). The myth of clinical judgment. *Journal of Social Issues, 44* (1), 127–140.

Bina, M. (1995). Mainstreaming, schools for the blind, and full inclusion: What shall the future of education for blind children be? In J. M. Kauffman & D. P. Hallahan (Eds.), *The illusion of full inclusion: A comprehensive critique of a current special education bandwagon* (pp. 269–273). Austin, TX: ProEd.

Borland, J. H. (1996). Gifted education and the threat of irrelevance. *Journal for the Education of the Gifted, 19,* 129–147.

Brantlinger, E. (1997). Using ideologies: Cases of non-recognition of the politics of research and practice in special education. *Review of Educational Research, 67* (4), 425–459.

Brantlinger, E. (2003). *Dividing classes: How the middle class negotiates and rationalizes school advantage.* New York: Routledge/Falmer.

Brantlinger, E. (2004). Confounding the needs and confronting the norm. *Journal of Learning Disabilities, 37* (6), 490–499.

Brasch-Librach, P. (1992, June 16). Inclusion: Mixing pupils who have handicaps with others helps many to improve. *St. Louis Post-Dispatch,* p. 1.

Bratcher, J. (1988, August 18). Ruling spurs school probe of disabled bias. *Chicago Defender,* p. 6.

Brett, J. (2002a, May 30). Kids who bring uncommon gifts: Students learn from peers with special needs. *Atlanta Journal and Constitution,* p. 1JF.

Brett, J. (2002b). The experience of disability from the perspective of parents of children with profound impairments: Is it time for an alternative model of disability. *Disability and Society, 17* (7), 825–843.

Britzman, D. P. (2000). "The question of belief": Writing poststructural ethnography. In E. A. St. Pierre & W. S. Pillow (Eds.), *Working the ruins: Feminist poststructuralist theory and methods in education* (pp. 27–40). New York: Routledge.

Brown, M. (1955, May 21). Letter to the editor. *New York Times,* p. 16.

Brown v. Board of Education (1954). 347 U.S. 483.

Buck v. Bell (1927). 274 U.S. 200.

Buckley, S. (1993, June 12). Making room in the mainstream: Down's syndrome student turns trepidation to triumph in Potomac. *Washington Post,* p. A1.

Campbell, J. & Oliver, M. (1996). *Disability politics: Understanding our past, changing our future.* New York: Routledge.

Carey, A. (2003). Beyond the medical model: A reconsideration of "feeblemindedness," citizenship, and eugenic restrictions. *Disability & Society, 19* (4), 411–430.

Carr, M. (1993). A mother's thoughts on inclusion. *Journal of Learning Disabilities, 26* (9), 590–592.

Carrier, J. (1986). *Learning disability: Social class and the construction of inequality in American education.* New York: Greenwood Press.

Castro, A. N. (1954, July 16). Says segregation dangers democracy. *Atlanta Daily World,* p. 4.

Charleston, W. V. (1955, June). *Southern School News,* p. 8.

Christensen, C. & Rizvi, F. (Eds.). (1996). *Disability and the dilemmas of education and justice.* Philadelphia: Open University Press.

Clarke, I. (2001, May 8). Rewriting special education rules: Is the debate about rules or children? *Michigan Chronicle,* p. A7.

Clarke, K. & Holquist, M. (1984). *Mikhail Bakhtin.* Cambridge, MA: Harvard University Press.

Clotfelter, C. T. (2004). *After Brown: The rise and retreat of school desegregation.* Princeton, NJ: Princeton University Press.

Collins, K. M. (2003). *Ability profiling and school failure: One child's struggle to be seen as competent*. Mahwah, NJ: Lawrence Erlbaum.

Collins, P. H. (1991). *Black feminist thought: Knowledge, consciousness & the politics of empowerment*. New York: Routledge.

Collins, P. H. (1998). *Fighting words: Black women and the search for justice*. Minneapolis, MN: University of Minnesota Press.

Collins, P. H. (2000). *Black feminist thought: Knowledge, consciousness & the politics of empowerment* (2nd edition, revised). New York: Routledge.

Comment on Park decision. (1955, June). *Southern School News,* p. 16.

Confederate Democrat. (1954, June 8). [Letter to the editor]. *Atlanta Constitution*, p. 4.

Conroy, J. W. (1999). *Connecticut's special education labeling and displacement practices: Analysis of the ISSIS data base*. Unpublished report, Center for Outcome Analysis, Rosemont, PA.

Cornell, A. E. (1954, October 29). Integration will work just like prohibition. *Atlanta Constitution*, p. 4.

"Corrections." (1994, July 26). *New York Times*, p. 2.

Council for Exceptional Children. (1993). *CEC policy on inclusive schools and community settings*. Reston, VA: Author.

Council for Learning Disabilities. (1993). Concerns about the full inclusion of students with learning disabilities in regular education classrooms. *Learning Disability Quarterly, 16*, 126.

Court order gets varied reaction from region's newspapers. (1955, June). *Southern School News*, pp. 8–9.

C. P. T. (1955, Aug. 22). Pulse of the public. *Atlanta Constitution*, p. 4.

Crenshaw, K. W. (1998). Color blindness, history and the law. In W. Lubiano (Ed.), *The house that race built: Original essays by Toni Morrison, Angela Davis, Cornel West and others on Black Americans and politics in America today* (pp. 280–288). New York: Vintage.

Crenshaw, K. W., Gotanda, N., Peller, G., & Thomas, K. (Eds.). (1995). *Critical race theory: The key writings that formed the movement*. New York: The New Press.

Cumming, D. (2003, April). How the South covered desegregation. *The American Editor*. Retrieved August 25, 2004 from http://www.asne.org/index.cmf?ID=4572.

Danforth, S. (2002, June). *What happens when "bad" kids become a medical problem?: A historical review of the critical literature on attention deficit hyperactivity disorder*. Paper presented at Second City Conference on Disability Studies in Education on Education, Social Action, and the Politics of Disability at National-St. Louis University, Chicago.

Danforth, S. (2004). The "postmodern" heresy in special education: A sociological analysis. *Mental Retardation, 42* (6), 445–458.

Danforth, S. & Smith, T. J. (2005). *Engaging troubling students: A constructivist approach*. Thousand Oaks, CA: Corwin Press.

Darke, P. (1998). Understanding cinematic representations of disability. In T. Shakespeare (Ed.), *The disability studies reader: Social science perspectives* (pp. 187–216). London: Kissell.

Darling-Hammond, L. (2003, February 16). Standards and assessments: Where we are and what we need. *Teachers College Record*. Retrieved from http://www.tcrecord.org. ID Number: 11109.

Davies, B. (2000). *A body of writing*. Lanham, MD: AltaMira.

Davis, L. J. (1995). *Enforcing normalcy: Disability, deafness and the body*. London: Verso.

Davis, O. L. (2004). Fifty years past . . . and still miles to go: Curriculum development and the *Brown v. Board of Education. Journal of Curriculum and Supervision, 19* (2), 95–98.

Davis, R. H. (1954, June 17). Professor in Liberia should tell students of high living standard of American Negro. *Atlanta Constitution,* p. 4.

de Beauvoir, S. (1952/1989). *The second sex* (H. M. Parshley, Trans.). New York: Vintage.

DeCuir, J. T. & Dixson, A. D. (2004). "So when it comes out, they aren't that surprised that it is there": Using critical race theory as a tool of analysis of race and racism in education. *Educational Researcher, 33* (5), 26–31.

DeFord, S. (1998, February 8). Inclusive classrooms. *Washington Post,* p. W8.

Delgado, R. & Stefancic, J. (2001). *Critical race theory: An introduction.* New York: New York University Press.

Delgado-Bernal, D. (2002). Critical race theory, Latino critical theory, and critical raced-gendered epistemologies: Recognizing students of color as holders and creators of knowledge. *Qualitative Inquiry, 8* (1), 105–126.

Delpit, L. (1995). *Other people's children: Cultural conflict in the classroom.* New York: New Press.

Diana v. California State Board of Education. (1970). No. C-70, RFT, Dist. Ct. No. Cal.

Dolan DNA Learning Center, Cold Spring Harbor Laboratory. *Image archive on the American eugenics movement.* Cold Spring Harbor, NY: Author. Retrieved August 30, 2004 from http://www.eugenicsarchive.org/eugenics/ [image archive].

Dorn, S., Fuchs, D., & Fuchs, L. (1996). A historical perspective of special education reform. *Theory into Practice,* 35 (1), 12–19.

Drake, St. C. (1956, March 18). Letter to the editor. *New York Times,* p. 10E.

Dunn, L. M. (1968). Special education for the mildly retarded: Is much of it justifiable? *Exceptional Children, 35,* 5–22.

Dwyer, J. (2003). Disease, deformity, and defiance: Writing the language of immigration law and the eugenics movement on the immigrant body. *Mellus, 28* (1), 105–121.

Dyer, R. (2002). The matter of whiteness. In P. S. Rothenburg (Ed.), *White privilege* (pp. 9–13). Cranbury, NJ: Worth Publishers.

East Tennessee views on school issue. (1956, July). *Southern School News,* p. 7.

Editorial excerpts from the nation's press on segregation ruling. (1954, May 19). *New York Times,* p. 20.

Education of All Handicapped Children Act. (1975). P.L. 94–142, U.S.C.

Ellison, R. (1952). *Invisible man.* New York: Random House.

Emerson, C. & Holquist, M. (1986). Speech Genres & Other Late Essays. Austin, TX: University of Texas Press. (V. W. McGee, trans).

Equal education for all. (1954, May 19). *Washington Post,* p. 14.

Estrada, L. (1996, September 10). Parents' suit seeks to return autistic son to Loudoun Schools. *Washington Post,* p. B05.

Evans, S. (1996, March 17). Opening the door: Schools trying for 'inclusion' in line for extra state aid. *Atlanta Constitution,* p. 4H.

Expand inclusion in proper way. (2002, January 20). *Chicago Daily Herald,* p. 14.

Family's battle. (1993, July 28). [Editorial]. *New York Times,* p. 5.

Faragoa, J. (1999, June 27). Essay on special education used false pretenses. *New York Times,* p. 15.

Fear and obsession pose worst integration danger. (1955, September 30). *Atlanta Constitution.* p. 4.

Ferguson, D. L. (1995). The real challenge of inclusion: Confessions of a "rabid inclusionist." *Phi Delta Kappan,* 77 (4), 281–287.

Ferguson, P. M. (2001). *On infusing disability studies into the general curriculum. On point: Brief discussions of critical issues.* Washington, DC: Special Education Programs (ED/OSERS).

Ferguson, R. F. & Mehta, J. (2004). An unfinished journey: The legacy of *Brown* and the narrowing of the achievement gap. *Phi Delta Kappan, 85* (9), 656–669.

Ferri, B. A. (2004). Interrupting the discourse: A response to Reid & Valle. *Journal of Learning Disabilities, 37* (6), 509–515.

Ferri, B. A., & Connor, D. J. (2004). Special education and the subverting of Brown. *Journal of Gender, Race, & Justice, 8* (1), 57–74.

Ferri, B. A., Connor, D., Solis, S., Valle, J., & Volpitta, D. (2005). Mediating discourses of disability: Teachers with LD revising the script. *Journal of Learning Disabilities, 38* (1), pp. 62–78.

Ferri, D. A. (2002, January 1). Letter to the editor. *Plain Dealer,* p. B8.

Fierros, E. G. & Conroy, J. W. (2002). Double jeopardy: An exploration of restrictiveness and race in special education. In D. J. Losen & G. Orfield (Eds.), *Racial inequity in special education* (pp. 39–70). Cambridge, MA: Harvard Education Press.

First year 'A success.' (1955, June). *Southern School News,* p. 10.

First year of desegregation is analyzed at school. (1956, February). *Southern School News,* p. 3.

Flanders, A. (1955, July 22). Georgians should not deny themselves basic personal freedom and principles. *Atlanta Constitution,* p. 4.

Fleischer, D. & Zames, F. (2001). *The disability rights movement: From charity to confrontation.* Philadelphia: Temple University Press.

Focus on Education. (1956, December). *Southern School News,* p. 8.

Ford, D. Y. (1998). The underrepresentation of minority students in special education: Problems and promises in recruitment and retention. *Journal of Special Education, 32* (1), 4–14.

Ford, J. W. (1954, October 9). Question of color. *Richmond Afro-American,* p. 4.

Foucault, M. (1980). *Power/Knowledge* New York: Pantheon Books.

Foucault, M. (1982). The subject and power. In H. Dreyfus & P. Rabinow (Eds.), *Michel Foucault: Beyond structuralism and hermeneutics* (pp. 208–226). Brighton: Harvester.

Foucault, M. (1990). *The history of sexuality: An introduction, Volume I.* New York: Vintage Books.

Foucault, M. (1994). *The birth of the clinic: An archaeology of medical perception.* New York: Vintage Books.

Foucault, M. (1995). *Discipline and punish: The birth of the prison.* New York: Vintage Books.

Franklin, B. M. (1987). The first crusade for learning disabilities: The movement for the education of backward children. In T. Popkewitz (Ed.), *The foundations of the school subjects* (pp. 190–209). London: Falmer.

Freeman, M. (1993). *Rewriting the self: History, memory, narrative.* New York: Routledge.

Fresh Thinking on Special Education. (1996, November 26). *New York Times,* p. A20.

Friend of the court. (1954, Nov. 26). *New York Times,* p. 28.

From Kinston, Tennessee. (1955, January 6). *Southern School News,* p. 1.

Fuchs, D., & Fuchs, L. (1995). Inclusive schools movement and the radicalization of special education reform. In J. M. Kauffman & D. P. Hallahan (Eds.), *The illusion of full inclusion: A comprehensive critique of a current special education bandwagon* (pp. 213–242). Austin, TX: ProEd.

Gabel, S. (2001, April). *What is Disability Studies?* Paper presented at the Membership Meeting of the Disability Studies in Education SIG of AERA, Seattle, WA.

Gabel, S. (2002). Some conceptual problems with critical pedagogy. *Critical Inquiry, 32* (2), 177–201.

Gabel, S. & Danforth, S. (2002). Disability studies in education: Seizing the moment of opportunity. *Disability, Culture and Education, 1* (1), 1–3.

Gallagher, D. J. (1998). The scientific knowledge base of special education: Do we know what we think we know? *Exceptional Children, 64* (4), 493–502.

Gallagher, D. J. (2001). Neutrality as a moral standpoint: Conceptual confusion and the full inclusion debate. *Disability and Society, 16* (5), 637–654.

Gallagher, D. J. (2004). Preface. In D. J. Gallagher, L. Heshusius, R. P. Iano, & T. M. Skrtic, *Challenging orthodoxy in special education: Dissenting voices* (pp. vii–x) Denver, CO: Love Publishing.

Gannon, S. (2002). *Writing memory.* Unpublished doctoral dissertation, Queensland, Australia, James Cook University.

Gardner, H. (1983). *Frames of mind: The theory of multiple intelligences.* New York: Basic Books.

Garland, R. (1995). *The eye of the beholder: Deformity and disability in the Graeco-Roman world.* Ithaca, NY: Cornell University Press.

Garland-Thomson, R. (1997a). *Extraordinary bodies: Figuring physical disability in American culture and literature.* New York: Columbia University Press.

Garland-Thomson, R. (1997b). Integrating disability studies into the existing curriculum: The example of 'Women and Literature' at Howard University. *Radical Teacher, 47,* 15–21.

Garland-Thomson, R. (2002). The politics of staring: Visual rhetorics of disability in popular photography. In S. L. Snyder, B. J. Bruggemann, & R. Garland-Thomson (Eds.), *Disability studies: Enabling the humanities* (pp. 56–75). New York: Modern Language Association.

Garrett, R. (1954, December 18). Letter to the editor. *Richmond Afro-American,* p. 4.

Gartner, A. & Lipsky, D. K. (1987). Beyond special education: Toward a quality system for all students. *Harvard Educational Review, 57* (4), 367–395.

Georgia editors view ruling as judicial common sense. (1955, June 3). *Atlanta Constitution,* p. 4.

Georgia is building and equalizing schools. (1954, March 30). *Atlanta Constitution,* p. 4.

Georgia v. U.S. (1954, November, 5). *New York Times,* p. 20.

Gerrard, L. C. (1996). Inclusive education: An issue of social justice. *Equity & Excellence in Education, 27* (1), 58–67.

Gest, J. (2002, February 9). Integrating disabled students. *Los Angeles Times,* p. 23.

Gilroy, P. (2000). *Against race: Imagining political culture beyond the color line.* Cambridge, MA: (Belknap Press) Harvard University Press.

Gledhill, C. (1997). Genre and gender: The case of soap opera. In S. Hall (Ed.), *Representation: Cultural representations and signifying practices* (pp. 337–386). London: Sage.

Globetti, E., Globetti, G., Brown, C. L., & Smith, R. E. (1993). Social interaction and multiculturalism. *NASPA, 30* (3), 209–218.

Godfrey, N. (1999, June 18). Resegregation in the schools hurts all students. Letter to the editor. *New York Times,* p. A34.

Goertzel, T. (n.d.). The myth of the bell curve. Retrieved November 11, 2004 from http://www.crab.rutgers.edu/~goertzel/normalcurve.htm [article].

Goffman, E. (1963). *Stigma: Notes on the management of spoiled identity.* New York: Simon & Schuster.

Goodman, W. (1994, September 7). Disabled: Public or special school? *New York Times,* p. C18.

Goodman, W. (1996, May 11). The problems of special education [Television review]. *New York Times,* p. 44.

Gordon, B. M. (1990). The necessity of African-American epistemology for educational theory and practice. *Journal of Education, 1* (3), 88–106.

Gordon, M. M. & Roche, J. P. (1954, January 3). Enforcing racial segregation. *New York Times,* p. E6.

Gordon, W. (1954, May 18). For the Negro, there will be no violence. *Atlanta Daily World,* p. 4.

Gould, S. J. (1996). *The mismeasure of man.* New York: W. W. Norton.

Grady, C. (1989, December 21). Students speak out: Is 'mainstreaming' mentally and physically handicapped students a good idea? *Washington Post,* p. M6.

Greene, M. (1992). The passions of pluralism: Multiculturalism and the expanding community. *Journal of Negro Education, 61* (3), 250–261.

Greenville News (excerpt). (1955, June). *Southern School News,* p. 9.

Gregory, G. H. & Chapman, C. (2002). *Differentiated instructional strategies: One size doesn't fit all.* Thousand Oaks, CA: Sage.

Guglielmo, J. & Salerno, S. (2003). *Are Italians white? How race is made in America.* New York: Routledge.

Guskey, T. R. & Huberman, M. (Eds.). (1995). *Professional development in education.* New York: Teachers College Press.

Hahn, H. (1997). New trends in disability studies: Implications for educational policy. In D. K. Lipsky & A. Gartner (Eds.), *Inclusion and school reform: Transforming America's classrooms* (pp. 315–328). Baltimore: Paul H. Brookes.

Hall, S. (1997a). The work of representation. In S. Hall (Ed.), *Representation: Cultural representations and signifying practices* (pp. 13–74). London: Sage, in association with Open University.

Hall, S. (1997b). The spectacle of the 'other'. In S. Hall (Ed.), *Representation: Cultural representations and signifying practices* (pp. 223–290). London: Sage.

Hall, S. (1997c). Introduction (Ed.). *Representation: Cultural representations and signifying practices* (pp. 1–12). London: Sage, in association with Open University.

Halliburton, C. D. (1955a, April 19). Fear of intermarriage not supported by the evidence. *The Philadelphia Tribune,* p. 4.

Halliburton, C. D. (1955b, July 16). Power of superiority myth waned much, but not dead. *Philadelphia Tribune,* p. 4.

Hamilton, P. (1997). Representing the social: France and Frenchness in post-war humanist photography. In S. Hall (Ed.), *Representation: Cultural representations and signifying practices* (pp. 75–150). London: Sage.

Hancock, D. G. B. (1953, December 12). Segregation has failed in both of major objectives. *The Philadelphia Tribune,* p. 4.

Hancock, D. G. B. (1954, November 13). Troublesome struggle seen in desegregation move. *The Philadelphia Tribune,* p. 4.

Hand is their man. (1954, September 14). *The Chicago Defender,* p. 9.

Haney-Lopez, I. A. (1996). *White by law: The legal construction of race.* New York: New York University Press.

Harry, B. (1992). *Cultural diversity, families, and the special education system: Communication and empowerment.* New York: Teachers College Press.

Hartz, G. (2000, January 11). Inclusion or exclusion? It all depends. *Christian Science Monitor,* p. 13.

Haug, F. (1999). *Female sexualization: A collective work of memory.* New York: Verso.

Hayward, L. & Kane, J. (2000, June 16). Close the cupboards and all they stand for. *The Times Educational Supplement* [UK], p. 18.

Head, L., Head, A., Hall, M., & Hall, K. (1996, October 13). Fairfax's exclusive public schools. *Washington Post,* p. C8.

Hernandez, R. (1999, June 12). Under federal threat, Albany seeks to overhaul special education. *New York Times,* p. B1.

Herrnstein, R. J. & Murray, C. (1994). *The Bell Curve: Intelligence and class structure in American life.* New York: Simon & Schuster.

Heshusius, L. (2004). From creative discontent toward epistemological freedom in special education: Reflections on a 25-year journey. In D. J. Gallagher, L. Heshusius, R. P. Iano, & T. M. Skrtic. *Challenging orthodoxy in special education: Dissenting voices* (pp. 169–230). Denver, CO: Love Publishing.

Heubert, J. P. (2002). Disability, race, and high-stakes testing of students. In D. J. Losen & G. Orfield (Eds.), *Racial inequity in special education* (pp. 137–166). Cambridge, MA: Harvard Education Press.

Hochschild, J. L. (1984). *The new American dilemma: Liberal democracy and school desegregation.* New Haven, CT: Yale University Press.

Holladay, S. (1998, February 7). Learning-challenged kids shouldn't be in regular classrooms. *Roanoke Times & World News,* p. A7.

Hollander, E. D. (1954, May 30). Corning's school plan. *Washington Post,* p. 4.

Hollowell, D. L. (1955, April 2). GEA teacher vote termed selfish move. *Atlanta Constitution,* p. 4.

hooks, b. (1981). *Ain't I a Woman: Black women and feminism.* Boston: South End Press.

hooks, b. (1994). *Teaching to Transgress: Education as the practice of freedom.* New York: Routledge.

Hosp, J. L. & Reschly, D. J. (2004). Disproportionate representation of minority students in special education: Academic, demographic, and economic predictors. *Exceptional Children, 70* (2), 185–199.

Hubert, J. P. (2002). Disability, race, and high-stakes testing of students. In D. J. Losen & G. Orfield (Eds.), *Racial inequity in special education.* Cambridge, MA: Harvard Education Press.

Hughes, L. (1954, August 14). Simple casts a dark eye on that first day in school. *Chicago Defender,* p. 11.

Hunter, M. S. (1995, January 16). All children need to be able to compete. [Letter to the editor]. *Washington Post,* p. A22.

Huston, L. A. (1956, March 13). 92 Negroes act as principals. *New York Times,* p. 2C.

Imparato, A. J. (2001, January 28). Aid disabled students. *New York Times* (London Ed.), p. 14.

Individuals with Disabilities Education Act (IDEA). (1990). P.L. 101–476, 20, U.S.C. 1400 *et seq.*

Inson, P. (2000, July 21). Talkback. *Times Educational Supplement,* p. 33.

Integration seen as disadvantageous. (1954, May 29). *Atlanta Constitution,* p. 4.

Interview with Mr. Gibson (school board member). (1956, August). *Southern School News,* p. 14.

Irons, P. (2002). *Jim Crow's children: The broken promise of the Brown decision.* New York: Viking.

Jackson, E. O. (1954, July 4). The tip off. *Atlanta Daily World,* p. 4.

Jackson, G. (1956, March). Christian principle. *Southern School News,* p. 9.

Jacobs, J. (1999, January 31). Close to home. *The Washington Post,* p. B8.

Jacobson, L. (1993, September 29). Counting special kids in 'Inclusion' plan helps pupils learn from each other. *Atlanta Constitution,* p. J1.

Jacobson, L. (1994, May 9). Disabled kids moving into regular classrooms. 'Inclusion' is on, but critics call it unfair. *Atlanta Constitution,* p. C1.

Johnson, C. (2001, June 15). [Letter to the editor]. *San Francisco Chronicle,* p. 2.

Johnson, E. B. (1955, July 2). Not getting away. *Richmond Afro-American,* p. 4.

Johnson, H. J. (1954, July 5). Baptist minister says Atlanta pastor wrote wisely and kindly on voluntary segregation. *Atlanta Constitution,* p. 4.

Kamin, J. & Berger, B. (2001). Still waiting, after all these years. . . . Inclusion of children with special needs in New York City Public Schools (report). New York: Least Restrictive Environment Coalition.

Karagiannis, A. (2000). Soft disability in schools: Assisting or confining at risk children and youth? *Journal of Educational Thought, 34* (2), 113–134.

Kastens, T. Y. (1995, January 4). My children have a civil right to learn. *Washington Post,* p. A15.

Katsiyannis, A., Yell, M. L., & Bradley, R. (2001). Reflections on the 25th anniversary of the Individuals with Disabilities Education Act. *Remedial and Special Education, 22*(6), 324–334.

Kauffman, J. M. (1989). The regular education initiative as a Reagan-Bush education policy: A trickle-down theory of education of the hard to teach. *Journal of Special Education, 23* (3), 256–278.

Kauffman, J. M. (1999). Commentary: Today's special education and its messages for tomorrow. *Journal of Special Education, 32* (4), 244–254.

Kauffman, J. M. & Hallahan, D. P. (1995a). Toward a comprehensive delivery system for special education. In J. M. Kauffman & D. P. Hallahan (Eds.), *The illusion of full inclusion: A comprehensive critique of a current special education bandwagon* (pp. 157–191). Austin, TX: ProEd.

Kauffman, J. M. & Hallahan, D. P. (Eds.). (1995b) *The illusion of full inclusion: A comprehensive critique of a current special education bandwagon.* Austin, TX: ProEd.

Kelebay, Y. G. (1992). Multiculturalism on the mind. *Canadian Social Studies, 26* (3), 98–99.

Kelly, R. (1955, January 22). Letter to the editor. *Richmond Afro-American,* p. 4.

Kendall, G. & Wickham, G. (1999). *Using Foucault's methods.* Thousand Oaks, CA: Sage.

Kent, B. (1998, October 25). Special schools? Ballot issue could set tone. *New York Times,* p. 6.

King, M.L. (1963). Letter from Birmingham City Jail. Retrieved July 19, 2005 from http://teachingamericanhistory.org/library/index.asp?document=100 [letter].

Kliebard, H. M. (1995). *The struggle for the American curriculum: 1893–1958.* New York: Routledge/Falmer.

Kliebard, H. M. (1995). *The struggle for the American curriculum: 1893–1958* (2nd ed.). New York: Routledge.

Kliewer, C. & Drake, S. (1998). Disability, eugenics, and the current ideology of segregation: A modern moral tale. *Disability and Society, 13* (1), 95–111.

Kluth, P., Straut, D. M., & Biklen, D. P. (2003). *Access to academics for ALL students: Critical approaches to inclusive curriculum, instruction, and policy.* Mahwah, NJ: Lawrence Erlbaum.

Kohl, H. (1967). *36 Children.* New York: Signet.

Kozol, J. (1991). *Savage inequalities: Children in America's schools.* New York: Crown Publishers.

Kozol, J. (1995). *Amazing grace: The lives of children and the conscience of a nation.* New York: Harper Perennial.

Kremen, J. (1997, February 19). Mindless cuts in special education. [Letter to the editor]. *The Washington Post*, p. A20.

Krock, A. (1956, March 27). 'Gradual' in the frame of history: II. *New York Times*, p. 34.

Kudlick, C. J. (2003). Disability history: Why we need another "other." *American History Review*, *108* (3), 28 pages.

"Kudos to our exceptional children." (1987, May 7). *Chicago Defender*, p. 17.

Kwate, N. O. A. (2001). Intelligence testing and race: Intelligence or misorientation? Eurocentrism in the WISC-III. *Journal of Black Psychology*, *27* (2), 221–238.

Lahey, D. A. (1954, May 21). Integration in Georgia: Will ruling be "An Abstraction?" *The Washington Post*, p. 23.

Lane, H. (1995). The education of deaf children: Drowning in the mainstream and the sidestream. In J. M. Kauffman & D. P. Hallahan (Eds.), *The illusion of full inclusion: A comprehensive critique of a current special education bandwagon* (pp. 289–292). Austin, TX: ProEd.

Larry P. v. Riles. (1979 & 1986). C-71-2270 FRP. Dist. Ct.

Lather, P. (1997). Creating a multilayered text. In W. G. Tierney & Y. S. Lincoln (Eds.), *Representation and the text* (pp. 233–258). Albany: New York State University Press.

Lather, P. & Smithies, C. (1997). *Troubling the angels: Women living with HIV/AIDS*. Boulder, CO: Westview Press.

Lawrence, C. R., III. (1993). If he hollers let him go: Regulating racist speech on campus. In M. J. Matsuda, C. R. Lawrence, R. Delgado, & K. W. Crenshaw (Eds.), *Critical race theory, assaultive speech, and the first amendment* (pp. 53–88). Boulder, CO: Westview Press.

Learning Disabilities Association of America. (1993). Position paper on full inclusion of all students with learning disabilities in the regular education classroom. *Journal of Learning Disabilities*, *26* (9), 594.

Lehman, H. H. (1954, August 1). Much still to be done: Report shows progress on the civil rights front. *The Washington Post*, p. 6.

Leo, J. (1994, June 27). Mainstreaming's 'Jimmy's problem.' *U.S. News & World Report*, p. 22.

Lesko, N. (2001). *Act your age! A cultural construction of adolescence*. New York: Routledge/Falmer.

Levine, M. & Reed, M. (1999). *Developmental variation and learning disorders* (2nd ed.). Cambridge, MA: Educators Publishing Service.

Lewin, T. (1997, December 28). All in One: Where all doors are open for disabled students. *New York Times*, p. 1.

Librach, P. (1992, March 2). Inclusion: Mixing pupils who have handicaps with others helps many to improve. *St. Louis Post-Dispatch*, p. 1.

Lidchi, H. L. (1997). The poetics and politics of exhibiting other cultures. In S. Hall (Ed.), *Representation: Cultural representations and signifying practices* (pp. 151–222). London: Sage.

Lieberman, L. M. (1985). Special education and regular education: A merger made in heaven? *Exceptional Children*, *51* (6), 513–516.

Ligget, H. (1988). Stars are not born: An interpretative approach to the politics of disability. *Disability, Handicap and Society*, *3* (3), 101–104.

Linton, S. (1998). *Claiming disability*. New York University: New York University Press.

Lipsky, D. K. & Gartner, A. (1996). Inclusive education and school restructuring. In W. Stainback & S. Stainback (Eds.), *Controversial issues confronting special education: Divergent perspectives* (pp. 3–15). Boston: Allyn and Bacon.

Lipsky, D. K. & Gartner, A. (1997). *Inclusion and school reform: Transforming America's class-rooms*. Baltimore: Paul H. Brookes.

Lorde, A. (1984). Sister Outsider. Freedom, CA: Crossing Press.

Losen, D. J. & Orfield, G. (Eds.). (2002). *Racial inequity in special education*. Cambridge, MA: Harvard Education Press.

Losen, D. J. & Welner, K. G. (2002). Legal challenges to inappropriate and inadequate special education for minority children. In D. J. Losen & G. Orfield (Eds.), *Racial inequity in special education*. Cambridge, MA: Harvard Education Press.

MacMillan, D. L. & Reschly, D. J. (1998). Overrepresentation of minority students: The case for greater specificity or reconsideration of the variables examined. *Journal of Special Education, 32* (1), 15–24.

Malcomb, E. F., Jr. (1954, November 14). Letter to the editor. *Washington Post*, p. B4.

Malveaux, J. (2001). Sanger's legacy is reproductive freedom and racism. *Women's eNews*. Retrieved July 18, 2004 from http://www.womensenews.org/article.cfm/dyn/aid/618 [article].

Mandell, D. S., Listerud, J., Levy, S. E., & Pinto-Martin, J. A. (2002). Race differences in the age at diagnosis among Medicaid-eligible children with autism. *Journal of the American Academy of Child and Adolescent Psychiatry, 41* (12), 1447–1453.

Mariage, T., Paxton-Buursma, D. J., & Bouck, E. C. (2004). Interanimation: Repositioning possibilities in educational contexts. *Journal of Learning Disabilities, 37* (6), pp. 534–549.

Martin, E. W., Martin, R., & Terman, D. (1996). The legislative and litigation history of special education. *Special Education for Students with Disabilities, 6* (1), 25–39.

Martin, W. E. (1998). *Brown v. Board of Education: A brief history with documents*. Boston: Bedford St. Martin's.

Marx, K. (1959). *Capital: The communist manifesto and other writings*. New York: The Modern Library.

Mason, B. (1994, June 9). Special education: Warehousing black youths. New Pittsburgh Courier, p. A9.

Matsuda, M. J., Lawrence, C. R., Delgado, R., & Crenshaw, K. W. (Eds.). (1993). *Critical race theory, assaultive speech, and the first amendment*. Boulder, CO: Westview Press.

Maushard, M. (1994). Parents' views on success of inclusion. *Baltimore Sun*, p. 1B.

McMahon, E. (2002, May 1). Mainstreaming children. *New York Times*, p. 24.

McMullen, V. B. (1994, January 1). From the people [Letter to the Editor]. *St. Louis Post-Dispatch*, p. 7B.

Mickelson, R. A. (2001). Subverting Swann: First and second-generation segregation in the Charlotte-Mecklenburg schools. *American Educational Research Journal, 38* (2), 215–252.

Miller, K. (2002, February 16). Mainstreaming disabled kids isn't cheap, easy. *The Los Angeles Times*, p. B23.

Missouri. (1955, June). *Southern School News*, p. 19.

Mitchell, A. S. (1955, June 18). *Atlanta Constitution*, p. 4.

Mitchell, D. T. & Snyder, S. (2003). The eugenic Atlantic: Race, disability, and the making of an international eugenic science, 1800–1945. *Disability & Society, 18* (7), 843–864.

Mondale, S. & Patton, S. P. (Eds.). (2001). *School: The story of American public education*. Boston: Beacon Press.

Moore, S. & Hayasaki, E. (2002, February 1). The challenge of special education. *Los Angeles Times*, p. 1.

More time needed. (1956, June). *Southern School News*, p. 9.

Morgan, D. (1980, July 28). Blacks, whites, critical of Cleveland's desegregation effort. *Washington Post,* p. A6.

Morris, H. (1954, August 28). [Letter to the editor]. *Richmond Afro-American,* p. 4.

Morris, J. (1991) *Pride against Prejudice: Transforming attitudes to disability.* Philadelphia: New Society.

Morris, M. (2001). Multiculturalism as jagged walking. *Multicultural education, 8* (4), 2–8.

Morris, P. (Ed.). (1994). *The Bakhtin reader: Selected writings of Bakhtin, Medvedev, and Voloshinov.* New York: Edward Arnold.

Morrow, V. (1954, June 19). Letter to the editor. *Richmond Afro-American,* p. 4.

Mostert, M. P. (2002). Useless eaters: Disability as genocidal marker in Nazi Germany. *Journal of Special Education, 36* (3), 155–168.

National agenda for achieving better results for children with disabilities. (1993). *U.S. Department of Education.* pp. 6–8 [Forum briefing materials].

National Alliance of Black School Educators. (2002). *Addressing overrepresentation of African-American students in special education.* Arlington, VA: Council for Exceptional Children.

National Education Association. (2003). *Status of the American public school teacher, 2000–2001.* Washington, DC: NEA Research.

National Joint Committee on Learning Disabilities. (1993). A reaction to full inclusion: A reaffirmation of the right of students with learning disabilities to a continuum of services. *Journal of Learning Disabilities, 26* (9), 596.

National Parent Network on Disabilities. (1993). Statement on fully supported inclusive education. *Coalition Quarterly, 11* (3), 24.

Nealon, P. (1991, February 24). *Boston Globe,* p. 1.

Negro responsibility. (1957, February). *Southern School News,* p. 15.

Negro school dedication is educational milestone. (1954, February 1). *Atlanta Constitution,* p. 4.

Nothing to fear. (1956, February). *Southern School News,* p. 15.

Oakes, J. (1985). *Keeping track: How schools structure inequality.* Binghamton, NY: Vail-Ballou Press.

Oakes, J., Wells, A. S., Jones, M., & Datnow, A. (1997). Detracking: The social construction of ability, cultural politics, and resistance to reform. *Teachers College Record, 98* (3), 482–510.

Oakes, J & Lipton, M. (1999). Teaching to change the world. Boston, MA: McGraw-Hill.

O'Brien, T. (1955, July 2). Thurgood shocked? *Richmond Afro-American,* p. 4.

O'Keefe, D. (1994). Multiculturalism and cultural literacy. *International Journal of Social Education, 9* (1), 66–80.

Oliver, M. (1996). *Understanding disability: From theory to practice.* New York: St. Martin's Press.

O'Neil, J. (2002, April 14). Q & A: A better *IDEA. New York Times,* p. 17.

Opposing forces. (1955, April). *Southern School News,* p. 13.

Orfield, G. (2000). Policy and equity: Lessons of a third of a century of educational reforms in the U.S. In F. Reimer (Ed.), *Unequal schools, unequal chances: The challenge to equal opportunity in the Americas* (pp. 401–426). Cambridge: Harvard University Press.

Orfield, G. (2001). *Schools more separate: Consequences of a decade of resegregation.* Harvard Civil Rights Project. http://www.civilrightsproject.harvard.edu/research/deseg/separate_schools01.php.

Orfield, G. (2004). *Brown* misunderstood. In J. Anderson & D. N. Byrne (Eds.), *The unfinished agenda of Brown v. Board of Education* (pp. 153–164). Hoboken, NJ: Wiley.

Orfield, G. & Eaton, S. E. (1996). *Dismantling desegregation: The quiet reversal of Brown v. Board of Education*. New York: The New Press.

Osher, D., Woodruff, D., & Sims, A. E. (2002). Schools make a difference: The overrepresentation of African American youth in special education and the juvenile justice system. In D. J. Losen & G. Orfield (Eds.), *Racial inequity in special education* (pp. 93–116). Cambridge, MA: Harvard Education Press.

Oswald, D. P., Coutinho, M. J., & Best, A. M. (2002). Community and school predictors of overrepresentation of minority children in special education. In D. J. Losen & G. Orfield (Eds.), *Racial inequity in special education* (pp. 1–13). Cambridge, MA: Harvard Education Press.

Oswald, D. P., Coutinho, M. J., Best, A. M., & Singh, N. N. (1999). Ethnic representation in special education: The influence of school-related economic and demographic variables. *Journal of Special Education*, 4 (32), 194–206.

Out of step with trends. (1954, September 18). *Atlanta Daily World*, p. 6.

Parents protest plan to close two special-needs schools. (1991, March 7). *Washington Post*, p. A1.

Parochial school report given. (1955, June 8). *Southern School News*, p. 14.

Parrish, T. B. (2002). Racial disparities in the identification, funding, and provision of special education. In D. J. Losen & G. Orfield (Eds.), *Racial inequity in special education* (pp. 15–37). Cambridge, MA: Harvard Education Press.

Parrish, T. B. & Hikido, C. (1998). *Inequalities in public school district revenues* (NCES 98–210). Washington, DC: U.S. Department of Education, National Center for Education Statistics.

Patterson, J. T. (2001). *Brown v. Board of Education: A civil rights milestone and its troubled legacy*. New York: Oxford University Press.

Patton, J. M. (2004). The disproportionate representation of African Americans in special education: Looking behind the curtain for understanding & solutions. In S. Danforth & G. D. Taff (Eds.) *Crucial readings in special education* (pp. 164–172).Upper Saddle River, NJ: Pearson/Merrill.

Patton, S. & Mondale, S. (Producers) (2001). *School: The Story of American Public Education*. Chevy Chase, MD: Stone Lantern Films.

Paul, P. V. & Ward, M. (1996). Inclusion paradigms in conflict. *Theory Into Practice*, 35 (1), 4–11.

Pearce, L. (1994). *Reading dialogics*. New York: Edward Arnold.

Pelkey, L. (2001). In the LD bubble. In P. Rodis, S. Garrod, & M. L. Boscardin (Eds.), *Learning disabilities and life stories* (pp. 17–28). Needham Heights: Allyn & Bacon.

Perricone, M. A. (1994, January 11). Benefits of mainstreaming [Letter to the Editor]. *Newsday* (Nassau and Suffolk edition), p. 29.

Pfeiffer, D. (1994). Eugenics and disability discrimination. *Disability & Society*, 9 (4), 481–499.

Phillips, J. T. (1954, May 27). St. Loius Physician Lauds Court Ruling. *Atlanta Daily World*, p. 4.

Ponton, C. D. (1954, November 3). Desegregation and the South. *New York Times*, p. 28.

Prelude to freedom. (1954, May 29). *Chicago Defender*, p. 11.

Prendergast, C. (2002). The economy of literacy: How the Supreme Court stalled the civil rights movement. *Harvard Educational Review*, 72 (2), 206–229.

Price, J. & Shildrick, M. (1998). Uncertain thoughts on the dis/abled body. In M. Shildrick & J. Price (Eds.), *Vital signs: Feminist reconfigurations of the bio/logical body*. Edinburgh: Edinburgh University Press.

Proctor (1995). The destruction of 'Lives Not Worth Living.' In J. Terry & J. Urla (Eds.), *Deviant bodies: Critical perspectives on difference in science and popular culture* (pp. 170–196). Bloomington: Indiana University Press.

Publisher itemizes his opposition to school bias. (1953, July 14). *Atlanta Daily World*, p. 2.

Punshon, M. C. (1954, June 3). Observing segregation ruling. *New York Times*, p. 26.

Rabinow, P. (1984). *The Foucault reader*. New York: Pantheon.

Raps court, press, NAACP. (1956, December). *Southern School News*, p. 5.

Raps Supreme Court. (1956, December). *Southern School News*, p. 7.

Raye, E. (1955, April 30). Patriotism first. *Richmond Afro-American*, p. 4.

Reback, M. (1994). Swept away by the mainstream. *Washington Post*, p. A17.

"Reforming special education." (1995, May 26). [Editorial]. *New York Times*, p. A26.

Reforming special education. (1998, August 4). *New York Times*, p. 18.

Reid, D. K. & Valle, J. (2004). The discursive practice of learning disability: Implications for instruction and parent school relations. *Journal of Learning Disabilities, 37* (6), 466–481.

Renner, M. J. (1994, January 1). [Letter to the Editor]. *St. Louis Post-Dispatch*, p. 7B.

Revell, P. (2001, November 13). Education: On or out? Who is special? *Guardian* (London), p. 6.

Reynolds, M. C. (1989). An historical perspective: The delivery of special education to mildly disabled and at-risk students. *Remedial and Special Education, 10* (6), 7–11.

Reynolds, M. C. & Birch, J. W. (1977). *Teaching exceptional children in all America's schools*. Reston, VA: The Council for Exceptional Children.

Rich, A. (1980, Summer). Compulsory heterosexuality and lesbian existence. *Signs: Journal of Women in Culture and Society, 5*, 631–660.

Richardson, L. (1994, April 6). Minority students languish in special education system. *New York Times*, p. A1.

Richardson, L. (2000). Skirting a pleated text: De-disciplining an academic life. In E. A. St. Pierre & W. S. Pillow (Eds.), *Working the ruins: Feminist poststructuralist theory and methods in education* (pp. 153–163). New York: Routledge.

Rosenberg, G. I. (1993, June 25). Mainstreaming isn't for everyone [Letter to the Editor]. *Washington Post*, p. A24.

Rucker, C. M. (1954, June 7). Says court decision was dictated abroad. *Atlanta Constitution*, p. 4.

Ruppmann, J. (1991, November 7). Where disabled do best. *Washington Post*, p. A16.

Russell, M. (1998). *Beyond ramps: Disability at the end of the social contract*. Monroe, ME: Common Courage.

Sailor, W. (1991). Special education in the restructured school. *Remedial and Special Education, 12* (6), 8–22.

Salend, S. J. (2001). *Creating inclusive classrooms: Effective and reflective practices* (4th ed.). Upper Saddle River, NJ: Merrill Prentice Hall.

Salend, S. J., Duhaney, L. M. G., & Montgomery, W. (2002). A comprehensive approach to identifying and addressing issues of disproportionate representation. *Remedial and Special Education, 23* (5), 289–299.

Sanders, B. (1954, May 29). Letter to the editor. *Richmond Afro-American*, p. 4.

Sanger, M. (1922). *The pivot of civilization*. Retrieved July 15, 2004 from http://www.womensenews.org/article.cfm/dyn/aid/605/ [excerpt].

Sapon-Shevin, M. (1987). The national education reports and special education: Implications for students. *Exceptional Children, 53* (4), 300–306.

Sapon-Shevin, M. (1996). Beyond gifted education: Building a shared agenda for school reform. *Journal for the Education of the Gifted, 19*, 194–214.

Sapon-Shevin, M. (2000). Schools fit for all. *Educational Leadership, 58* (4), pp. 34–39.

Sapon-Shevin, M., Dobbelaera, A., Corrigan, C., Goodman, K., & Mastin, M. (1998). Everyone here can play. *Educational Leadership, 56* (1), 42–45.

Saulter, J. P. (1954, December 18). Decision from heaven. *Richmond Afro-American*, p. 4.

Schattman, R. & Benay, J. (1992). Inclusive practices transform special education in the 1990s. *The School Administrator, 49* (2), 8–12.

Schley county educator proposes school plan. (1954, May 21). *Atlanta Constitution*, p. 4.

School boards and schoolmen. (1956, December). *Southern School News*, p. 15.

Schools for disabled children. (1996, July 10). *Washington Post*, p. A16.

Second year is harder: Faculty of Missouri school reviews two years of desegregation. (1956, July). *Southern School News*, pp. 1, 5.

Segregation groups went to capital. (1956, March 13). *New York Times*, p. C6.

Selden, S. (1999). *Inheriting shame: The story of eugenics and racism in America*. New York: Teachers College Press.

Selden, S. (2000). Eugenics and the social construction of merit, race, and disability. *Journal of Curriculum Studies, 32* (2), 235–252.

Selletti, R. (1994, January 3). Disabilities no barrier [Letter to the Editor] Newsday (Nassau & Suffolk edition), p. 33.

Semmel, M. I., Gottlieb, J., & Robinson, N. M. (1979). Mainstreaming: Perspectives on educating handicapped children in the public schools. In D. C. Berliner (Ed.), *Review of research in education* (vol. 7, pp. 223–279). Washington, DC: American Educational Research Association.

Shakespeare, T. (1998). Choices and rights: Eugenics, genetics, and disability equality. *Disability & Society, 13* (5), 665–681.

Shapiro, A. (2000). *Everybody belongs: Changing negative attitudes toward classmates with disabilities*. New York: Routledge/Falmer.

Shapiro, J., Loweb, P., Bowermaster, D., Wright, A., Headden, S., & Toch, T. (1993, December 13). Separate and unequal. *U.S. News & World Report*, pp. 46–60.

Shohat, E. (1999). Talking visions: Multicultural feminism in a transnational age. Cambridge, MA: MIT Press.

Shore, D. (1994, May 13). Classroom inclusion helps children with disabilities. *Atlanta Constitution*, p. A13.

Sicker, T. (Executive Producer) (2002, March 27). *Misunderstood minds: Understanding kids who struggle to learn*. [Television broadcast]. Kirk documentary group and WGBH Foundation: Boston.

Simpson, R. (1954, May 22). Nation can pray, wait for democrats. *Atlanta Constitution*, p. 4.

Singer, A. (1992). Multiculturalism and democracy: The promise of multicultural education. *Social Education, 56* (2), 83–85.

Skrtic, T. M. (1991a). *Behind special education: A critical analysis of professional culture and school organization*. Denver, CO: Love Publishing House.

Skrtic, T. M. (1991b). The special education paradox: Equity as a way to excellence. *Harvard Educational Review, 61* (2), 148–206.

Sleeter, C. E. (1987). Why is there learning disabilities? A critical analysis of the birth of the field with its social context. In T. S. Popkewitz (Ed.), *The foundations of the school subjects* (pp. 210–237). London: Palmer Press.

Sleeter, C. E., Gutierrez, W., New, C., & Takata, S. (1995). Radical structuralist perspectives on the creation and use of learning disabilities. In T. M. Skrtic (Ed.), *Disability and democracy: Reconstructing (special) education for postmodernity* (pp. 153–165). New York: Teachers College Press.

Slow learner plan urged. (1956, July). *Southern School News,* p. 6.

Smith, A. (2001). A faceless bureaucrat ponders special education, disabilities, and white privilege. *Journal of the Association for Persons with Severe Handicaps, 26* (3), 180–188.

Smith, C. J. (1954, July 13). Letter to the editor. *Atlanta Daily World.* p. 4.

Smith, D. J. (1999). Thoughts on the changing meaning of disability: New eugenics or new wholeness? *Remedial and Special Education, 20* (3), 131–132.

Smith, E. G. (1955, April 30). Letter to the editor. *Richmond Afro-American,* p. 4.

Smith, L. (1954, June 6). Letter to the editor. *New York Times,* p. E10.

Snyder, S. L. & Mitchell, D. T. (2002). Out of the ashes of eugenics: Diagnostic regimes in the United States and the making of a disability minority. *Patterns of Prejudice, 36* (1), 79–103.

Solorzano, D. G. & Yosso, T. J. (2001). From racial stereotyping and deficit discourse toward a critical race theory. *Multicultural Education, 9* (1), 2–8.

South reacts quietly to high court ruling. (1955, June 1). *New York Times,* p. 30.

South's editors hail mild court ruling, see delays. (1955, June 1). *Atlanta Constitution,* p. 24.

Souto, B. (1996, May 8). To become independent adult [Letter to the Editor]. *The Washington Post,* p. A24.

Special care for special education. (1996, November 9). *New York Times,* p. 22.

Special focus on special kids. (1996, June 19). *St. Louis Post-Dispatch,* p. 6B.

Spelman, E. (1997). *Fruits of sorrow: Framing our attention to suffering.* Boston: Beacon.

Stacey, G. & Tulenko, J. D. (Executive Producers). (1996, May 12). *The Merrow Report* [Television broadcast]. New York, Public Broadcasting Service.

Stainback, W. & Stainback, S. (1984). A rationale for the merger of special and regular education. *Exceptional Children, 51* (2), 102–111.

Steinberg, J. N. (1954, June 4). New Experience. *Washington Post,* p. 28.

Stokes, T. L. (1954, May 20). Court decision is a signal for work. *Atlanta Constitution,* p. 4.

Strausberg, C. (1991, December 10). Special ed program integrates disabled. *Chicago Defender,* p. 6.

Strausberg, C. (1992, May 27). Disabled kids' status questioned. *Chicago Defender,* p. 3.

Strong, H.H. (1954, June 29). Atlantan says pastor was hardly justified in twisting scripture to make his point. *Atlanta Constitution,* p. 4.

Students speak out: Is 'mainstreaming' mentally and physically handicapped students a good idea? (1989, December 21). *Washington Post,* p. M6.

Study made of child behavior in St. Louis' mixed classes. (1956, March). *Southern School News,* p. 12.

Supreme court decision needs planning study (1954, November 9). *Atlanta Constitution,* p. 4.

Supreme court reaffirms a principal: Leaves implementation to communities. (1955, June 1). *Atlanta Constitution,* p. 4.

Tanaka, G. (1997). Pico College. In W. G. Tierney & Y. S. Lincoln (Eds.), *Representation and the text* (pp. 259–304). Albany: State University of New York Press.

Taschereau, A. (1954, May 27). Terms high court decision "About 80 years late." *Atlanta Daily World,* p. 4.

Taylor, S. J. (1988). Caught in the continuum: A critical analysis of the principle of the least restrictive environment. *Journal of the Association for Persons with Severe Handicaps, 13* (1), 41–53.

The decision of a century. (1954, May 18). *Atlanta Daily World,* p. 4.

Thomas, G. & Loxley, A. (2001). *Deconstructing special education and constructing inclusion.* Buckingham, England: Open University Press.

Thomas, S. (1995, April 8). Educators explore new frontier in special education delivery. *Indianapolis Recorder,* p. A1.

Thornton, K. (2000, Aug. 11). Staff not prepared for SEN influx. *The Times Educational Supplement* (London), p. 6.

Thousand, J. S., Villa, R. A., & Nevin, A. I. (Eds.). (2002). *Creativity & collaborative learning: The practical guide to empowering students, teachers, and families* (2nd ed.). Baltimore: Paul H. Brookes.

Threlkeld, G. W. (1954, June 14). Court decision upset domestic tranquility. *Atlanta Constitution,* p. 4.

Tollin, M. (Director). (2004). *Radio.* Columbia-TriStar.

Tomlinson, C. A. (2001). *How to differentiate instruction in mixed ability classrooms* (2nd ed.). Alexandria, VA: ACSD.

Torres, C. A. (1998). Democracy, education, and multiculturalism: Dilemmas of citizenship in a global world. *Comparative Education Review, 42* (4), 421–447.

Transfer of disabled student rejected. (1988, October 6). *Washington Post,* p. B6.

Tyack, D. B. (2001). Introduction. In S. Mondale and S. B. Patton (Eds.), *School: The story of American public education* (pp. 1–8). Boston: Beacon Press.

Udvari-Solner, A. (1996). Examining teacher thinking: Constructing a process to design curricular adaptations. *Remedial & Special Education, 17,* 245–259.

U.S. Department of Education. (2000). *Elementary and secondary school civil rights compliance report: Projected values for the nation and individual states, 1998.* Washington, DC: U.S. Government Printing Office.

United Cerebral Policy Associations. (1993). *Policy on full inclusion of individuals with disabilities.* Washington, DC: Author.

United States Constitution Amendment XIV. (1968) Retrieved December 5, 2004 from http://www.law.cornell.edu/constitution/constitution.amendmentxiv.html.

Valencia, R. R. (1997a). (Ed.), *The evolution of deficit thinking.* London: Falmer.

Valles, E. C. (1998). The disproportionate representation of minority students in special education: Responding to the problem. *Journal of Special Education, 32* (1), 1–4.

Varenne, H. & McDermott, R. (1998). *Successful failure.* Boulder, CO: Westview Press.

Villa, R. A. & Thousand, J. S. (1995). *Creating an inclusive school.* Alexandria, VA: Association for Supervision and Curriculum Development.

Vogel, T. (Ed.). (2001). *The Black press: New literary and historical essays.* New Brunswick, NJ: Rutgers University Press.

Volmer, R., Jr. (1955, June 4). Letter to the editor. *Richmond Afro-American,* p. 4.

Wagner, M. (1991). *Youth with disabilities: How are they doing? The first comprehensive report from the National Longitudinal Transition Study of Special Education Students.* Menlo Park, CA: SRI International.

Walker, R. C. (1955, July 5). Calls segregation moral, social issue. *Atlanta Constitution,* p. 4.

Wang, M. C., Reynolds, M. C., & Walberg, H. J. (1986). Rethinking special education. *Educational Leadership, 44* (1), 26–31.

Ware, L. (2001). Writing, identity, and the other: Dare we do disability studies? *Journal of Teacher Education, 52* (2), 107–123.

Warner, M. (Ed.). (1993). *Fear of a queer planet: Queer politics and social theory.* Minneapolis: University of Minnesota Press.

Washer, M. & Blackorby J. (1996). Transition from high school to work or college: How special education students fare. *The future of children: Special education for students with disabilities.* 6(1), 103–120.

Watts, I. E. & Erevelles, N. (2004). These deadly times: Reconceptualizing by using critical race theory and disability studies. *American Educational Research Journal, 41* (2), 271–299.

Wax, M. L. (1993). How culture misdirects multiculturalism. *Anthropology & Education Quarterly,* 24 (2), 99–115.

We can learn from children. (1954, Jan. 2). *Chicago Defender,* p. 11.

Wells, A. S., Holme, J. J., Revilla, A. T., & Atanda, A. K. (2004). Against the tide: Desegregated high schools and their 1980 graduates. *Phi Delta Kappan, 85* (9), 670–679.

West, C. (1993). *Race matters.* Boston: Beacon Press.

Wharton, J. (2000, March 3). Make the school fit the child: Opinion. *New York Times Educational Supplement,* p. 17.

What they say. (1955, April). *Southern School News,* p. 13.

What they say. (1955, June). *Southern School News,* p. 5.

What they say. (1955, July). *Southern School News,* p. 5.

What they say. (1956, January). *Southern School News,* p. 5.

What they say. (1956, February). *Southern School News,* pp. 7, 15–16.

What they say. (1956, April). *Southern School News,* pp. 9, 14–16.

What they say. (1956, June). *Southern School News,* pp. 3, 5, 9.

What they say. (1957, January). *Southern School News,* pp. 3, 14.

What they say. (1957, February). *Southern School News,* p. 15.

Wilgoren, D. (1994, December 27). In autism case, hearing is over, but battle isn't. *Washington Post,* p. D1.

Wilgoren, D. & Pae, P. (1994, August 28). As Loundon goes, so may other schools: Case could influence future of 'inclusion' of disabled students. *Washington Post,* p. B1.

Wilkins, R. (1995). Dream deferred but not defeated. *Teachers College Record, 96* (4), 614–618.

Will, M. C. (1986). Educating children with learning problems: A shared responsibility. *Exceptional Children, 52,* 411–415.

Williams, J. (1987). *Eyes on the prize: America's civil rights years, 1954–1965.* New York: Viking Penguin.

Wilson, P. K. (2002). Harry Laughlin's eugenic crusade to control the "socially inadequate" in Progressive era America. *Patterns of Prejudice, 36* (1), 49–66.

Wrong, D. (2000). Adversarial identities and multiculturalism. *Society, 37* (2), 10–14.

Wurtzburg, G. (Producer/Director). (1992). *Educating Peter* [Motion picture]. United States: Aquarius.

Yatron-Kastens, T. (1995, January 4). My children have a civil right to learn. *Washington Post,* p. A15.

Yates, R. B. (1956, March 29). Letter to the editor. *New York Times,* p. 26.

Yell, M. L., Rogers, D., & Rogers, E. L. (1998). The legal history of special education: What a long, strange trip it's been! *Remedial and Special Education, 19* (4), 219–228.

Young-Hawthorne, J. (1990, November 8). Mainstreaming handicapped schoolchildren. *Los Angeles Times,* p. B6.

INDEX

Italicized page numbers indicate illustrations.